TRAFFORD

My Mother is a Tractor

"Shunning thousand-mile walks, the martial arts, *zen* and forays into art and culture in favour of beer, day-trips and *karaoke*, Nicholas Klar's *My Mother is a Tractor* offers a disturbingly realistic look at life in Japan. This book is a refreshing break from the more epic and pretentious travelogues…this is also what makes it a must read. The book's message, or warning, is simple: This is life in Japan. Enter at your own risk. Enjoy your stay."

Dwayne Lively, *The Crazy Japan Times*

www.crazyjapan.com

"*My Mother is a Tractor* contains the wry insights of a former teacher on the JET scheme - Nicholas Klar who has written about his experiences. Required reading for anyone contemplating JET-hood or thinking of teaching English in Japan."

Jan Dodd, co-author, *The Rough Guide to Japan*

www.jandodd.com

"*My Mother is a Tractor* is a witty and light account of one man's time in Japan. It is neither an academic tome nor the last word on the topic--and it stakes no claim to either. Rather, it documents Klar's own fortunes--and misfortunes--as he takes off for, adjusts to, and ultimately must bade farewell to Japan. Never pedantic, always open: a good summer read."

C. Ogawa, *Japan Visitor*

www.japanvisitor.com

- Sapporo
- Sendai
- Omi
- Kanazawa
- Tokyo
- Hiroshima
- Nagoya
- Osaka
- Fukuoka

Nicholas Klar

My Mother is a Tractor

A Life in Rural Japan

Trafford Publications

© Copyright 2005 Nicholas Klar
All rights reserved. No part of this publication may be reproduced, stored in a retrieval system, or transmitted, in any form or by any means, electronic, mechanical, photocopying, recording, or otherwise, without the written prior permission of the author.

Note for Librarians: A cataloguing record for this book is available from Library and Archives Canada at www.collectionscanada.ca/amicus/index-e.html
ISBN 1-4120-4897-4

Printed in Victoria, BC, Canada. Printed on paper with minimum 30% recycled fibre. Trafford's print shop runs on "green energy" from solar, wind and other environmentally-friendly power sources.

Offices in Canada, USA, Ireland and UK
This book was published *on-demand* in cooperation with Trafford Publishing. On-demand publishing is a unique process and service of making a book available for retail sale to the public taking advantage of on-demand manufacturing and Internet marketing. On-demand publishing includes promotions, retail sales, manufacturing, order fulfilment, accounting and collecting royalties on behalf of the author.

Book sales for North America and international:
Trafford Publishing, 6E–2333 Government St.,
Victoria, BC v8t 4p4 CANADA
phone 250 383 6864 (toll-free 1 888 232 4444)
fax 250 383 6804; email to orders@trafford.com
Book sales in Europe:
Trafford Publishing (uk) Limited, 9 Park End Street, 2nd Floor
Oxford, UK ox1 1hh UNITED KINGDOM
phone 44 (0)1865 722 113 (local rate 0845 230 9601)
facsimile 44 (0)1865 722 868; info.uk@trafford.com
Order online at:
trafford.com/04-2705
10 9 8 7 6 5 4 3 2 1

Nicholas Klar is peripatetic soul, hailing originally from Adelaide, Australia. He has lived in four different countries, studied in Australia and the U.S., and has travelled widely through Asia and the Pacific. His most recent incarnation is as a History teacher at an international school in Shanghai, China where he lives with his wife, Mami and daughter, Youki. His only real claim to fame at this time is being the only person in the whole of Shanghai without a mobile phone. He has had several short stories, travelogues and essays published previously but 'My Mother is a Tractor' is his first full-length book. His ambition is to be very rich without ever having to actually work for it...and to never hear the words "Hey, let's climb Mount Fuji" again.

This book is dedicated to the memory
of my late father, Brian
- a raconteur supreme with a
bottomless pit of tales to tell,

plus,

The kind folk of Omi,
Niigata Prefecture, Japan

A word of thanks

A tome such as this one is a collection of many experiences that have all intersected with mine at some time – for better or worse. Therefore I must acknowledge with a hearty *arigato gozaimasu* and a deep bow all the following people who made this book possible. In no particular order – to those who helped me during or after my sojourn, made me laugh (or cry), provided me with material to work with (either unwillingly or unknowingly), and/or generally got me through my *ni-nen* (two years) and beyond.

My many fellow JET's and *compadres* – too numerous to name here,

The countless resident kind souls of Omi and Niigata – likewise,

Good friends and colleagues Dennis, Paul, Mary and Marie, plus Alasdair for their early encouragement,

Libby and the venerable Colin for sage advice and assistance with editing,

My students in Shanghai - whose assignments lay unmarked, and my daughter Youki – who squirmed on my knee or missed many *dakko* altogether, whilst I busied myself with late revision,

Dwayne Lively, Jan Dodd and Ogawa-san for their time, advice and pre-reviews of the book,

My wife Mami for her unfailing faith, her correction of my poor spelling and usual acceptance of some of my more contentious observations, her always helpful suggestions, but mostly for clearing up so many of my cock-ups in general and still accepting me throughout the whole process,

All those on my ever-so-cocked-up reference list,

My stomach especially thanks Yamada-san for her delicious *ramen*.

And if I missed anyone I humbly apologise – but cannot provide you with any expensive whisky for compensation…

Chapters

1. Prologue
2. Why Japan…? An Introduction
3. I Don't Need To Study Japanese
4. Business Class??!
5. Economic Bubbles And The Salaryman's Vomit
6. *Karaoke* and Barbecued Carrots… Exploring Tokyo
7. The Ghosts Of Dead Fish
8. It's *Gomi* Day!
9. Bureaucrats, The YMCA And Mr. Meat Warehouse
10. Ode To My *Jitensha*
11. C'mon Train. Dancing On The Bridge
12. Naked Boys And Yen
13. Eat, Drink, Man, Sumo
14. Do You Play Sex? Raw Eggs For Breakfast
15. Women Chattering At The Well
16. Hot As Molten Lava!
17. Oh, So THAT Was A Hostess Bar.
18. Oops! I Think I Killed My Boss
19. Gifts From The Omi *Gomi* Guy
20. Junkie Jellybeans And Dancing Elvises
21. *Bōnenkai*, Plus Wielding The *Mochi* Mallet
22. The Yakuza Ramen Bar
23. *O-Yuki*, Or The Fine Art Of Coping With Cold Niigata Weather
24. *Matsuri* Month Madness
25. A Tale Of Two Capitals
26. That's….Ummm…Shampoo
27. The Five Levels Of Drinking

28. Marching To A Different Beat
29. Are We There Yet? A Pilgrimage To Fuji-San
30. Those Awful Five Letters
31. Sleeping On Concrete – No More Ferries Tonight
32. A Cow Fell From Where!?
33. Japanese Dead Heads
34. It's English Jim, But Not As We Know It…
35. Oh My God! It's An Eyeball!
36. 'Love Select' And 'Memory Notes'
37. Toilets, Smoking And Cults
38. Ground Zero And The Road To Mecca
39. The Toilet Sled And Free Whisky
40. Victims Of Fashion
41. What Do You Do With A Drunken Sailor?
42. The Ghosts Of Children Past, Or Ode To My *Jitensha* II
43. Going From Bad To Worse
44. A Very Public Intercourse?
45. "The Time Has Come, And So I Face The Final Curtain…"
46. Farewell, Blue Sea, Farewell
47. A Post-Script: Same Stuff, Different Day

Appendix: References

1: Prologue

If you believe everything you read, better not read.

- Japanese Proverb

In high school I was voted 'Most likely to be abducted by aliens'. Well, I wasn't abducted - I went freely of my own accord. My destination was Japan, and it was certainly me who was the alien. I still have a copy of my baby pink-coloured 'alien card' to prove it. When I first landed at my junior high school in rural Japan I found on my desk a disparate collection of three hundred and fifty summer writing assignments to be marked by me. Every vacation period the students were set an English assignment, and my predecessor had decreed the topic for that summer would be 'My Family'. Hence the title of this book came from one student's evaluation of his/her mother. To this day I'm still not sure what was meant by it. A derivation of 'attractive'? A miscued reading of the dictionary? I don't know, but I solidly laughed my way through a great number of the assignments and made a list, now lost, of the more humorous statements.

I studiously recorded most of my comings and goings in a semi-regular diary. It didn't start out as an idea for a book. It was just my personal musings. However the words started to stack up, so one day I sat down to rewrite them and what you now hold in your hands is the result. Naturally, some names have been changed to protect my insurance and personal safety records.

I didn't set out in this account to affront and more than often my observations are conveyed firmly tongue-in-cheek. I'm sure a Japanese person could write a just as an eclectic account about the cultural incongruities of Australians, my wife in particular. This was just my life as it happened. Okay...maybe it includes bits of other people's lives too. If I offend anybody by what is contained herein I apologise profusely from the bottom of my toilet slippers. If you have spent any time in Japan I'm sure you will relate to many of my experiences. If you are intending to visit this ancient land of the rising sun I hope some of my more bizarre tales will not discourage you. Despite its perceived contradictions Japan is an utterly amazing place that must be experienced. *Gambatte!*

Lastly to all the people that were part of my life, both *nihonjin* and *gaijin*, I thank you for being part of this incredible time in my life. This book is for you. Well, most of you. I couldn't have done it without you.

2: Why Japan? An Introduction

Doing is a mistake. Not doing is a huge mistake

- Japanese Proverb

Until the 1990's the only ideas I had about Japan were formed by the TV series 'Shintaro' that my brother Peter and I had religiously watched as children, and also my father's reminiscences of WWII. Particularly the one where they overran a Japanese base and the fleeing soldiers of the Emperor left behind crates of *sake*. Apparently the Australian war effort in New Guinea was put back by about three days while Dad and his mates lay puking amongst the jungle growth and got over their hangovers.

The first idea I ever actually had about going to Japan was during a university workshop. At the time I was studying in California and was checking out possibilities of working overseas. The speaker urged us to check out the Japan Exchange and Teaching (JET) Program, which I decided was good advice, and in due time I called the office in Los Angeles. However I was politely told by the person on the other end of the phone that, "It's only for Americans". Two friends of mine applied and got accepted. I guess it was fortunate that they were American. In fact as far as I know they still are.

At the completion of my study I packed my bags and headed home to Australia. But I was still thinking about Japan. To be quite honest I didn't have a burning desire to go there. Yet I'd never had a real urge to visit America either, but I'd gone and thoroughly enjoyed myself - apart from the night I got cornered drinking cheap vodka with Igor the Slovenian. Still that's another story - but it starts out with "Hey Nic, zis boddle iz huge and iz only $5!" And maybe I did enjoy myself, but the brain cells containing those particular memories have long since gone to brain cell heaven. Or maybe purgatory given the strength of the ingredients.

I enquired again with the Japanese Embassy in Canberra who assured me that Australians were in fact not excluded, just a minority. Something to do with balance of trade I think. Even during the 'bubble' years of Japan's mighty economy Aussies always enjoyed a trade that was long on the credit side. I duly completed my forms, arranged my references, composed an eloquent essay about just how very interested I was in Japan, posted all of them off, and told my friends to expect me. Then I waited for the phone call that never came. All I received was a letter that can be summed up with the solitary word – 'rejection'.

I covered my disappointment well with a tirade of profanities and ill feeling, and then promptly marched off to the employment office. I was offered a managerial job interstate and spent the next year honing my people skills in a cold mountain town. Sick of cold weather and small towns I decided to apply to JET again, but with decidedly less ardour. I also applied to return to university for teaching studies and was accepted. I handed in my resignation and almost completely forgot about Japan until two weeks before I was to leave, when I received an interview invitation for three weeks hence.

Because I had applied to the Melbourne office I had to take my interview there. Now being on a student budget I had to catch the overnight bus from Adelaide rather than fly - my previous preferred mode of transportation. I was placed at the front of the bus right below the air conditioner and next to a large swarthy, sweaty man of Mediterranean heritage. My new companion, replete with studded belt and restless sleep habits, was apparently a bouncer in a Kings Cross nightclub. By the time we hit the Spencer Street bus station in Melbourne I didn't feel in the best shape for a potentially life changing interview.

My friend Mark met me there and we had breakfast before he had to leave for work. I consumed a large amount of coffee in an attempt to appear coherent, and then changed into something more befitting than my casual bus wear of track pants, t-shirt, and sleep drool. I was striding boldly down Queen Street on my way to the Japanese Embassy when I chanced across $30 lying on the footpath. I stopped and looked around. There was no one nearby so I picked it up and put it in my pocket. It was obviously a good sign - the road to the embassy was lined with money!

The interview went exceedingly well and in April I received my posting to Omi-machi (Blue Sea Town) in Niigata Prefecture. I couldn't find it on a map, nor was it mentioned in any travel guides. The only reference anywhere of Omi that stopped it from being entirely anonymous was in 'Debt of Honour' by Tom Clancy where it talks about a secret American mission as it crosses the Japanese coast between Omi and Ichiburi. Actually it says 'Ichifuri', but they obviously misread the *kanji*. Still, it didn't matter. That's where I was going, and regardless of any spelling mistakes, I was on my way...

3: I don't need to study Japanese...
Getting Organised

Darkness reigns at the foot of the lighthouse - Japanese Proverb

After getting my acceptance in April the pace began to increase in May. I received my contract (which I temporarily misplaced), a language program (which I chose to ignore for the time - and eventually forevermore), various information, and a letter from Shanti, the teacher I was replacing. I was to hate Shanti. Everyone else loved him. In contrast to my tenure he studiously studied Japanese, ingratiated himself with management, and never seemed to complain.

My placement at Omi was confirmed - a small cold town two hundred and fifty kilometres north-west of Tokyo and nowhere near where I wanted to be in Kyushu. Shanti did mention that he was happy there, so that was positive. Though not <u>actually</u> knowing him who could be sure? With a surname like Escevado he could be a Colombian drug lord on the witness relocation program for all I knew.

However I wasn't really sure about the dormitory accommodation I was being set up in at the local chemical and cement company. What really worried me was when Shanti commented; "You get to eat a lot of different foods you wouldn't normally be able to". I wasn't sure if I was ready for that kind of adventure. Also Omi sounded to me like a much smaller Japanese version of the town I'd only rid myself of a few months before. At least it was on the coast - but surrounded by mountains. I wrote back to Shanti and asked for more information but all I was supplied were two very quick and rough notes in illegible handwriting. He must have written them at a time when the crack was just kicking in or he wanted to go to medical school and was just practicing writing prescriptions. This was definitely going to be a voyage of self-discovery.

A month out from leaving saw me no closer to studying my language program and vigorously pulling strings in regard to my accommodation. The town claimed there were no apartments to rent there. This proved false because as the final month dawned Shanti contacted me to say that I had been given an apartment instead of a dorm. That was pretty pleasing. I had no desire to live in a small box with men reeking of cement and chemicals. My taste buds also breathed a sigh of relief. The complication was that I had told them I needed an apartment so my girlfriend could visit. Why I was even thinking of extending the relationship beyond take off day still remains a mystery to me. Probably because I was too weak to back up my promise of leaving day finality to her. I thought we had agreed on a finite relationship. I believe the first conversation after I received my acceptance went,

"So we can either break up now or in June. What do you think?"
But she was working hard on trying to change my mind.

Regardless Shanti stated that if she was going to visit she couldn't be my 'girlfriend', but had to be my 'fiancée'. This was something that would haunt me for a long time. I would be questioned for months after I arrived about my wedding plans - even for a long time after we had finally broken up. The news did spread quickly in some quarters. Three single women joined my adult class within a fortnight of the news of our break up. The more immediate effect prior to leaving was on my poor besotted girlfriend who now wanted to believe that we were engaged rather than about to break up. Oh what a tangled web we weave...

On holiday for a few days we stopped in a roadhouse for lunch. The midday news had a report on the huge floods affecting Japan. Niigata prefecture was mentioned. Could the town be washed away before I even arrived there? Maybe they would just give me a year's salary and I wouldn't have to go. I kept my eyes on the news for the next few days but there was no further mention. Neither did the town contact me, but that might be hard when it's a few metres underwater, or maybe not even there anymore.

The reality of leaving sunk in when my ticket arrived, courtesy of 'Kinki Travel'. That was the name they used in Japan anyway. In Australia it was 'Kintetsu Travel'. The agent confided to me that it had been called 'Kinki' in Australia too until they got sick of being over-run with enquiries from dirty old men looking for tours to places like the Philippines and Thailand.

I still had a million things to do with only three days left. I blew the dust of my language program and put it in my carry on bag. By now I was rationalising that I'd have about eight hours to finally study it on the plane. I had my farewell party on the last Saturday night - my third one in four years. My family goodbye was on the Sunday, and finally a JET alumni farewell on the second last night.

With the hours ticking down my girlfriend was sick with a sore back, plus all kind of other ailments and complaints. And after that the pleading began.

"Yes, I know you said it was only temporary..."
"I thought you'd change your mind..."
"You can't leave me now..."
And then of course, the desperate line of last resort,
"I think I'm pregnant..."
The last clutches of a drowning woman. Sorry baby, I'm gone...

4: Business class??! Time to go...

We've arrived, and to prove it we're here. - Japanese proverb

I ran out of time on the last night and was still packing my bags at 11:30pm. It was then up at 5:30am to catch the 'red-eye' flight to Melbourne. I had to be present for an orientation there with people from the embassy, which was to be the first of three boring orientations I would endure over the next couple of weeks. From there it was on to Sydney. I admit to having some doubts on the plane up. This was not helped by the worst landing I'd ever experienced in my life. To make matters worse my luggage forlornly appeared in several pieces on the conveyor (*see:* completely trashed) and I spent forty five minutes sticking it back together with bright orange airline tape before getting on the bus to the Sheraton. I got there so late the program leader was worried that I had got the jitters and bolted. Apparently it's not unknown to have people bail at the airport. And the trauma was not yet over. After another 5.30 start and no breakfast supplied we had to endure check in. I unfortunately stood in the line of the check-in lady who was either having a bad day, or suffering from PMS, or both. Eventually I came off $290 lighter for my sin of excess baggage. About the only one to do so.

The biggest shock was when we were handed business class tickets and discovered 'what lies on the other side of that curtain they pull across the aisle'. Those who fly economy would know what I mean. Then again how many business class travellers are going to buy a book like this? I finally got Japanese seaweed crackers for breakfast at 10.00am, along with a vodka and orange. Thinking back it's probably not that strange in Japanese culture. Then again maybe it's the same in Australia - except without the crackers.

About eight hours air time later we glided down through the Tokyo smog to Narita and disembarked to a blast of summer humidity. Enduring a ridiculously long wait at immigration I was the second last person off the plane through the gates. After eventually organising my bags, which now felt like they contained moon rocks, we were faced with the long bus ride from Narita to our hotel in Tokyo. Finally after checking in, throwing my bags (or what remained of them) on the bed, and a quick shower I headed out into the Shinjuku night for a bite with two other Aussies - Jodie and Sarah. The adventure truly begins...

5: Economic Bubbles and the Salaryman's Vomit...

What do we want our kids to do? Sweep up around Japanese computers?
- Walter F. Mondale

We walked out from our hotel, the very salubrious Hyatt, that was most recently made famous by the movie 'Lost in Translation'. A word of thanks to Japanese taxpayers is appropriate at this point as I will never be able to afford to stay there myself, nor fly business class most likely. As we wended through Shinjuku station we found the hundreds of homeless living in cardboard boxes. These men, but no women, I guessed were an obvious sign of the recent economic decline in Japan after the bursting of the 'bubble economy'. Since I arrived in Japan the problem has not improved but become even greater and more institutionalized. In Kawasaki, outside of Tokyo the homeless have, "erected scores of wooden shacks, neatly spaced, with locks and, sometimes, ornamented windows and doors. As a sign of the suburban life many had led, some have transformed tiny patches of land into gardens. Many keep dogs and have bicycles. Others sit in lawn chairs in front of their shacks, reading novels." These homeless have become easy targets for Japan's newly disaffected youth and assaults are soaring. Youth arrested have apparently told the police that they were "killing time," "getting rid of stress" and "disposing of society's trash."

On the other hand, some families on ever-reducing low-incomes are experiencing such extreme poverty that there have even incredibly been some cases of people dying from malnutrition. One such case was reported in February 2005 when a 27-year-old mother and her three-year-old son were found starved to death in their apartment near Tokyo. Police sadly reported that there was no food left in the apartment and the woman only had a sparse eight yen left in her purse.

Students of economics will remember how Japan's economy never missed a beat after the stock market crash of 1987 that had sent other major economies into a tailspin. Bloated by the excesses of towering land prices, political kickbacks, and money leant to dubious projects and criminal gangs, Japan Inc. was considered to be on its way to being the world's number one economy. Japan could do no wrong and the idea was floated that corporate Japan could

"...wind up owning the Grand Canyon, the Lincoln Memorial, and the New York Stock Exchange - and still have enough left over to buy Latin America." Though why they would want to do any of that is beyond me. Just chalk it up to notions of insecure paranoia. The covers of TIME screamed headlines like, 'Super Japan', 'Yen Power' and 'How to cope with Japan's business invasion'. History shows that the 1990's, now known as Japan's 'lost decade', brought something very different. By 1992 TIME's covers now led with headlines such as, 'Japan's Recession, Why the powerhouse will never be the same', 'Japan's new anxiety' and 'The mighty fall'.

This was perhaps to the relief of some of the other major economic powers. This was most noticeable in America where business and political leaders spent most of the 1980's frothing at their mouths and reading a steady stream of best-selling books on Japanese management that were cranked out faster than Toyota minivans. Nowadays they are blaming the Chinese instead. However I have yet to see any management books based on the financial sophistication or enlightening precepts of The Great Leap Forward, Cultural Revolution or crowd-control in Tiananmen Square.

I read recently that Japan's economy of the early 21st Century was likened to a driver thrown from a speeding car. As the country's politicians and bureaucrats, playing the metaphorical role of paramedics, attend to the driver at the side of the road, they have many difficult decisions in their treatment. There are just so many complex choices to be made, and done in the right order, if the patient is to survive. Some sceptics may insinuate a priest and last rites may be more appropriate. Nonetheless, by 2005 the share market had begun to sputter to life and some optimism was returning at last.

However with continuing economic fears and concerns about the soundness of financial institutions, the Japanese appear to be hoarding more money under their futons. The amount of cash in circulation reached a record ¥75.5 trillion (USD$70 trillion) at the end of 2002, central bank figures showed. The total number of bank notes on issue amounted to ¥13.03 billion. According to the Nihon Keizai News, if this money was stacked it would be 345 times taller than Mount Fuji and if lined up end to end, it would go around the globe about fifty times.

Mixed amongst the homeless this night were *salarymen* (office workers and businessmen) obviously just too drunk or broke to go home. One lay on his back on a bench - his tie askew, his briefcase still firmly clutched in his fist and…his front covered in vomit. Even on a Sunday night there were many of these *salarymen* (and their accompanying O.L.'s – office ladies) out late in their suits drinking and standing around. To the uninitiated (e.g., me) it resembled an invasion of Asian Mormons.

In the days of the booming 'bubble economy' *salarymen* would work hard for at least ten hours, usually more, and then stay out even later with their colleagues drinking and talking shop. Traditionally the three words they would utter, and nothing else, to their devoted spouses when they eventually came through their highly mortgaged front door, or if, in the case of the previously mentioned souls, would be *meshi, furo, neru* (meal, bath, bed). If feeling particular chatty they might also add *biru, terebi* (beer, TV - usually baseball). Since the collapse of the economy in the 1990's women have stampeded out of the kitchen and into the workforce, no longer happy to practice *gaman* (self denial) and be dependent upon the patronage of what used to be called the *nure ochiba zoku* ('wet leaf tribe').

However it often seems that the Japanese would rather let their economy stagnate than send their women up the corporate ladder. Traditionally Japanese companies hire almost exclusively men to fill career positions, reserving short term and casual places, mostly clerical tasks and tea serving, for women. Resistance to expanding women's professional and/or managerial roles remains high in a country where the economic status of women trails far behind that of women in other advanced economies. Whilst forty percent of Japanese women now work - a figure that reflects their rapid, recent entry into the job market - they hold only about nine percent of managerial or authoritative positions in industry compared to about forty-five percent in America. To top it off, women's wages are only about sixty-five percent of those of their male counterparts, one of the largest gaps in the industrial world.

Nonetheless, despite the seeming non-threat from the fairer sex, this has caused quite some consternation in such a male dominated society. One example of this ascendancy was that it took more than thirty years to legalise birth control pills, yet only a few months to approve Viagra. Yet, if you saw some of the men who buy the product you might wonder why. In a metaphorical sense I think it would be similar to sticking a new flagpole on a condemned building.

Also, with the collapsing status of the Japanese corporate warrior and its promise of lifetime employment, *salarymen* must stretch themselves to simply avoid being sacked. *Salarymen* used to be so devoted to their employers they would report for work through snow, sleet and brain surgery. It reminded me of a former fellow employee. One morning the phone rang out and the ensuing conversation went something like this,

"Hi Nic, it's Mark. I won't be able to come in today."
"What's the problem?"
"I had an accident on my motorcycle on the way in."
"So, are you okay?"
"I don't know. I'm waiting for the ambulance to arrive…"

It was not difficult to envisage Mark pulling his torso, trailing its bloody and bleeding stumps, across the road to a public phone and calling work with his one remaining limb. Back in Japanese society, in light of the vast sea-change that is now occurring, the groups of dark-suited company men that are seen everywhere striding in packs, chain-smoking and heads bowed, are now viewed as *iketenai* (uncool) and *nasakenai* (clueless).

Young men in particular are now rebelling against the traditional 'give it all for the corporation' type sacrifices of their fathers and grandfathers, and having a succession of jobs, many of them casual and part-time. These 'rebels' are referred to as *freeter* – a combination of 'free' and *arbeiter*, the German word for 'worker'. But increasingly, the members of this swelling army of temporary workers is realising that 'freeterism' is a most likely in reality a sugar-coated way of marginalising Japan's new generation and cutting wages and benefits. At least there's a substantial chance it's better than having the chance to die from *karoushi* (overworking), as too many Japanese *salarymen* still do, or having to recite endlessly, "My dream is to be a tiny cog in a huge and honourable machine".

Reports state that a decade ago, four job openings awaited each graduate of a Japanese high school that was looking for work. Since that time the number of job-seeking high school graduates has plummeted by two-thirds (roughly four hundred thousand people) because of falling birth rates. Despite this, there is now barely one opening for each student who wants a job. In the late 1990's, ninety percent of Japanese high school students who sought work after their March graduation had a job lined up by late January. However by 2002 the job placement rate had fallen to 75 percent, the lowest on record. Now it is not uncommon to see university graduates taking positions that once went to high school leavers. The whole Japanese concept of collective good and *wa* (harmony) appears to now being slowly being sacrificed on the new altars of individualism, materialism and personal happiness.

Despite all this Japan is still the world's second largest economy, a veritable country mile ahead of the third placegetter, Germany. Not that Germany is without its own economic troubles. In fact Japan could remain in a withering economic funk for a further few years, even endure another deep recession or two, and the worst case scenario might be that it slips to Number Three – not exactly the end of the world you would think. The Japanese are talented beyond belief and anyone can have a bad decade, or two.

6: Karaoke and barbecued carrots...
Exploring Tokyo

The crow that mimics a cormorant is drowned - Japanese Proverb

Before I stray too far down the path of a scholarly exposition on the 'new' Japan (if I haven't already), and say something stupid, or even worse - remotely intelligent, I best get back to where I started the previous chapter, and that was the three of us walking around Tokyo. We finally stopped at a fast food place called 'First Kitchen', ate some kind of chicken thing, then sat outside on a bench watching the hub-bub of humanity pass around us. Tokyo was then, and still is, a fascinating cauldron of humanity.

I was sharing the room with Adrian, a fellow South Australian. Adrian had requested as remote an area as possible like rural Hokkaido, Japan's northernmost major island. In fact he received a posting in Chiba - only about fifty kilometres from Tokyo and near to Narita, the international airport. I would learn much about the joys of Japanese bureaucracy over the next two years and this was a good example. Adrian apparently only lasted until November. In the morning as I awoke the fairytale lights had turned into the grim reality of a dirty smog that envelopes the city, swallowing any distant building. No sights of Mt. Fuji today. No matter - this was Tokyo, a city of history and legends, and I was happy to see it in any of its manifestations. As Adrian joined me at the window he could not believe it was smog but I assured him it was.

How did I know so much about smog? Simple really - I'd been to Los Angeles where they have it down to an art form. When I was flying into LAX for the first time it was the middle of summer but there seemed to an inordinate amount of cloud around. Suddenly it struck me - it must be the famous Los Angeles (*motto:* 'Drive you turkey, we hate public transport') smog. I leaned over to the man sitting across from me and asked,

"Is this the famous LA smog?"

To which he replied in a deep drawl, "Don't ask us, we're from Texas!"

I pondered on this for a second or two, then responded, much to the big Texans ire,

"Oh, so you're just one of the guys who supply the oil for it..."

The orientations we were forced to attend in Tokyo were, let's speak bluntly now, boring with a capital B. Lots of speeches and things already known. I was to learn very quickly that these things are woven into the very fabric of Japanese society in an attempt to maintain *wa*. I don't know about that, but I do know that every other meeting I went to in Japan was also boring. No wonder the Japanese have the obligatory *enkai* (drinking party) after each one where they consume lavish amounts of liquor. Maybe they should try drinking before...

On my second night I went for a wander way past Shinjuku and maybe a little surprisingly ended up being the only *gaijin* around. A lot of the locals looked at me wondering what a *gaijin* was doing way out there by himself. Years later I realised that I had actually been wandering around Kabuki-cho, the very *risqué* red light district of Tokyo. So everyone probably thought I was a randy American sailor. Working up some bravado I went into Macdonald's by myself and was glad they had pictures I could point to. I wanted a chocolate milkshake but bought a coffee flavour instead (no, no, *chyokorieto*!) before heading back to the Hyatt.

When I got to the dining room late the next morning the ravenous hordes had generally departed so I sat next to a fellow Australian Karen and, not wanting to make myself noticed, ate a dessert and bread rolls that had been left by someone else. Just as I finished those a waiter came out and enquired, "Do you want *blekfastu?*" The word "yes" had scarcely rolled off my tongue before a plethora of staff had descended, and I had a veritable feast placed in front of me. Having to run off to a workshop I bolted it down in about three minutes flat. Too fast apparently because shortly afterwards I had my first attempt at a Japanese squat toilet. It's not one I wanted to repeat much.

Another point of Japanese toilet life I never got used to the cleaning ladies that walked around you while you stood at the urinal in a public toilet! <u>Note for potential travellers:</u> As toilet paper in public toilets is a rare beast it's best to keep a packet of tissues in your backpack at all times. They give plenty of them away in major cities, and if you're bored anytime you can use the number on the wrapper to call one of the local schoolgirls. Lest I stray too much on all things toilet, I will discuss more on this later in Chapter 37.

The last night in Tokyo there was a bash at the Australian Embassy. Presumably having to show that they were the lapdogs of Japanese economic might we weren't given anything to drink after arrival but were instead subjected to ninety minutes of boring speeches and information. The food wasn't bad but I didn't want to try the barbecued carrots - what a bizarre concept. These guys had obviously stayed too long and started to go feral. A group of a dozen or so of us settled in for the night before being pushed out the door. One employee got particularly upset about our impromptu indoor cricket game. What were they thinking? They get us all drunk, and then don't expect us to behave in a like manner...? I think it was Phillip Adams who once noted that young Australians travelling abroad tended to see the world as an extended pub-crawl - with behaviour to match.

On the way back to the subway two fellow Aussies, Shane and Charles, also took up the local custom of peeing in the street. This was really one of those cultural anomalies I found difficult to get my head around. It's okay to take a pee in public but not to blow your nose or eat while walking. We ended up in an apparently well-known bar called 'Pronto' which some locals didn't like and left. Hey, what do you know, it was my first experience of '*gaijin* fear'. When we began to sing the barman yelled at us (I'm told), "Stop making so much noise, you are not wanted here!"

So much for our first attempt at being ambassadors. Undeterred, and encouraged by previous performance, we moved onto...a *karaoke* lounge! About twelve people squeezed into a very small room singing everything from The Carpenters to Petshop Boys. Back at the Keio Plaza Hotel around 2.00am, and collapsed on the foyer stairs, some Canadians tried to convince us to come to a gay bar. With a twenty-minute walk and a 6.30am start I decided against it and struggled back to the Hyatt.

7: The Ghosts of Dead Fish...
Off to *inaka*

Try anything once, except incest and country dancing – Stephen Fry

Wake-up came far too early the next morning. I finished my packing and struggled down to the restaurant for a breakfast that contained some indiscernible ingredients, or maybe it was just the hangover. Jill, the Niigata prefectural contact person made sure we arrived early. We were meant to arrive in the lobby at 8am but didn't leave till after 9am. Hence the majority of us stood around too bleary eyed and hung-over to be excited about leaving. At this time all conversations generally consisted of mostly "Hey" and "ugh".

I sat in the car park outside in the sun drinking coffee trying to soak up some Vitamin E with Anne, who was posted to Niigata as well, while we waited. Later on Anne was to go on to teach playwriting in Ohio before finally landing a job as a scriptwriter on the smash hit TV series '24'. They even named a character after her. To our dismay, rather than organise a bus to Tokyo station the bright and chipper Jill, who obviously didn't go out carousing the night before, made us walk to Shinjuku station and connect on the subway to Tokyo station. After hanging on grimly to the overhead straps on the commuter 'Yamanoate Line' for half an hour we finally transferred at Tokyo, were bundled onto the Joetsu *shinkansen* (bullet train) and were away. The train didn't look that modern and I was quite sure it wasn't moving at bullet speed - but I think given my condition it was maybe just my perception.

As we moved out of Tokyo it was good to see blue sky and the countryside was very pretty. Fellow new teachers were getting off at various stations on the way to Niigata City. My stop was Nagaoka along with several others. Just before the train arrived, James - the British guy next to me, and I started to go into what most esteemed psychiatrists would instantly diagnose as 'denial'. We began to laugh and joke loudly, and construe Monty Python type scenarios on what would happen when we got off the train, or even indeed if we didn't! I decided I would mug the conductor, who was wearing what we considered a tasteful white captains uniform, change clothes and spend the rest of the year stalking the aisles of the bullet train. We figured we expended enough nervous energy to keep an average Japanese town lit for several days.

We were not the only ones. Most of our companions were nervous and when the train pulled into Nagaoka we could not delay the inevitable. At least I had the biggest welcome sign, complete with an intricately painted picture perfect right down to my baby blue eyes. It seems strange but in fact most *gaijin* teachers have blue eyes. No wonder that they like you to send pictures with your résumé. It seems the right 'look' is often much more important than the substance.

Three gentlemen from the Board of Education in Omi met me, and bowed deeply whilst offering their business cards. Only one of them spoke passable 'Ingurish'. Gripped by fear, I could not remember my greeting, that I had only just bothered to try and learn on the train, but it seemed to matter little to the happy threesome. We climbed into a waiting car but stopped on the outskirts of town for lunch at a place called Casa. I tried to impress them with my foreign language skills, and they seemed appreciative to know that it meant 'house' in Spanish. I later found out it means a close approximation of 'umbrella' in Japanese - one of the thirteen or so words I actually learnt in two years. With all the rain in Niigata I guess it was a pretty key word. I was not hungry and only ate some horrible aniseed jelly that I ordered thinking it was chocolate, and an ice cream soda that had a flavour I could not describe.

From Nagaoka the journey took about two and half-hours, but seemed much longer at the time, and conversation was difficult. Later I was told that they had never heard an Australian accent before, which didn't help at all. Along the way they informed me that that evening they would be having a welcome dinner for me.

"Do you mean an *enkai*?" I asked.

A distinct murmur went round the car.

"You know about *enkai*?" one replied, quite astounded.

I had made my first good impression.

Enkai in Japan are a cultural institution - basically dinner along with a lot of drinking. And I mean a lot. *Enkai* represent a place and time in Japan where normally unacceptable behaviour such as fawning, grovelling, speaking honestly, alcoholism, sexual harassment, vomiting, blowing your nose, and speaking in English, becomes quite okay. This is probably due in part to the large amount of alcohol imbibed by the participants – and because one is drunk you are not held accountable for your actions. I presume it would be perfectly okay to, in the space of one evening, abuse your superiors, grope the waitress and pee in the corner, and the next day everything would be hunky-dory. I never did stretch the envelope quite that far. For many Japanese, particularly *salarymen*, *enkai* seem to occur on a daily basis. If you were to put an entry for drinking in a Japanese-English dictionary I think it would probably resemble something like:

Drinking (du-ri-n-ki-n-gu) *see:* Enkai, Beer, Whisky, Sake, Vomit, Salarymen, Vending machines, Sexual harassment, or Karaoke

Finally we crossed the Hime River into Omi. The town had a huge sign saying, "Welcome to Omi-machi. Abandon all hope all ye who enter in." Well, maybe not. But sometimes I was to feel that it could have been appropriate. My first impression was almost like a town in the developing world. Steamy weather soaked into my pores. Jungle type growth cascaded down the mountainsides. Narrow streets meandered past small houses, dirty apartment blocks, and tiny shop fronts filled with expensive things.

For those at this stage grasping for maps (if the one provided is not comprehensive enough) or thirsting after details geographic - Omi is about two hundred and fifty kilometres north-west of Tokyo. It's located on the Japan Sea coast on the southern-western border of Niigata Prefecture tightly pinched in on its opposite flanks by the North Alps. The area also includes two small village areas, Oyashirazu and Ichiburi, located around six and thirteen kilometres respectively further down the coast from Omi. Formerly a municipal town in it's own right, it was squeezed into a merger with its neighbours, Itoigawa City and Nou Town, in March 2005.

The town gateway

Omi is a classic case of rural decline that is now rapidly affecting Japan like so many other nations. In the last thirty years the population has decreased from around 17,000 to a level of just over 10,000. After graduating from high school most young people are forced to move to major population centres for university study or in search of work. This is reflected in the population, with the majority of residents aged over 35. Concurrently the number of students attending Omi *chugakko* (where I would be based) has fallen from 568 to 344 in the last fifteen or so years.

As the situation continues to worsen so has local business. There are only a few small local shops, supermarkets and restaurants surviving, and no real entertainment facilities (movie theatre, bowling alley, amusement arcade, etc.). With the declining population many such facilities, such as the movie theatre and baseball stadium, have been closed and demolished in recent years. The main employer in Omi is Denka Ltd., with two large factories producing cement and chemicals. The other major provider of jobs is the town and governmental agencies with one civil servant for every 76 residents. However, given its location, the upcoming arrival of the Hokuriku *shinkansen*, the price of housing in major cities, plus the imminent retirement of the post-war generation, it may in time become a favoured destination with 'sea-changers' – a fad that does not yet seem to have hit Japan.

Our first stop was the Town Hall where the Board of Education is, and where I was to be based until school starts. I was shown my desk, albeit a temporary one until I was packed off to the school, then expected to give a small speech to my fellow workers, which is the normal cultural practice. All I could blurt out in English was that I was happy to be in Omi and looking forward to working with them, plus, "I don't know what else to say!" Perhaps I should have learnt some more Japanese - or in fact <u>any</u> Japanese.

From my introduction at the office I was taken back to my apartment to drop off my things. As we rounded the corner of Route 8 I saw two blocks. All I could think was "Please God, don't let it be the one on the right" - but unfortunately it was! It appeared as a big slab of concrete, and very dingy on the outside. It was on the third floor and contained basically very little. But no time to sort out, I was taken back to the office and sat at my desk with nothing to do. I fiddled with a Japanese word processor for awhile without understanding a thing before they felt sorry for me and asked a girl from another department to come talk to me. I don't know which department she came from but she spoke quite good English. After she left I never saw her again.

Another girl, whose name was Tomoe, also spoke to me for awhile in the hall just before I left. I guess she made an immediate impression because she did not possess the normal stereotypical build of a Japanese woman. We did see each other reasonably regularly before she got married and moved out of town shortly before I also left. The Board of Education office was not air conditioned at that time and made me glad I'd packed lots of deodorant. They couldn't believe how much I sweated. Neither could I...

After work I was taken to a local restaurant for a welcoming *enkai*. I was told that Mr. Kinokawa, the head of the Board of Education (hence, my boss), was sick in hospital. I was to visit him soon and pay my respects. I was not told what he was suffering from, but when I eventually did meet him I presumed (at that time) it was probably due to him consuming the profits of the part-time liquor outlet that I was told he ran from the front of his house. He was so pale I thought he was either already deceased and returned as a ghost, or that he was using the same potion as Michael Jackson. More on Kinokawa–san later. Anyway, I was promised there would be another party as soon as he recovered.

To start the evening I was presented with a bottle of Jose Cuervo Gold Tequila, because on the long car trip down I had said I didn't drink beer, plus a huge bouquet of flowers. Apparently they had sent one of the OL's out scouring for several hours trying to find the tequila. I thought it an excellent welcoming gift, except when it seemed they thought I should drink the whole bottle that night.

Right at the start of the night I made my first cultural *faux pas* - one of many I guess. After all the drinks are poured the Japanese have a toast of '*kanpai!*' and then drink together

"Nic-san, what do you say for a toast?" I was asked. I pondered a moment.

"Well, usually 'cheers', or 'bottoms up', or maybe even 'chin chin'"

The room went silent for a clearly definable moment. Some time later I found out the Japanese slang for 'chin-chin' and realised I had proposed a toast by shouting 'penis'...

The meal that night was huge, mostly Japanese of a style that I had not encountered before, apart from some chicken pieces and potato wedges. I considered that it would be culturally respectful to at least sample as much as possible, and as I kept on having strange substances put in front of me I, for better or worse, kept on consuming them - while trying to keep a straight face. After everyone had drunk too much, which is the usual thing as you quickly find out I was mostly just laughing and smiling as everyone spoke Japanese. I did keep hearing my predecessor's name a lot and I'm sure there were a lot of comparisons going on.

I tried to do everything right and seemed to make a favourable impression - especially with my use of chopsticks. The disposable variety of chopsticks (*hashi*) are commonly used at restaurants in Japan, and also as I later found out, China. Their enthusiasm for these is only slightly more than the Australian obsession for barbeques, plastic cutlery and paper plates from which everything either dribbles or falls off the side. So how many rainforests die for *hashi* each year? Without thoroughly researching anything I would take a stab most of Sarawak and Borneo plus parts of the Amazon Basin and New Guinea Highlands. To their credit most of the people I worked with or taught in Japan would bring their own chopsticks for lunch in a small case (*hashi bako*) and I soon found myself doing the same.

After the dinner I was taken back and abandoned outside my depressing concrete digs. I staggered up the stairs, unpacked (*see:* strewn around), and after some deep concentration finally rolled out my futon in anticipation of a good nights sleep. Unfortunately the *saké* and tequila, along with the ghosts of dead fish, came back to haunt me till early in the morning. I narrowly avoided an out of stomach experience and spent a restless night in my new home. Later I was posed the question "Do tequila and *sushi* mix?" Now with some experience I could answer truthfully "No. Except when they come out."

Bleary eyed and feeling like death warmed up I arose in the morning to the realisation I had forgotten to iron my last clean shirt. I gave up, wore my dirty one, and arrived two minutes late for work. They didn't seem to hold it against me - but seeing I did the same the following day maybe they did. It was really part of an effort to get them used to my idea of punctuality.

8: It's *Gomi* Day…! Settling in.

Getting money is like digging with a needle. Spending it is like water soaking into the sand
- Japanese Proverb

During the next couple of days I got taken on a couple of shopping trips, one for house wares and another for food. I was hoping they would buy me a bit more than what had been supplied, which was very little, but no such luck. They bought me a gas cooker, as Japanese households don't come with stoves, but anything else had to come out of my pocket. I was hoping they would at least purchase me a microwave and gas water heater for the kitchen, which Japanese households also don't come with, but soon realised I had fat chance of that. For such a rich town they had incredibly short pockets. Probably finances were my biggest source of angst with the town, and were to result in a penultimate battle *royale* shortly before I left.

So, it was the days of the 'super yen' and I had arrived with pathetic Aussie dollars (a.k.a. the South Pacific *peso*) in my pockets - and not too many of them. How to cope? Fortunately it was 'Gomi Day' shortly after I arrived. Every three months the town had a day for large garbage (*gomi*). I was to look forward to Omi *gomi* days. I even had a little song, "It's Omi Gomi Day, It's Omi Gomi Day…" You must note that times were still reasonably good in Omi around the time I was there and some good stuff was discarded regularly. The ruling Liberal Democratic Party (LDP) was throwing billions of yen into projects in rural areas to stoke the economy, and of course retain their hold on the voting imagination of the public. Omi at this time was building a huge music hall, auditorium, museum and library near the town hall. Not bad for a town of around 10,000 people…

At the time of writing it was noted that Japan's farmers could only produce about forty percent of the nation's needs, even below the government's own target of fifty percent, as compared to 1960 when Japan supplied seventy nine percent of its food. The rest, of course, is imported - much of it under strict quotas or high tariffs. Rice, the national grain, is still protected mainly by paying subsidised farmers to grow it through a tariff set at a stiff 490 percent. On a couple of trips to Thailand I actually brought back bags of rice with me. Talk about coals to Newcastle. Apart from the fabulous savings I loved the look on local's faces when I told them how much I had paid for it.

Rural reality is that all of Japan's primary industries - agricultural, forestry and fisheries - have declined dramatically in the past forty odd years - from 32.6 percent of the working population in 1960 to 4.4 percent in 2000. By 2001 agricultural production in rural Japan was down to 1.3 percent of GDP from 9.0 percent in 1960. However what has grown in the non-urban areas, in almost inverse proportion to demographics, is the size and clout of Japan's highly organised agricultural and rural establishment (*see:* lobby group). This requires the LDP to actually demonstrate that it is supporting rural residents if it wants to remain in power. Hence the manna from heaven in my little town.

My first Saturday in town I got up early and embarked on what I later realised was a fruitless and idiotic search for an English newspaper. I gave up on my quest when I noticed all this great 'garbage' lying around and quickly decided to score some. It was amazing how many stereos and TV's had been thrown out. I was actually hoping to find a new fridge. The apartment only possessed a tiny little bar fridge that barely functioned in the humidity of Omi. The day before I had lashed out with my meagre funds on a small container of ice cream for ¥1,000 and later found it turned to milkshake. The really sad part was that it was good old-fashioned three-flavour ice-cream, not the fancy-pants variety you find in Tokyo.

Apparently at places like 'Ice Cream City' in Namco Nanja Town in Tokyo you can find an extraordinary range of flavours that include, Raw Fish, Horseflesh, Goat, Whale, Shark Fin, Noodle, Oyster, Abalone, Seaweed, Curdled Bean (a.k.a. *natto*) Lettuce and Potato, Tomato, Sesame, Soybean and Dried Kelp Spinach, Silk, Chicken, Tulip, and lastly Garlic – which is named after Dracula. Ha, nice marketing touch there.

In the regard to refrigeration my luck wasn't in but certainly proved so in other ways. I walked home with some chairs, which washed up well, and carted a nice <u>pink</u> desk home on top of my granny bike, which I carried up to the third floor by myself.

People must have thought strangely of the new *gaijin* in town. Certainly my new neighbours in 'Cellblock H' showed me some glances askew. Especially when I carted everything up by myself. Most of my furnishings over my two-year tenure were to come from the '*gomi* shop' which made for a rather eclectic, but I prefer to call it a Bohemian, style of furnishing.

Seeing there was no hanging space I had to set up a makeshift wardrobe with two small bookshelves and a rusty old pole from the jungle out the back. The apartment actually had enormous amounts of cupboard space - just no wardrobes. This of course was all absolutely normal Japanese housing but still a mystery to me at the time. The place was bigger than average apartments and had wonderful sea views. Pity the balcony faced Highway 8 instead of the ocean. Omi meant 'blue sea' in Japanese and that was certainly the case. I had no air conditioning, but hey, being Australian the thought of winter caused me more concern.

I sat and reflected upon my current fortune. I was over fifty kilometres from the last bastion of civilisation (McDonalds), at least ninety minutes from a city of any major proportion - to my way of thinking, more than six hours separated me from the nearest international airport, a place to find cappuccino might as well as been on Pluto and I was the only westerner in town. Things could maybe get lonely. But I could gaze straight out my front windows at the ocean, and to the rear the mountains. Millions of Californian realtors would kill for this sort of view. Maybe, just maybe, things were going to be okay.

The view from the back

And the view from the front

9: Bureaucrats, the YMCA and Mr. Meat Warehouse

The less people know about how sausages and laws are made, the better they'll sleep at night. -
Otto von Bismarck

In the morning I finally received my first piece of mail. I opened it excitedly only to find that it read, "Congratulations, you may already be a winner..." With no let up in the hot sticky climate I was making use of the beach and had been swimming everyday. The Sea of Japan is lovely - despite its lack of surf and the presence of stony beaches. Maybe I was spoiled growing up in Australia but I do like not having to reach for a bottle of Betadine every time I come home from the beach. At least you don't have to watch out for hypodermic needles in Japan. Either way, I decided one of my first purchases should be a sturdy pair of sandals, if I could find my size.

I was also having just a wee bit of trouble with the whole slipper concept too. For those not in the know, in Japan you're generally not allowed to wear your shoes inside, but must wear the slippers provided. These come in sizes 3-6, which always leaves about ten centimetres of your sock feet hanging off the back. These slippers are specially designed to help you 'slip', e.g. down stairs. Once inside and wearing your slippers you must be aware of what I once saw referred to by Dave Barry as, 'the invisible slipper border checkpoint'. This is a point in the building where for some reason you must change slippers, or abandon them altogether. This is especially so when entering the restroom. Toilet slippers come with higher heels so that, I presume, drunken males will naturally lean toward the bowl and avoid 'spillage'. Just like in the west the Japanese male attaches a sprinkler to his knob before he goes out drinking. I once met someone who wanted to climb Mt. Fuji in toilet slippers. I thought that was pretty stupid. You know, wanting to climb Mt. Fuji. More details on that in Chapter 29. Even some fastidious car owners declare their vehicles *do-kin* and make passengers change into slippers before getting in.

After three nights of being taken out to eat I finally cooked my first major meal - macaroni and bolognaise sauce, which were one of the few recognisable things I could find in the local 'Hapi' supermarket down the road. I subsequently woke up in the night with stomach cramps but I'm not sure if it was that or one of the alien substances that I had ingested over the preceding days.

This was also the time that I began my first real struggle with bureaucracy, something that the Japanese have down to an art form. My phone was not connected yet and for some reason I was to have a different number from my predecessor. I rang NTT (the telephone company, or should I say monopoly) from a phone box on the Friday morning and they said they wouldn't accept credit cards for the overseas calls I wanted to make. I tried with a pocketful of coins on Friday night at a couple of public phones (one was even marked IDD) but it seemed Australia was not on their Top Forty list. Later I found out that you have to use a special grey phone for overseas calls, and the nearest one of those was about five kilometres away at the port in neighbouring Itoigawa. My phone finally was connected a week later.

On a later trip back to Japan my application for a visa went something like this,

I put in my visa application and passport with a supposed two-day turnaround. Yeah, the American embassy told me that too with my student visa a few years previously. A couple of days later the phone rang and a Japanese voice asked for 'Mr. Nikorasu'.

"I'm sorry, we need a return date."

"But I'm buying a return fare in Japan."

"Oh yes, we understand (<u>I remember those words</u>!), but we need a return date."

A long conversation ensued which I knew I wouldn't win. All they wanted was *tatemae* - a show of a return date, whether it actually existed or not.

The next day I cut and pasted a fax from my agent in Japan and posted it to them. Two days the later the phone rang for 'Mr. Nikorasu' again.

"Your details do not match."

"Yes, I'm leaving earlier. I rebooked my dates."

"Oh yes, I see. But we need full details."

GRRR. By this time I had booked all my flights using some frequent flyer points to get home. I typed out all the details in length and faxed it off. After ten days there was no reply, so I faxed again asking what the delay was.

A few hours later and the telephone rings to life again...

"Hello, Mr. Nikorasu, we are still waiting for your details."

"But I faxed them ten days ago."

"Ah yes, but that was to another section."

"But you just got my last fax."

"Yes, but they get very angry if they must bring it over" (*Note:* this is about a thirty-second walk)

"So, they didn't give you my other fax?"

"No, we are very sorry."

(With frustrated air) "Well, what's the visa section fax and I'll send it there."

"I'm sorry we do not have a fax. You must post it…"

I posted it off the next day. I called them three days later and they said they would be sending the visa out the next day. I collected all my tickets, kept my fingers crossed and finally received it with about three days left.

Once again I was forced to ask the rhetorical question - how did Japan get to be such an economic superpower?

At least it was by economic means, with a large dosage of American intervention in the form of aid and defence assistance, and not by military conquest. I was reminded of this when I was taken to the Mayor's office to be introduced and pay my respects. I could say little, but couldn't help thinking about Basil Fawlty's exhortation, "Don't mention the war!" So I didn't - but the mayor did. Doing some research I found out that there had been Australian POWs 'working' in Omi during the war. From an historical sense this really intrigued me. I couldn't find out any more real information about the matter so I decided it best not to pursue it further.

School did not start for some time so I was left sitting bored at my desk in the Board of Education office each day with little to do. I just mostly wrote letters, played computer games and thought nefarious thoughts about a couple of the office girls. I also thought of doing some Japanese study, however briefly, but couldn't get motivated. In the end I left the tape running through on my Walkman, put my feet up on the desk and hoped, as have thousands of lazy students before me, it would just somehow cerebrally soak in.

I loved lunchtimes there. At noon a musical tone would sound throughout the building. They would turn the lights off, put the radio on and eat lunch at their desks. Some would even put their heads down on the desk and nap. I was given lunch most days when I first arrived. I wasn't really sure where it came from or who paid for it - but later found that my budget was the most likely candidate, probably along with everyone else's meal. One lunch was so big I had leftovers in the fridge for days. At the end of the lunch break another tone sounded, the lights went back on, the radio was turned off, the computer games ceased, and it was back to work. For someone who seems to now consistently work through his short lunchtime this memory is still a fond one.

Around this time there were deep discussions in the office on how I should be formally referred to. The Japanese, perhaps more than any other people, have long taken notice of social standing in their language. As an example - French speakers must decide between the familiar '*tu*' and the formal '*vous*' in addressing someone in the second person, but in Japanese there are a multitude of ways to say I or you, dictated by age, circumstance, gender, social position and other factors. Verb endings, adjectives and entire words also can differ according to the situation. This is serious stuff and mistakes have been deadly. Way back in 1975 it was reported that two workers, Kunihiro Fukuda,

30, and Tomohiko Okabe, 27, were having a drink in a Tokyo bar. The story goes that "...although Mr. Okabe was younger, he had entered the company first and had taken to addressing his colleague in a manner usually reserved for someone younger, calling him Fukuda instead of Fukuda-san. Mr. Fukuda protested. But Mr. Okabe said, "What's wrong if a senior guy calls his junior in this way?" Enraged, Mr. Fukuda grabbed his colleague by the neck and beat him to death".

It was never to be that hairy for me but after some serious discussion it was considered that the best way to refer to me would be *Nikorasu-sensei*. *Sensei* is the honorific term for teacher, plus a few other occupations, and 'Nikorasu' is the phonetic spelling of my name in Japanese. I told them that plain 'Nic' (or 'Niku') would suffice, but these suggestions were ignored. I would discover late one night in the midst of a drinking session that there were very sound reasons for this. In a literal translation *niku* means meat. Hence *niku-san* means Mr. Meat. In some cases this might be considered a real advantage. But wait, this gets better. My surname comes out in Japanese as '*Kura*'. Combined with my first name I would be known as 'meat warehouse' or 'meat saddle'. Some *gaijin* friends seized upon this revelation with glee and referred to my abode as 'The Meat Locker'.

In Itoigawa I found myself at a pseudo-department store, then known as 'Nichii', and decided to browse around. In the distance I spied a petite blonde-haired woman. Knowing this to be an unlikely sighting in these parts I was intrigued and drew closer. As I did so I realised that it was Wendy, one of the two new teachers living in Itoigawa. It was with great relief to finally speak to someone who could communicate in better than broken English. We unburdened ourselves with a brief recap of each other's stories, both good and bad. Deciding it would take too much time, we sallied forth back to her place for coffee.

She and Rananda, the other new teacher, lived in the same tiny apartment building. Although both British Wendy and Rananda were like chalk and cheese, and their spats would often prove an amusing respite from other cares. It was at this time that I discovered that I was the only foreign male teacher in the area, the only other four *gaijin* in the area being female. Over the next year it was never decided whether I was the token male in the group, or an honorary female.

This particular night Rananda and Wendy were going out to explore the town by themselves and they, maybe in pity, invited me along. We wandered around looking for a particular bar where the host was supposed to speak English but couldn't locate it. For awhile we drifted around the streets unsure of where to go, and then at one stage looked up to see lights on top of a building. We rode the elevator up which some drunks had vacated as we got on and who had gesticulated to us in some strange manner. Upon arrival we found a rooftop bar which was a bit like a beer garden. We ordered drinks somehow - none of us having the remotest grasp of the language, and for some reason I was brought a full bottle of whisky. Not sure what the protocol was I decided to play it safe and began to consume the contents in as short a space of time as possible. A short while later the bar owner hurried over, and apologising profusely, removed the offending bottle from my grasp. I think they just may have got me confused with someone else. In Japan regular clientele will buy full bottles and leave them with the barman until their next time in. With the lack of foreign males in those parts I wondered how they could be confused. Or maybe it belonged to an itinerant male sailor who occasionally came through the local port.

Around 11pm we got kicked out at the closing and now fortified by the strength called alcohol we crashed through the doors of a...*karaoke* bar. The drunks at the bar, who appeared to have never set eyes on white folk before, joyously welcomed us. They even insisted on us singing – despite the bar not actually having any English songs. We tried a woeful version of YMCA ("Hey you don't <u>really</u> need to know the words to that!") but it fell pretty flat when we realised soon into our presentation that there were other words apart from "YMCA! YMCA!" Finally about 2am our new friends bid us farewell and we stumbled outside seeking to ascertain the direction of 'home'. We thought it was an expensive night - even <u>after</u> our new friends had coughed up for at least half of our bill, but we would soon learn. After bidding goodnight to the girls I located my bike and rode carefully in the direction of what I hoped was Omi…

10: Ode to my *jitensha*

All who wander are not lost. - JRR Tolkien

At the end of my second week I had my first Friday afternoon off and was informed, much to my delight, I would have every Friday afternoon off. I decided to try out the old *jitensha* (bike) left to me in the apartment and headed to Itoigawa, the next town over. But maybe I should tell you about my bike experiences first....

I fell in love with mountain bikes years ago. I was living in Santa Cruz, California and everybody was riding them. Considering the terrain of the campus where I was studying this was not surprising. I acquired my first mountain bike, a Giant 'Iguana', through a back scratching deal with a friend who was shortly to embark on an internship to Ireland. I simply had to go to her ex-boyfriend's place, break his thumbs, re-arrange his face, and then steal her bike back. Okay, that's a lie. I just had to give him the impression that I was the new ardour in her life, and that her bike was now a required commodity which I would be minding for her. Fortunately he was a good six inches shorter than me so he didn't have any qualms about that. He was also pretty spun out on some illegal substance when I knocked on the door. He probably thought the next day, "Hey, like, where's the bike man?"

As soon as I went back to Australia I traded in my old ten speed racer and bought an 'Iguana' of exactly the same style and colour. After graduation and my move interstate to near the Australian Alps I spent many weekends discovering its back tracks and unspoiled landscapes. When I left there and went home to university for grad work I was now minus a car. Hence the Iguana became my sole transport. As I prepared to leave for Japan I dismantled it, put it in storage, and bid it a fond farewell, as my meagre baggage allowance would not allow it to accompany me. Having been assigned to Omi, sandwiched between the sea and mountains, was a definite bonus for someone like me who loved sailing as much as mountain biking. Not that I ever saw anything remotely resembling a sailing boat in Omi while I was there. But I eagerly looked forward to buying myself a new bike in Japan - the land of techno-wizardry. So many inventions pour out of this land it's hard to keep track of. The one I liked the most were the underpants you could wear for six days in a row. The concept went something like this – you rotated them 120 degrees for three days, turned them inside out, and then repeated the process for another three days. On the seventh day one rested and washed I suppose.

I had noted on my JET application about my interest in cycling. Obviously having paid attention to this, upon arrival my supervisor proudly handed me my 'assigned bike' - a five year old *mama chari* (granny bike) with rusty chain. "Okay", I thought, "this will do for a few days till I find myself something a lot better". With some leisure time on my hands I shocked the town by riding the old bike to Oyashirazu in my first week - the gruelling distance of some seven kilometres, via the winding and narrow Route 8. But I dared not attempt much more than that.

After a couple of weeks I was still riding the *mama chari* and still no closer to a new bike. I had dropped hints to the Board of Education, but no one had listened. No shop in my small town stocked mountain bikes. I rode to Itoigawa and finally found a shop that stocked them. I then realised exactly how much taller than the average Japanese I was as the proprietor showed me bikes that looked more like they needed training wheels. In my non-existent Japanese I thanked him for his time, rode home on the increasingly gruesome granny bike, then threw myself on the bed and cried till I dehydrated.

I took a trip to Joetsu City and couldn't find anything with a price tag that had less than six zeros on it. Enquiries on the internet turned up naught. Finally the local English conversation teacher mentioned she had a friend who might be able to order me one from a catalogue. I picked one with the largest frame I could see and crossed my fingers. Even at what seemed an exorbitant price. But I was becoming desperate.

A couple of days hence I attended a seminar in Takada. Another teacher turned up with exactly the same bike I had ordered. He let me take it for a spin and all I could think was, "Oh no Koji". Well, not that actual expression because I didn't know it yet, or even what a Koji was. That's just a metaphor for what my thoughts were - but hopefully you get my drift anyway. It was far too small for me. After the seminar we had the obligatory *enkai*, and later we drifted down Nakamachi toward a *karaoke* bar.

As I stumbled down the road in a drunken haze I passed Maruishi Cycles - a small shoebox of a bike store. I blinked and rubbed my eyes. Was that a mountain bike sitting out the front all by itself? A <u>real</u> mountain bike? A real *gaijin* <u>size</u> mountain bike. I moved closer and checked. Lawdy, lawdy, it was. I hadn't drunk too much *sake*. Well, actually I had - but that didn't impair my judgement in this case. This lonely looking machine was covered in cobwebs and dirt, it had flat tyres and other signs of a long wait for a new owner. But there it was - a genuine 'Scott, Made in USA!' mountain bike. I approached the owner who was just closing up shop and asked him in slurred broken Japlish how much. "*go-sen*" came the reply. Huh? I asked him to write it down. ¥5,000 the paper said. In an instant my fingers flashed toward my back pocket as I thought, "Please, don't let me have drunk my money away!" My prayers were answered. I handed over the cash out of my wallet and the good shop owner set about adjusting everything to suit my size and pumping up the tyres.

I'm not sure why it was so cheap. I think either, A) he was scared of the drunken *gaijin* and wanted to be quickly rid of him, or B) no Japanese person could get their leg over the seat, making it effectively dead stock to be let go at a large discount.

The next morning I called to cancel my catalogue order. Too late, it had already arrived. No cancellation allowed. That's not the way Japanese do business, supposedly. Through some quick phone calls I managed to on sell it to Joanne, another newly arrived teacher. I proudly cleaned my 'Scott, Made in USA!' and thus began a new love affair. My only one. Well, in that context it could be said.

I fitted all kinds of snazzy appendages, and rode my bike everywhere. I discovered new tracks and new ways of getting places. I rode to and from Joetsu City a few times. I began riding to my visit schools seven and thirteen kilometres away and when my town found out I was promptly banned from doing so because it was considered *abunai* (dangerous). Even when the snows arrived in January I would ride to school most days. I was taken aside by a teacher and had the inherent dangers pointed out to me. I told them it was okay because I had 'snow tyres'. With a knowing nod, and a quick *wakarimashita* (I understand), it was then okay with them too.

I rode around nearby Sado Island twice. The second time I missed the ferry by a few minutes and slept on the concrete outside the terminal overnight waiting for the first boat out in the morning. I was the only transport on board and all the port employees waiting to direct traffic off the ferry laughed as a lone *gaijin* on his bike came rumbling out from the hold. My students admired my dexterity of being able to ride through the rail underpass near the school without having to push up one side, and tried to emulate me on their *mama chari*.

My gruesome *mama chari* was now mainly used for shopping trips or left at the *eki* (train station) when I went away for weekends. It was borrowed by Tom, a friend from the next town, about a year after I arrived and later it vanished from out the front of Itoigawa *eki*. Its *gomi* pile replacement, which was in much better condition, did the same a few months later from Omi *eki*. The new bike I had on sold to Joanne disappeared from outside her adult English class one night, but after an 'intensive' police search was recovered from a *gomi* pile a few weeks later. As far as I know Maruishi-san (the bike shop owner in Joetsu) is still plying his trade on Nakamachi, and still afraid of drunk *gaijin* perusing his stock.

Anyhow – I digress, more on the bike later. I was coping okay with the humid weather - when I didn't have to dress up, which was pretty much most of the time. I was hoping I would score an air conditioner during the *gomi* collection but no such luck. However, months later I discovered that I had a storage space in the basement. Amongst all the rubbish and assorted porno mags left behind by the previous occupant there was also an air conditioner. After my previous experience in the office I went out and bought a new short sleeve shirt at Nichii - which was a cheap shirt at an expensive price. Fortunately they had one in my size - just.

It's about here that I have to tell you about Kinya Yamagishi, my liaison from the Board of Education. It had fallen somehow upon his shoulders to take care of anything in relation to the resident English teacher, in this case me. Kinya-san, as he was affectionately known by many, was a hardy soul with a heart of gold. Like most middle-aged males in the town, he did not mind a cigarette, plus a drink or three. Despite the salaryman hours he worked, Kinya was a true family man with two lovely teenage daughters and a thoughtful spouse. He would often go far beyond his call of duty and I must've caused him grief on more than one occasion I fear.

After a couple of weeks Kinya-san, his wife, and Mrs. Asaba - an office lady from the board who had bought me the tequila for my welcome *enkai*, came around to cook me a meal. From what I gathered there was a *matsuri* (festival) taking place on the beach in front of my apartment and I would get a ringside view of the *o-hanabi* (fireworks). They set up a cooker on the coffee table and proceeded to conjure up an enormous meal. Actually I first thought it was a coffee table and later discovered that in Japan it's really the dining table. The food they cooked was delicious. Lots of meat and sauce and vegetables, but nothing too strange or inedible. Of course it was all washed down with copious amounts of alcohol. I couldn't believe how much these people drank. One friend was taken out and left in a haze so often he referred to his primary occupation as 'indentured drinker'. Courtesy of Sydney Airport Duty Free I introduced them to Southern Comfort which didn't seem to affect Mrs. Yamagishi or Mrs. Asaba - until they tried to stand up.

Kinya-san and Mrs. Asaba (plus the Southern Comfort)

At 9pm the fireworks started which were a delight. Mainly I would guess because I've never had fireworks outside my window before. I would have liked to walk down the beach to see more of the *matsuri* but I think the others just wanted to prostrate themselves on the *tatemae* mats. I was left with plenty of beer, *saké*, *sushi*, etc., in my tiny fridge and also was given a bottle of bourbon as a gift. My alcohol collection was beginning to get very large. After they left on unsteady legs I went for a walk down to the beach but most of the festival stuff was being packed up by then. The next day I spent in recovery mode and getting ready to head off to Niigata City on the Monday for a prefectural orientation. My diary entry read, "Bet it's boring..."

11: C'mon train. Dancing on the bridge...

If something goes wrong...blame the guy who can't speak English.
- Homer Simpson

I had been in Omi two weeks and finally settling in a little bit. Despite a lot of early teething problems I was enjoying myself. Many nights I found myself looking out my kitchen window at the sunset thinking how lucky I was. During summer the sun would set in a golden orange orb over the distant Noto Peninsula. Almost like something out of "Apocalypse Now"...but without the napalm.

On the Monday of my third week I was awake at 5.10am to bright sunshine. I wish they had daylight saving in Japan. Call me picky, but the sun coming up as early as 4am tended to bother my sleep patterns somewhat. But getting up so early this day meant I was actually ready on time to go to the conference in Niigata City. Well in fact I was even early, something very distinctly unlike me. Setsuko Watanabe, who was to be my school supervisor, drove me up to Niigata City rather than taking the chance of me losing myself somewhere along the two hundred and fifty odd kilometre journey.

Actually this orientation wasn't as boring as the one in Tokyo - I was even able to duck out and do some exploring, though we were not actually meant to. We stayed in the Niigata Kyoiku Centre that was way out amongst the rice paddies bordering Niigata City and in some ways resembled a prison farm. This was particularly so in regard to the rules which included a curfew of 10pm. If you were late you got a stern talking to from a short bald Japanese man with a big flashlight. Not that you could understand what he said anyway, but the language of discipline and/or anger can at times seem universal.

The first night we had a beach party at Kobari which was entertaining with swimming, drinks, a BBQ and dancing. It probably would have been better if someone had brought more than two CD's. I couldn't help noticing a couple of the local bikini clad beauties. It was not so much their attractiveness that caught my eye, but their long white fluffy socks and high heels as they tottered down the beach. These socks have been *de rigeur* for Japanese teenage females now for some years. The socks don't have any elastic so they are kept up with 'Sock Touch'. This is another of those amazing Japanese inventions. High school girls, who refuse to wear anything other than short skirts that end somewhere about the belly button, always carry this. It looks akin to a glue stick and its contents are stuck on the leg above the ankles to make sure their oversize socks don't fall down. Presumably these girls legs are always well waxed. Otherwise this useful item may also double for personal jobs like bikini lines.

Tuesday night we went to a famous *matsuri* in Niigata. I'm not sure of its name but the tourist blurb referred to it as "A large ballad draining". Perhaps 'draining beer' might be more appropriate. First stop was the Niigata International Friendship Centre where we were kitted out in traditional Japanese *yukata*. The intention from there was to go out and try some traditional Japanese dances with about 30,000 other people on the Bandai Bridge. Most of us before setting out were thinking, "This must be a bloody big bridge."

Of course you couldn't go anywhere in Japan without booze. Each different group wheeled a float along in front chockfull of beer and other 'relaxants'. We were allocated our own trolley, but tragedy struck at the first gutter when the wheels collapsed under the weight. Some hardy volunteers offered to carry the contents instead, and then as the night progressed demonstrated how to dance with a fan in one hand and a six pack under the other arm. In the end we weren't allowed anywhere near the bridge and got stuck dancing incompetently somewhere in a back alley.

Our little dancing group wasn't going anywhere in a hurry, so Steve, a British fellow newcomer, and I scuttled inconspicuously off down the road by ourselves and found a Mexican restaurant. When we shuffled back, roughly forty minutes later, our group had moved about fifty metres. Many of our compatriots had disappeared into nearby bars and coffee shops having become disillusioned with their progress and repeating the exact same steps in fairly much the same place.

The *matsuri* ran late and before we realised it had to make a dash for the last train. The locals were treated to the sight of about hundred *gaijin* running madly past them down city streets en route to the *eki*. I lost the sash that held the cloth together and ran wildly through the streets with only my shorts on and the *yukata* billowing in the breeze. We apparently set a new record at the centre, fifty-seven people late in one night! The little bald man was kept very busy remonstrating as we trickled in. One bloke (Jack, the mad Canadian) supposedly got lost, took a wrong turn, and almost spent the night sleeping in a rice paddy. Not many of us actually believed that story. Remember that name because it will feature later. Jack was like a puppy dog. He was adorable and well loved, but always seemed to be getting into trouble.

The conference finished on Wednesday at lunchtime but unfortunately nobody in Omi remembered to come and collect me as they'd promised. Another teacher was meant to have made the journey but they apparently forgot he was still on vacation. This meant I was eventually left by myself sitting on the centre steps looking like a lonely Norman Rockwell boy as my peers were spirited away. After a couple of quick phone calls to the board of education in Omi the cavalry showed up about 2:30 in the form of someone's distant relative who studied at Niigata University. They had decided to put me on the train and this guy's job was to get me to the station. He bundled me into his car and then I was treated to a mad rush down narrow back roads in order to make the train on time.

As is the case with many of the locals his car was full of soft toys. Japan, it sometimes appears, has given up on airbag technology. Instead most Japanese have chosen to opt for soft toys to cushion the blow of their skull breaking apart on the car dashboard. Why else would Japanese cars contain so many soft toys in every conceivable crevice or space? Personally I find the thought of a soft fluffy Snoopy covered in blood and impregnated with bone shards quite revolting. He didn't inspire me with confidence as he clicked his tongue, scratched his head, talked to himself, and made several fast u-turns. But he came through for me and saw me onto the train with five minutes to spare.

Once aboard I spent ages looking for my seat. I showed my ticket to several people who just muttered and pointed further down the carriage. Eventually I gave up and just plonked myself in a vacant seat hoping it would be okay. Along the way I discovered I was in the unreserved section. No wonder people didn't understand me. It was an express train so I had to get off in Itoigawa where I was met by a very repentant Kinya-san with a gift of selected pastries and a lot of apologetic bowing.

Discussions about baseball had been going on in the office since I arrived. The Japanese are totally enamoured with the sport and were glad to hear that I had some experience in it. In fact baseball is more of a religion and Hideo Nomo, the LA Dodgers pitcher (at that time anyway), its deity. By 2004 it was a holy trinity that also included Hideki Matsui of the New York Yankees and Ichiro Suzuki of the Seattle Mariners, both of whose every move was closely scrutinized by every single media outlet in Japan. Every news bulletin you could get reports like, "This is Ichiro parking his car" and "It was reported that Matsui took a dump after a large meal of spaghetti".

In vain hope I was asked by Kinya-san, "Are you a pitcher?" He was then doubling as manager of the local team and was obviously searching for some relief in regard to their aging forty-two year-old hurler. I confessed that it was not my *forte* and the spark of optimism sadly disappeared from his eyes. That night he appeared on my doorstep with an invitation to come out with the team. I could only watch from the bench as Omi demolished an invitation team from the Denka factory 13-0. Omi take their baseball very seriously and many years ago were even host to a semi-professional team. That night I was told that later in the month I was going to Niigata City with the team for the Niigata prefectural championships where Omi was to have the honour of representing the local Joetsu region. In what capacity I was tagging along in I was completely unsure of at this time.

12: Naked boys and ¥en...

When the character of a man is not clear to you, look at his friends
- Japanese Proverb

On the Saturday following orientation I was up fairly early which was not good considering the day I had ahead. I had, obviously during a time of drunken weakness, invited a bucket-load of people to a 'beach party', some of whom I could not even remember. Most likely because of the plethora of brain cells that I had left in the vicinity of Kobari Beach and the Bandai Bridge. Nonetheless, quite a number trickled in over the afternoon. We spent a few hours at the beach and the large group of *gaijin* caused somewhat of a stir amongst the locals. Lots of kids were walking back and forth, probably in an attempt to identify which one was to be their new *sensei*. Some of the boys played in the water in front of us and whilst doing so a couple of them decided to do backward flips and show us their party sausages. What this was meant to prove I'm not totally sure, but I knew then that I was going to be in for a heck of a year.

About midnight, and with everyone being well lubricated, it was decided that a skinny dip was the go. I unfortunately lost my shorts to the incoming tide and was forced to wander bare-assed up and down the beach in my t-shirt till my friend Alan found them. Even at that time of night there were still people on the beach and I hate to think what kind of impression we were giving. Still, if it's common practice for 12-year-old boys to flash their new teacher, I guess our behaviour was not too out of character.

Shortly thereafter, and presuming that I would attend fully clothed, Kinya-san had all his family around along with me for the *Obon* festival. Each year in August families make their way home to ancestral towns to greet the souls of departed relatives, or something like that, and he kindly invited me around to get loaded with them - as is the case with all celebrations in Japan.

The cultural immersion continued unabated as the following Monday afternoon I was taken to a 'coming of age' party at the town hall. This function entails the mayor inviting all the young people in the district who have reached the ripe age of twenty years old to a celebration. There are a few drinks and nibbles, plus the mayor has to give the usual long-winded address. In recent years older Japanese have complained how young people have begun to misbehave rather badly at these kind of functions. Well, nothing too over the top occurred this day, and it was pretty boring really, but interesting to see the parallels of Japanese twenty year olds - some trendies, some extroverts, wallflowers, geeks, etc., etc. At the end they gave out three prizes - what for I don't know. I was hypothesizing it was for nicest suit, biggest breasts, and most conservative (viz, old people would never complain about their behaviour).

Kinya-san and his affable work colleague Mizushima-san continued to do their best to show me many of the local sights and also keep me busy. Well, there was not much to do in the office and it was quite obvious I wasn't going to try and do anything useful – like study Japanese. One day they took me for a drive up to the 'Fossa Magna' geological museum near Itoigawa, which was fairly interesting. The highlight was the fossilised dinosaur poo, which I'd never seen before. At least not that I was aware of. I could best describe it as round stones that look like they had come from a very large and long-constipated rabbit. The next time I caught up with Wendy and Rananda they mentioned they had also been taken there. What was the first question out of their mouth? "Did you see the fossilised dinosaur poo?" These ancient excreta have obviously taken on a stature of legendary proportions in those parts.

Coming back from our viewing of the aforementioned stone faeces (great name for a rock band) we had lunch at a cafe called 'Bon Jour' on Highway 8 that I'd wanted to check out since I'd arrived. We all had pizza and for once it was role reversal time as the others struggled to eat their pizza with a fork. I now realised how I must look trying to eat Japanese food with *hashi* in front of them. Mizushima-san proved particularly non-adept, lifting each piece balanced on top of his fork then trying to suck/chew on it. I bet his dry cleaner was happy the next day.

During the week we went for an afternoon drive to visit Kinokawa-san in hospital and I was a little shocked on my first impression. He was very gaunt and pale and from what I make out he had some sort of head problem. When I asked what ailed him he just tapped his very bald head and said, "Brain". He spoke little English so there were quite a few awkward moments as we struggled to communicate. He asked what Japanese food I liked and so I just listed off as many names as I could remember. My reply included *ramen* so he insisted to Kinya-san and Mizushima that he be taken to the local shops. Bundled up in his dressing gown and shod with hospital slippers he coasted shakily down the aisles of the local supermarket surveying the comestibles on offer. He purchased ten packets of instant *ramen* and presented them to me in addition to the cheese and baked goods that he had already given me when I arrived. At least I wouldn't run out for awhile.

It was around this time that I discovered that Kinokawa had always insisted on the previous foreign teachers calling he and his wife *otōsan* (father) and *okasan* (mother). Apparently they often stayed around his place to get relief from the dormitory and I think Shanti used the Kinokawa's spare bedroom as a free 'love motel' with his Australian girlfriend. Legend had it that Shanti was so tight with his money that he would tape over the holes in his shoes and also cut his own hair. I later discovered that 'barber' and 'hospital' sound much like the same word in Japanese (*byoin* – depending on what syllabus you put the emphasis). It almost seems to cost as much for a haircut as a stay in hospital - but you don't get your hair blow-dried for an hour in hospital.

Kinokawa's wife was also very sick at the same time and staying at a different hospital a long way away. As mentioned, they had used to run a liquor shop from the front room of their house and the rumour was that they had probably consumed too much of the profits. I saw little of them for the first couple of months because of their sickness and we never became close. I guess having an apartment made things easier for me but they seemed to find it difficult that I didn't behave in quite the same way as the others, nor did I come by regularly. He finally retired the following year.

My theory on the major reason why previous teachers were all kept in the dormitory was because they were all single males. In Japan there are few single males that can cope by themselves. This explained why some of the ladies in the building brought me meals quite regularly in the first few weeks. I'm sure they were thinking to themselves, "That poor man, he must be wasting away in there by himself". I was quizzed in at the office about how often I ate out, how often I cooked, and what I cooked. When I told them I cooked for myself nearly every night I heard one of the office ladies utter *"sugoi"* (wonderful/amazing). I decided to play to the crowd and added, "Yes, and I also clean, and do my washing, and ironing..." which elicited even more profound cries of astonishment. The word travelled and meals stopped coming to my door. I was pleased that they had thought to be so concerned.

Money started to become pretty tight before my first pay arrived. I hadn't budgeted for all the things I had to buy for Casá del Klar, plus the ¥/A$ (a.k.a. 'Super Yen' / 'South Pacific Peso') exchange was absolutely horrendous. I hoped I could stretch my savings as far as the trip to Sado Island for the Earth Festival on the following weekend, and also that my first payday would come soon.

One night I got taken out to dinner to somebody's house. I was introduced but later could never remember his name, only that it was a fine elderly man and some members of his family. Kinya-san reminded me some time afterwards in conversation that the man was in fact his father. I was the first *gaijin* to visit his house and he remarked how very well mannered I was. Perhaps it was he who was being well mannered to say such a thing. I at least made one positive impression.

On a visit back some time after my departure Kinya-san informed me that his father had passed away just a few months before. He told me that his father had always been honoured to have me as a guest and, once again, how well I had behaved. It made me quite sad, but also reminded me once again how lucky I had been to have spent time with people like him.

Anyway, these impromptu gatherings (for me) happened quite regularly. On the night just discussed Kinya-san had mentioned that he would come to my apartment at 5:30, but nothing else. He ended up taking me to this *enkai* - and a lot of that seemed to happen. People would come to me either in the office or to my apartment and say, "Nic, you come now". I would just follow and wonder what was to come.

Friday morning Mizushima-san took me on a sightseeing outing to some spots just south of Omi. He taught me the word for dragonfly (*tombo*) and also showed me the favourite suicide cliff jumping spot in the area. That had me a little worried. Did any of the previous English teachers in the area meet a gruesome end? Or maybe have a secret lover's pact with the Maths teacher? Incidentally when I met Okimura the mathematics teacher I found she was pretty damn cute. But I wasn't about to jump off a cliff with her.

Back at the office I was counting the remaining dregs of cash for the trip to Sado Island when they asked how much I had. When I showed them the ¥8,500 in my wallet the staff all broke out in fits of laughter. One called the bank and asked if I could get an advance on my visa card, but no. Eventually Mizushima lent me ¥30,000 which seemed like an exorbitant amount to me, but just like petty cash to him. I looked in my dictionary and asked the word for interest rate, but he graciously laughed, waved his hand, and bade me good journey.

13: Eat, Drink, Man, Sumo

It's a long way after dark - Japanese Proverb

As I hopefully articulated somewhere prior, I love the train system in Japan. They are clean, punctual and you can get just about anywhere on them, or at least a substantial part of the way. Throughout Japan, and particularly in places like Niigata Prefecture, you can find old single lines that wind up over the mountains bearing ancient railcars made in the 1950's and 1960's. In most other countries these lines would've closed down years ago in a fit of government rationalisation or handed over to dedicated volunteers to run tourist trains. After Japan Railways (JR) was flogged off years ago some lines were indeed shut down but the majority still fortunately exist. I think I can safely say here too that Japanese people are also in love with their train system, as epitomised by the tear jerker movie 'Poppoya', starring the legendary Ken Takakura.

Barring a recent incident (2005) in Kyoto, they are also extremely safe, apart from when the drivers fall asleep. A *shinkansen* driver was once found asleep by the conductor after the train pulled into Okayama station. Apparently the train, which had been travelling at around 300km/h, was fortunately pulled up by a safety device coming into the station. There are also semi-regular suicide attempts where the terminally despondent throw themselves in front of speeding trains. JR at first tried to curb this practice by making the families pay for the 'clean-up'. When this failed to stop the many attempts they tried something more realistic like safety barriers.

You need to be aware that if you go to Tokyo during winter some commuter lines may have a problem. Their platforms are of a certain length, pretty much the same span as the trains that ply the line. All trains always pull up in exactly the same spot so you know where the doors will be to get on. This is exactly what you would expect from such an efficient system. Tokyo's subway system, at around 2,500 kilometres in length, is five percent longer than the New York City system. However, it carries <u>eight times as many people</u> each day. Pedestrian gridlock occurs every morning when rush hour trains unpack their millions. Even with that, commuters don't push and shove to get into or off the train, except maybe during those rush hours when there's so many bodies that a bit of argy-bargy is inevitable.

So what's the predicament in winter? Well, the same number travel on the trains but there is one major difference. Clothes. People wear more in the cold season so there is less room inside. So folks have to fit a little more snugly than usual - and sometimes they don't fit at all. The solution? Train 'stuffers'. These humble rail servants stand at the ready on the platform and whenever they see a group of people trying to jam into a carriage that is already full they assist, and this is not a joke, by pushing them hard inside. Then the doors can be closed and everyone can all be merrily on their way to work/school or back to their homes in the distant suburbs.

Being so close together there is also a problem with groping. Until the 1990's women and girls just seemed to put up with this kind of behaviour but are now becoming more strident in their calls to abolish this abhorrent practice. Various authorities have been working harder on this problem in recent years and some rail companies in major cities have introduced 'female only' cars on rush hour and late night runs. They have generally proved a success although some women do not use the cars because they have decided that in reality they hate all the gossip and bitchiness more than the groping. Maybe coming soon will also be - 'drunken *salarymen* only', '*keitai* (mobile phone) users only' and 'those afraid of *gaijin* only'.

To the newcomer in Japan the rail system is often a mystery to be unravelled, and so it was with Wendy, Rananda and I as we stared up at the timetables in Itoigawa *eki* (station) one mid-afternoon. At least they used roman numerals. In some small stations they still use the old Chinese number characters. One afternoon I got stuck somewhere outside of Niigata City waiting for a train to take me to the famous Shirane Kite Festival. Having little to do I spent what seemed like a few hours deciphering the timetable written in Chinese characters. It was good practice. Which I forgot soon of course.

We asked the JR attendant for timetables but he would only give the three of us one schedule. Maybe he saw us as a holy, indivisible, three in one trinity. After some debate, the three of us decided it would be best to catch the express to Naoetsu, from where we could catch a ferry to Sado Island for the annual 'Earth Festival'. The problem was that, once on the express, the very polite and efficient JR official informed us that he was very sorry but we needed to pay a substantial extra cost above the standard fare. We considered this awfully expensive for a twenty-minute time saving over the local train. We ranted about being ripped off but as time passed we realised it was nothing more than a lack of experience, or stupidity, or both. I'll go with the former for now.

From Naoetsu we decided to walk to the ferry terminal rather than take our chances with buses and perhaps be ruined financially or maybe end up in Hokkaido. There we caught up with many others from the Niigata conference. There were also a lot of other *gaijin* milling around in groups - obviously teachers from other prefectures. Mostly from Toyama and Nagano as I was to later find out. After a pleasant late afternoon cruise of approximately two and a half hours we disembarked into the small town of Ogi to meet up with yet a few others, making it appear that nearly the entire English teaching population of Niigata Prefecture had abandoned their posts for the weekend.

Up at the concert site we found admission each night cost ¥4,000. Rananda and I thought that was a tad rich, particularly in our financial circumstances, so we went for a walk instead. Supposedly it was just for the exercise but, although there was no verbal communication on this point, it was really to see if we could just sneak in for free somehow.

As we walked along the beach we thought we heard the concert taking place somewhere on top the adjacent densely forested hill so we looked for a way up from the beach. I found what I thought was a path but as I walked in further sank thigh deep in mud and lost both shoes. Rananda followed and almost did ditto. After extracting myself and rescuing my shoes from the bog (God knows how much a new pair would cost!) I found solid ground on one side and thus we decided to press on. Upwards we went along a long path eventually coming into Shiroyama Park - with a concert going on! We had come out about a hundred metres from the back of the stage. We decided there and then that the mud was worth it, made ourselves comfortable in the gathering darkness and watched for about an hour.

Taiko drumming, as exhibited by the famous 'Kodo' on this night, is a fabulous experience to behold. Just a couple of months later the town began a *taiko* group and I was invited to join by Yuko Tatebe, the local English language tutor and her husband Atsushi. I would have dearly loved to have done so, but the practice was two or three times a week and I felt I could never be that dedicated. If I had that much time I could've actually tried to do something useful – like learn some Japanese. I thought it would be really cool to play the big (*see:* bloody enormous) drum where the drum-stick is the same size as a baseball bat. Not only would it be good fun, but it would also serve to get rid of a lot of stress. One of my successors, plus an English teacher from Itoigawa, joined the group in following years.

Yuko and I became good friends and she was always quick to help whenever it was needed. Which was pretty often. They had me around to dinner many times and Yuko would regularly invite some of her students to join us. I think it was her who showed me the copy of a video that my predecessor Shanti had made about Omi. It showed the various highlights and things to do around town. At one stage there was a shot of the *eki* from the nearby bridge. Shanti's commentary at this point enthusiastically stated, "This is Omi station. Many trains stop in Omi." The problem was that as one watched this scene an express train hoved into view – then went straight through the station without stopping.

However, as I return back to the story, the interesting bit came when we wanted to leave the park. We had walked up in semi-light but when we started back down it was complete darkness. The only tool at our disposal was Rananda's lighter, which we utilised to find our way. We had visions of wandering off into the jungle and never being seen again. Headlines would blare, *'Freeloading English teachers disappear on Sado Island. North Korea suspected.'* We did almost get stuck in the mud again at the bottom but as you can guess we did return safely. If we didn't you wouldn't be reading this book would you? Thanks by the way. Don't forget to recommend it to all your friends and family. Christmas presents are a good idea too. Gift of knowledge and all that. It was a relief to hit the beach and we celebrated with a hug and ceremonial cleansing of the mud. After that we wandered into the marketplace where we bought some CD's, and ended up on a still night sitting on the lawn with cold drinks and stars overhead listening to Cuban music. Heaven.

After the concert we met up with others, some of whom were upset about our freebie. We were not sure whether they thought it was dishonest, or they were just p***** off because they'd ponied up big dough instead of getting in for free. Most people were going to a Buddhist temple to sleep but I decided against that, mainly for theological reasons, which I won't go into here, and slept on the grass in a local park for the night. I woke up early – I don't know what time because my watch had broken. It wasn't much use trying to keep sleeping with the sun up so early so I determined to walk to the beach about ten to twelve kilometres away where some fellow teachers were camped.

It was indeed a fine walk at that time of day. There were few people about, apart from some local farmers and bent-over *oba-chan* (elderly women) carrying sacks of rice on their backs like they must have been doing for most of their long lives. Further on I discovered a fifteenth century temple and wandered through enjoying the solitude and history that few others in my position would be lucky enough to discover. Much of that day was spent at the beach, apart from a brief sojourn into Ogi to see a Nigerian percussionist perform. He spent most of the concert telling all assembled that all we needed was love. Yeah, well the Beatles tried that too – just before they went into LSD and other such stimulants, then broke up and declared they hated each other.

We all got up early again on the Sunday. Well, once the sun comes up there's not much choice. Apart from Todd the Canadian who was so completely wasted from the night before that he slept in a coma type state until late morning. Along with the usual hangover attributes he finally awoke around 10pm with severe sunburn and a mouth full of sand.

Mind you, as you got to know Todd you realised this wasn't an unusual experience. This very funny and easy going Canadian man was a great believer of the motto, 'When in Rome...', particularly when it came to drinking in Japan. He was from a town somewhere up near Edmonton that he claimed was named 'Jerkwaterville'. Todd and I bonded well and were to share many experiences over the next two years - including an adventure on Mt. Fuji (see Chapter 29) and the invention of a whole new dialect that was referred to as *todo ben* (Todd dialect). Years later Todd was still stuck in Japan teaching English, but now with a lovely wife, a cute daughter and a nagging mother-in-law. Most astonishingly was his licensing as a Christian priest, allowing a bit of lucrative moonlighting on the side as a marriage celebrant.

After an early morning swim and jellyfish sting it was time for me to pack up and leave. With a bad case of sunburn on my pale white flesh I didn't really want to stay out in the open for much longer. We crammed into a slow local bus heading toward Ogi and then jumped on the ferry back. In a way it was really a waste going just for the festival and I vowed then to come back another time to see the sights. I did. And if you keep reading right through you can get to that very interesting part by about 10.00pm, or 10.30 of you have to nip out for a smoke, or hot chocolate, or both.

Back in Omi I emptied out all the sand from my backpack, washed my clothes, scoured a bit more mud, showered, and tried to take it easy including a quick nap. That wasn't going to be easy. After a short time I heard some music in the distance and when I looked out my front windows saw a procession of *kimono* clad ladies proceeding down the next street over from the highway. They were doing an intricate little dance with paper fans along the street in front of a car fitted with megaphones blasting the same song over and over again. I think it was the Omi town song. This I figured due to the fact the singer kept on mentioning 'Omi-machi' *ad-infinitum*. As the new resident *gaijin* I decided I best go look and put in an appearance. There was a small *matsuri* happening in a field where the dance led to so I just walked around bowing, smiling and trying to make a good impression. Whether I did or not is a moot point I guess. Back home I readied for the morrow, my first official day at the *chugakko* (junior high), and tried to work on a speech.

In the morning I nervously ventured up to the school and this time I was prepared. After initial introductions I gave my speech, all in Japanese mind you, but with all the blank looks coming back at me I have no idea how it went. I was surprised because even with holidays there were still a heap of kids at school, all involved in various club activities. I thought this strange but soon found out it was quite normal practice. It's probably good for the kids, even better for the parents, but hell for the teachers. All the students had studiously been doing essays over the holidays and these were left on my desk to mark - about 350 of them!

I had an English Department meeting with Setsuko Watanabe and Shinichi Fukushima which went okay, apart from Setsuko's concerns about my accent. I couldn't do much about that. Many things seemed to worry Setsuko but nothing ever seemed to faze Fukushima. He was so laid back he was almost comatose. But he was also a fantastic teacher and impressed me greatly over my two years there. I think I can say truthfully that the man influenced quite a few of my teaching methods. Fukushima resembled a less-muscular Sylvester Stallone in many ways, and when I told him he took it as a compliment. I spent many an *enkai* loading him up with booze and trying to get him to yell, "Adrienne!" He finally did, not too long before I left Japan. Probably just to shut me up. I think it was the same night he got so carried away at *karaoke* that they threw him off the mike.

I left there early, as there was no need to stay, and went back to the Board of Education office. There I found that I was playing softball in a sports festival the next Friday in which I'm certain they had high expectations of me. I also got my first pay that day. I just wanted to go out and party! There was big time shopping that week I can tell you. The local 'Hapi' supermarket owner and staff would have been especially 'hapi'. On the Wednesday I visited a *shogakko* (elementary school) and *yochien* (kindergarten) at Ichiburi down the road about 13km. The following days I went visiting to all the other local schools and met some of the staff and kids. As part of my job I was to visit each one once a month on Wednesdays, teaching kindergarten in the morning and elementary in the afternoon.

Some proved quite amusing. At Omi *shogakko* my guide, Abe-*sensei*, couldn't speak English - like most staff at the schools. He took me on a tour through the 'rabbit warren' of classes, gym, hall, storage, and so on, and in one room there was teaching space for a disabled child. He couldn't convey it in words so he did it in actions and mannerisms. It was hilarious but I hopefully kept a straight face. At Omi *yochien* there were two funny incidents. Outside there were kids in the wading pool and some were rinsing themselves off. One kid managed to physically remove the tap and stood there watching the resultant gusher with an 'Oh, ****!' look on his face. At lunchtime another kid walked by smiling, totally oblivious to the prawn stuck up his nose! The kids there, like kids generally everywhere, are very cute. Call me biased, but I do think that little kids are especially cute in Japan, even if only in my neck of woods. I also spent more time at the *chugakko* but there wasn't much to do there - yet.

Outside of school my recalcitrant laptop computer and the continuing disintegration of my relationship were frustrating me, so anything I could keep busy with was a blessing. The former was much more of a problem for me than the latter though I must say. At the end of the week I had to give a speech to the Board of Education heads, which seemed to go off okay. At least this time I knew whom I was speaking to and why. A couple of times I had been told to give speeches to groups and I had no idea of who they were! At the end I had to rush back for the start of the sports festival at 5.30. It was fun and I acquitted myself reasonably well.

Naturally the real purpose of these gatherings is to maintain group harmony. And also get really loaded. At the *enkai* afterwards I made lots of friends with my bottle of tequila, including the mayor. I drank, ate, arm wrestled, sumo wrestled, and generally kept people entertained. One highlight was swanning around teaching people how to do tequila shots. It generally went this way. I would fill up their sake cup and they would then begin to sip it like *sake*.

"No, No!" I would cry, "like this!"

I would pick up the cup, cry "*salud!*", and knock it back.

They would follow by doing the same, chanting "saruda!", then choke horribly after swigging it down - as everybody else laughed. Finally Mizushima-san grabbed my arm and directed me on wobbly legs to the Mayor's table who apparently wanted to join in the fun.

"Hey Mr. Mayor", I slurred as I neared, "how are they hanging?"

Having no idea of what I said he smiled and instructed me to pour him a shot - which he downed like a vet.

Post *enkai* I ended up with some people in Itoigawa, who I didn't know and who didn't speak much English, in a *karaoke* bar. Luckily alcohol is a universal language. I couldn't find my wallet so everything was paid for me. After late night *ramen*, and missing out badly with one of the office ladies when she found out I had a 'fiancée', I was bundled into a taxi for the ride home and a good night's sleep. Needless to say, Saturday I awoke to a severe hangover and another stinking hot day.

At least heat was better than rain. *O ame* is a common expression in Niigata-ken, meaning 'big rain'. Anyone spending more than five minutes or so there will understand it well. The locals say that Niigata has four distinct seasons. I reckon that these could be called in English – 'Snow' (November-March), 'Rain' (September-October, April-June), 'Typhoon' (July), and 'Sweltering' (August). Strangely there are always complaints from the local authorities about water shortages. What I want to know is this - why is there a shortage of water in a place where it rains so much?

With the hot weather I decided to just take it easy and spend some time tinkering on my computer. <u>Bad move</u>! I was installing updates when the system froze. I exited and upon restart found my system had crashed. My computer (*see:* lemon) was to be a huge source of stress and discontent for the next three years or so as it constantly crashed or froze. Over that time I typed out a list of problems that extended for more than six A4 pages. In the end I was forced to sue the company to repair it properly because they would never accept that it could possibly be a complete s***box. I won't say what brand it was, apart from having something to do with fruit. Don't say I'm not a vengeful person.

I gave up on the computer when Rananda rang. She was going with Wendy up to Takada to meet some others so I decided to tag along. It was then that I remembered that I had left my bike at the Town Hall. But when I got there I couldn't find it. I thought this was fortuitous because I might now get a new one. No such luck unfortunately. The kindly caretaker had put it inside for me and dreams of Kinya-san wheeling in a new mountain bike disappeared.

By now my first month in Japan was drawing to a close. I had my bags packed ready to head to Niigata City for the baseball championships even though I was certain I was to just fulfil the role of team mascot.

14: Do you play sex? Raw eggs for breakfast

A humiliation in a trip can be thrown away - Japanese Proverb

I scurried down *Omi-dori* (Omi Avenue) to the town hall to meet the minibus that was taking the baseball team to Niigata City. Kinya-san had told me that they would pick me up from the school but I guess the plans were changed on me. I was never able to gain this special gift of E.S.P. that many Japanese seem to have. I would often have arguments with Setsuko that went along the lines of,

"…but I told you."

"No you didn't!"

"Yes, well sometimes we Japanese will communicate through gesture, or a third party"

"Take a long hard look. You will notice perhaps that I am not Japanese."

"Well, you need to learn…"

And so on, *ad infinitum* for two whole years. Setsuko was a truly lovely lady with excellent English skills and possessed the greatest of love and concern for her students. However she often seemed to be quite at the point of 'browning out' in her work. Either that or menopause. Just nine months after I left town she finally packed it all in and was intent on spending the rest of her working life as a home tutor.

Hot and sweaty, I bowed and apologised profusely as I found a vacant seat. I recognised a couple of faces from the sports festival and *enkai*, including Takeshi Shimada who had recently lent me an answering machine. Takeshi had been to visit my hometown Adelaide the previous year and was going again soon. His English was quite good and we were to become firm friends over my two-year tenure in Omi and beyond.

The team hotel was on the outskirts of Niigata near the baseball stadium and the nightly *enkai* was obligatory. To me it seemed hardly good form on the eve of an important championship. What seemed worse form to my hung-over *gaijin* sensitivity was the traditional Japanese breakfast in the morning - seaweed, sticky rice, a raw egg, and some unrecognisable vegetables to be washed down with green tea. Kinya-san and Takeshi explained to me that you put the rice and egg in a bowl together with soy sauce, and then mix them together.

Okay, I was willing to give it a try. After one mouthful I pushed the tray back, stood up, and asked with total cultural insensitivity, "Does anyone know where the nearest McDonalds is?" Where would the western traveller be without the golden arches that insidiously appear on corners in every major city of the world? Globalisation, and cholesterol, rules. Not that, I confess, I think terribly much of what one can purchase from McDonalds, nor do I care for many of their ethics or business practices. But in my position I was willing to compromise. Hunger and money can have a big impact on one's principles.

Unfortunately I soon discovered that they had not made that big an impact on the local neighbourhood where I was staying. Rather than starve I wandered off down the street and found a 'Lawsons' convenience store, then sat outside on the footpath munching on a pastry and coffee. By the time I arrived back the team was just about kitted up and ready to go. Once at the stadium my suspicions were confirmed and my presence was merely one of support. To add to this feeling of futility the whole day was excruciatingly boring and this was not assisted in any way when Omi lost the very first game. That knocked them out of the competition, which meant for the rest of the day we had to sit in the stands waiting for the closing ceremony. I went for a walk for a couple of hours rather than endure. The day dragged and it was a slow and silent trip home.

The two other foreign teachers in the local area, Maria and Jeet, had finally arrived back from their summer holidays. The next night they invited me out to a Japanese companion's place for dinner along with Rananda and Wendy. Jeet was an Indian/Canadian, as in those whose staple is curry - not buffalo, who had divorced and set off to Japan to sort out her life. We had a strange and often antagonistic relationship, but somehow managed to remain friends.

L to R – Myself, Rananda, Wendy (bottom), Maria (top), and Jeet

Maria was a space cadet from stateside and unfortunately held captive quite a few kangaroos in her top paddock. The Jeet/Maria fights provided alternative entertainment for me to the Wendy/Rananda bouts.

School formally started this week and at the Friday morning assembly I was introduced to the students with much clapping and camera flashes popping. I felt like a pop star. Japanese love their cameras. Whenever you take an informal picture of the Japanese at probably at least 90% of them are going to flash the 'V' sign – even more if they are under 25. At the same time a large percentage won't smile, even if they are having a good time, or are drunk, or both. I struggled to understand the meaning of this. I had to give an English speech, rather than the Japanese version I had prepared, to the students which fell very flat, judging once again by the sea of blank faces, ditto my first two lessons. "Oh well," I thought, "things can only get better from here". After a couple of weeks my lessons were just as boring as ever. I was shocked just how lively the kids were outside the class as compared to their behaviour within. It drove me crazy.

My confession here is that my only understanding of EFL teaching came from when I saw Harold Ramis trying to teach it in the movie 'Stripes'. I didn't really want to try and teach them, "Da Doo Ron Ron" for two years so I needed to get some ideas in a hurry. There is a presumption in Japan that native speakers study English the same way as the Japanese. That is, with a great focus on the grammar and rules, and little on the creative and communicative aspects. Fukushima and Setsuko would often ask me these detailed questions on grammar such as, "How do you say this in the passive voice?", or "How can the conjunction meet the verb in a poetic vindication?" Or other things like that. What was my response? Usually a blank look and the standard rejoinders,

1. "Don't ask me. I'm a History teacher", or
2. "Maybe this way…" – "Why?" – "Well…just because it sounds right, sort of…"

The following weekend saw a quite funky informal get together up north in Nagaoka, organised by JJ Thakkar who was somewhat of a local legend. JJ was a well-heeled young man on sabbatical from his headlong rush down the management track. After his first unhappy marriage finished he bought a duplex in Texas that overlooked the Enron office, perhaps to help him keep focus.

I arranged to meet Joanne on the train and she got on at Kakizaki where she had been posted. Canadian Joanne had been a spark in my life since we first arrived. We both shared a warped sense of humour and a love of things cinematic. In the first few weeks we spent many hours talking on the phone and keeping each other sane in our strange little towns. Some nights would find us rolling on the floor, separately of course, as we shared jokes and tales.

The phone calls lessened as Joanne began to see a bit of the mad Canadian Jack. Plus the insane phone bills didn't help either. Ours became one of those friendships that ebbed and flowed but fell into an easy familiarity whenever we saw each other. On the train up we shared experiences of our first few days at our respective schools. Joanne's most legendary *faux pas* went like this. Probably the most famous question a student can ask is, "Do you play sex?"

During one of her first intro/question times Joanne was asked, "What musical instrument do you play?"

Most Japanese have at least had a bash at some instrument in school so it's presumed *gaijin* are the same. "Well", Joanne answered, "I don't play it anymore, but I used to play sax".

The teacher rushed to interpret as the kids fell about laughing. To the novice it initially appears that sex in Japan only happens in love motels, after hostess bars, throughout *manga* magazines, and between 'fiancées' during and/or after *gaijin* parties - except in Nagano of course.

Fortunately, after arising late on Sunday, I discovered Monday was a holiday. Henceforth I determined it was 'Blow my pay cheque shopping in Joetsu' day. It started with high hopes - but ended as the logistical day from hell. I got going late and it was 12.30 before I even arrived at Naoetsu station and got on what I thought was the bus to the 'Wing Market' shopping mall. After about half an hour and with the fare indicator on the bus getting into four digits I decided it obviously wasn't. I pressed the stop button and alighted in the middle of rice paddies miles from anywhere - let alone Wing Market. Finding there was no bus in the opposite direction for over an hour I decided to walk and hail the next taxi. An hour later I was still walking, still in the middle of paddy fields, and still waiting for a taxi. I tried hitching but that proved similarly futile.

I eventually caught the return bus with the same driver rather bemusedly welcoming me back on the bus. As we moved back toward Naoetsu I spied the markets in the distance - or so I thought. After walking <u>again</u> for twenty minutes I began to think I must've been mistaken so I decided to hail a taxi. After some time I had seen only two cabs - both of which did not stop for me. So I determined to walk again in the general direction of where I thought the markets were. Four hours after alighting from the train, and totally exhausted, I was finally rewarded. I spent about an hour shopping up big time - a table, microwave, computer system disks, pin board, shirts, sleeping bag, et al...and emergency supplies in case of earthquake. Well, it <u>could've</u> happened – particularly in Japan. Joanne bagged me for months over my considered 'escape plan' and called me Colonel Klink. In truthfulness there was much more chance of dying of alcohol poisoning in Omi than an earthquake, but they were not unknown.

With my trolley loaded down I headed for the taxi rank and waited, and waited, and then waited some more. I went to a nearby shop and managed to communicate that I needed a taxi so they kindly called for me. I went outside and waited again till finally a taxi showed. I bundled everything in - and out again at the *eki*, then staggered up and down the stairs to the platform. The local train would be a long time coming so I decided to catch the express instead. The doors opened and as I tried to fling everything inside one bag dropped down in between the platform and the train. The one containing the expensive computer program! Fortunately it went no further than jamming beside a wheel. I reached down to retrieve it just as the stationmaster's whistle blew, so I threw it through the carriage door along with myself just as they closed. Indiana Jones had nothing on me. I had to get out at Itoigawa and catch a taxi home from there. Toting up my invoices as I sat on the *tatami* at home I was not surprised at all to learn that my travel expenses for the day came to a fairly hefty percentage of the total sum of actual goods purchased.

Nonetheless I set everything up then called Joanne to make sure she got home okay from Nagaoka. I collapsed into bed and the next morning was able to enjoy a civilised breakfast sitting at a table, rather than on the floor, whilst gazing out upon the beautiful Sea of Japan. After Omi I would <u>never</u> have such a gorgeous view out of my windows again.

I loved sitting at my kitchen table and just looking out at the view. There was never too much to see - except maybe for the glistening blue mass itself and the fantastic sunsets. I remember waking up very early one summer morning and through my window I could see the slow movement of small fishing boats passing by like ghosts in the night. In the stern of each stood a fisherman dimly lit by the glow of their acetylene lamp. It was almost surreal and it was experiences like this that were to make my time in Omi so special.

15: Women chattering at the well

One written word is worth a thousand pieces of gold. - Japanese Proverb

The start of the school year also meant the start of my weekly adult English class on Tuesday nights. It was called *Idobata*, an ancient Japanese word meaning 'women chattering at the well'. I'm not quite sure how they came up with the name but the class was certainly predominated by the fairer sex. A core group of them had been in the class ever since it started in the late 1980's with Chris, the first English teacher in Omi. For a fair percentage it was more of a social club, which in many respects made my teaching easier. They were never demanding,

My 'Idobata' class

keen to learn, and very generous. My first class went well, even though I had no idea of what I was doing. Although it must be said I would have no idea of what I was doing for a considerable length of time. Over the first few weeks the class numbered between twenty and thirty so I was certainly hoping some would drop out - which they did, either due to my teaching, or complete boredom, or both.

This week also saw my first official visit to the previously discussed *yochien* (kindergarten) and *shogakko* (elementary school). The kindy kids were just adorable. At lunch they played *janken* (a form of 'rock, scissors, paper') to see who would get to sit with me for the meal. The elementary kids were quite boisterous and after class asked to play basketball with me. They wanted me to slam-dunk but I said no - until I saw the height of the rings, which had been adjusted to about three inches above the level of my outstretched hand. I made quite an impression, especially with my reverse slam, and soon I was feeling thoroughly darker and claiming M.J. for initials. I did take a mental note that formal wear, especially the tie, was probably inappropriate wear for these kinds of visits.

At the end of the week there were no lessons again because there was a regional meeting for English teachers in Joetsu City. The meeting was fairly much on your ho-hum level, as usual, and then we headed out for the *enkai*. Afterwards we walked down Nakamachi to a local *karaoke* bar called 'Memory'. This bar was pretty well *gaijin* HQ in the area when it came to gatherings. The name of the establishment was definitely ironic. I mean, I left so many brain cells there I can hardly remember much of anything that ever went on at the place.

Karaoke is of course one of Japan's more interesting exports. It means 'empty orchestra' and they've even made Hollywood movies about it. When singing a song you are always accompanied by a film clip. Often these clips bear no relation to the song, particularly in the case of western songs. In a Japanese clip the woman will be a tender woman softly crying, or being in love. Western women are generally portrayed as Southern bimbos, usually blonde 1980's style in bikinis and/or various states of undress. They also tend to be doing things like showering, having pie fights, and covering each other in unidentifiable substances. When trying to put your heart and soul into 'Imagine' these visual distractions can be somewhat disconcerting.

I tried to catch the late train home but got lost on my new bike thanks to Steve's lousy instructions, once again out in some paddy fields, so rather than spend the night aimlessly riding in circles I gave up and rode back to the bar. Pete, the popular tall red-headed Scotsman from the local Catholic Church, and I seemed to be the ones doing most of the singing. Pete, Dale, Craig and I were the last ones to leave around 3am. We were followed part of the way by a young Japanese lady who had been abandoned in Memory by her friends. She had taken quite a shine to both Dale and I it seemed, but I wasn't going to fight over her.

Dale was extremely popular, not only with the local lasses, but also in Tokyo. His Japanese stretched just far enough to tell them the words they wanted to hear. Anything after that didn't matter much and it was actions that counted most. At one stage there was a rumour, and I can't confirm this, that he had a great scam going. There were two ladies in Tokyo that he was 'seeing'. When he went down to Tokyo he asked each to pay half his train fare there as it was so expensive. He would stay one night at one place, collect his money, get amorous, and then say he had to go back to Naoetsu the next day. He would then head over to the other place in Tokyo, collect his money, do some more 'business', then head back home. It was fairly obvious that the young ladies in question had no idea that Dale was getting free rides, to, from - and in - Tokyo

On the street corner I parted with Dale and the young lady, who appeared perplexed I was not continuing on with her, and crashed the night at the church in Pete's room. Dale assured me the next time I saw him that they hadn't actually got up to anything. I found this notion dubious as he also told me she had, however, apparently taken all of her clothes off, got down on all fours, and asked Dale to, "Do me like a dog."

In the morning I managed to get JR to let me on the train with my bike. If you carry a bike onto the train in Japan you really need to have it in a 'bike bag'. I think sometimes the locals just often gave up, or gave in, when I uttered the magic words *nihongo ga dekkimasen* (I can't speak Japanese). As I walked down the platform a complete stranger recognised me and bid me "Hello" as I went past. Was I starting to become paranoid? As time went by I would be going down Omi-dori or Highway Eight and people passing by would toot their horn or shout out the window. I would usually smile, wave, and think, "Who the hell's that?" It was just my lot in being the only foreigner in town.

That day I had to attend the school sports day. I must say that I found this somewhat dull too. At one stage I curled up under a tree and went to sleep. A pity because the students had obviously worked very hard getting ready for the day. Schools have their sports festivals early because they take so much work. After that it's noses into the books on a downhill run to entrance exams. The costumes, signs and cheering were all great, there were some fun parts, but I was too tired to really enjoy the spectacle.

It must be noted that it's not a sports day in the athletic sense, but more like picnic games and/or blood sports, plus a little bit of S & M. There seems to be a lot of props like tyres, ropes and chairs involved, as well as a frenzied throng of students carrying their peers around to undertake either aggressive or really inane acts. One team game that stood out involved groups of boys carrying around a fellow student on their shoulders. The one on the shoulders wore a headband and the objective was to remove the headbands of the their opponents on the other team's shoulders. Some students almost scalped each other in a frenzied attempt remove each other's headbands and bring glory to their team.

My only involvement for the whole day was participating in the teachers relay team in the final event, in which I singly failed to distinguish myself – but that is nothing unusual given my poor athleticism. Plus the fact I had to wear a very large hat with an even larger floral arrangement on the top could also be considered a handicap. I bet Carmen Miranda never won anything at her school sports days either.

I went home, had a quick nap to recover, and then headed to the *enkai* that was also doubling as my welcome dinner by the school staff. My main role was to smile a lot, drink a lot, and of course give what was, hopefully by now, my last speech. Given the previous night I contrived to get myself excused from the *karaoke* afterwards and I even managed to get home early.

I finally got some curtains to help keep the sun out in the morning. Mrs. Yamagishi (Kinya-san's wife) had kindly made some up for me as a gift, and she and her daughter came around one evening to put them up. They even brought me a pizza for dinner but just as they left I dropped it on the floor. I ate gritty pizza in a hurry and flew out for *Idobata* English class.

It didn't take people in town too long to work out that my favourite food was pizza. In most conversations and/or question times one of the opening gambits would be "What is your favourite food?" This information obviously got back to the local 'Hapi' supermarket that two or three weeks after I arrived started stocking fresh pizzas. The only problem was that they might have at least a dozen in stock and I would buy one or two a week only. I noticed they didn't seem to sell too many and the use-by date passed quickly. So then they must've figured that I didn't like that sort, so in addition they started stocking another brand. When they didn't sell much either it beget a price war. All through this I continued on only buying my one or two, because there's only so much pizza one is able to consume within a particular

Sports Day activities

timeframe. I think they finally got sick of taking a bath on them and within a few weeks all fresh pizza disappeared off the shelves forever.

Idobata classes were going okay but I think it was a bit basic for some. At least numbers were down by about a third. There were forty-three in total on the roll and I fretted about what to do if they all showed up at the same time. As time progressed it was obvious that many who were there at the beginning were merely onlookers curious to check out the new teacher. Some even came from as far away as Nou – more than twenty kilometres away. Within a couple of months the core group remained along with a handful of newer students.

My first visit to Tazawa *yochien* and *shogakko* I was vindicated wearing casual gear. The kids were all over me at the kindy. They even followed me into the toilet - including the girls, and they wouldn't go away! Either they were just playing or obsessed with finding out the size of a foreign 'chin-chin'. I don't know why it is, but many young children seem oddly fascinated with the size of certain anatomy. I read a tale of a Canadian teacher who recounted that he was in a local hardware store when a young boy, maybe eight or nine years old, walked up to him and said, "Ohhhh, *Amerika-jin, no chin chin oki-ne!*" ('Oh, an American, he has a big penis') – then grabbed his crotch. All this was done in the presence of his father. The father quickly ascertained that the *gaijin* was p***** off but simply looked away and ignored him. He also couldn't believe that kid had the nerve to call him American.

The head teacher at Tazawa *yochien* was an absolute sweetheart who was always trying to set me up with one of her teachers. Not that I minded, the teachers there were almost unanimously good looking. Unfortunately none of them spoke English and at this time I was still technically 'attached'. The kids at Tazawa were usually a rowdy lot and I could generally be assured of a headache for the rest of the afternoon. There were just so many of them too.

Down at the Board of Education Kinya-san presented me with an envelope containing ¥88,560. Apparently it was for 'costs' in Tokyo. I had hardly paid a cent, apart from some drinking sessions and a couple of train fares, but the town policy was to pay some sort of fixed amount for every day one of their employees was away. However, I was not complaining…

Nonetheless it was not to last long. I got the bill from Tomoe for the other bike that I had ordered and was going to on-sell to Joanne. The extras were nearly an additional ¥10,000. I had to pay Mizushima-san ¥6,000 for my re-entry permit. When I got home there was my international phone bill, mostly for the number of my neurotic 'fiancée' – another ¥30,000 gone. Then I put aside money I needed to give to Takeshi for stuff to bring back from Adelaide - another ¥10,000. There was not much left I'm afraid - barely a good night out in Tokyo, or even Niigata City. The next day my MasterCard bill arrived as well - ¥40,000, so in the end I came out behind. Little comes cheap in the Land of the Rising Sun.

I should mention at this time that there was a third teacher in the English department - Miss Matsuki. She was a sweet young lady and spoke quite good English, but with little confidence. Her homeroom was an awful class plagued by a gang of six cocky boys. Matsuki was small and young with a thin reedy voice. In other words no threat to anyone, let alone six aggressive adolescent boys. The foreign teachers were meant to allow the Japanese teacher to take care of discipline but it was obvious that this wasn't going to happen. I coped for several months, but when their antipathy turned into rudeness and antagonism I was forced to take direct action. One day I snapped. A particular boy, Shinichi, was a constant talker in class. I would ask him to stop, he would say sorry, and then he would be back at it again the next minute. This time I stood over Shinichi and with my finger in his face bellowed, contrary to what you are told in teacher's college, "Just shut-up!" A murmur went around the class. Shinichi cowered in terror and spoke little in class again, as did the other boys.

Their marks remained far below average but it was obvious that they had little interest in English anyway. Some of them sunk into such a shell that I would worry about their health. I would ask a question but the only response would be for them to stare at the floor, eyes glazed, not a muscle flinching.
I would ask again.
No response.

I might then turn to Matsuki and ask, "Could you check his pulse please?"
I heard one was intending to visit New Zealand so I asked him where he wanted to go. A little slower the second time.
No response.
As I tried to recall my knowledge of CPR, I turned to the teacher.

"Matsuki-sensei," I said, "please let him know that it will be okay if he's intending to go to somewhere like Dunedin." The irony of this was as good as lost.

"Are you sure he has a pulse?" I remarked as I left the room

I guess the question readers may ask, "Why didn't they just fail the little turds?" Well, nobody ever seems to fail in the Japanese education system. My friend Kevin taught a student in Nishikawa who scored '0' in five out six classes, and still they bumped him up to the next year. I think it has a lot to do not only with the Japanese group mentality but also with Buddhist principles of mercy – where there is no concept of failure. It was a pity that the only discipline they could understand was physical intimidation. But I wouldn't mess with someone who was at least half as big as me again either. They hadn't encountered that problem with Matsuki. There was an improvement in other student's work as the class flowed more smoothly from that point. Fortunately I didn't have any problems like it in any other class. For me it exemplified again the growing breakdown of *wa* in Japanese society as younger people begin to assert their own individuality. Of course there are pluses in this, but unfortunately many minuses too.

    I was still struggling to get all of the summer 'My Family' essays finished and still had three more classes to mark. Some of the things the students were saying were hilarious. One even claimed that, "My mother is a tractor". Another had a brother who was "sensitive to fashion", and yet another had a father whose job was a "commuter marriage". Fukushima and Setsuko told me to hurry up and finish. I guess I'd been preoccupied with other things. This included shopping every day because foodstuffs were going off in my tiny fridge rapidly. I couldn't freeze anything so I had to buy fresh food and eat leftovers quickly. I was told that it wasn't unusual to shop everyday in Japan. If they weren't going to fix or replace the fridge, which they never did, I was glad to be living not too far from the supermarket. One of the new British teachers who lived up north had to ride half an hour to her nearest supermarket. When the snows came she was forced to take taxis. One of the good things about Omi was that it was pretty easy to get around - and out of, which I decided at that time was a good thing to do regularly.

16: Hot as molten lava

No man is an island, but some of us are pretty long peninsulas
- Ashleigh Brilliant

One of the problems living where I did was that Niigata is a huge lengthy prefecture and being as far south as I was, I was extremely distant from most of it. Particularly the seemingly important bits. It took nearly three hours on an express train to get to Niigata City whereas it was only just over an hour by local train to Toyama City, the capital of Toyama Prefecture that bordered Omi on one side. If I got the right connection of train at Naoetsu it was still less time to get to Nagano City then Niigata. The Niigata prefectural government was extremely city-centric in that they seemed to have little consideration for those who didn't live in close proximity to the capital. Another resulting side effect of the prefectural size was that many cliques formed and people on the fringes, like me, could be easily forgotten.

On Sado Island I had met some people from Toyama who suggested I might like to come along to some of their social events given my proximity. I went down one Saturday considering it would also be a good opportunity to visit Kurobe Gorge, Unazuki Onsen and Kanazawa. I went to change trains at Kurobe but after alighting realised I should have gone one more station to Ouzu. The train from Toyama to Unazuki and Kurobe Gorge runs on a private line. The stations are next to each other at Ouzu, but equidistant in Kurobe. Could I be blamed? I thought, going to Kurobe Gorge – change at Kurobe. Made logical sense to me anyway.

I sat on the platform with an obvious bewildered look scouring my travel guide, which dispenses precious little advice on the whole area anyway. One of the station attendants took pity on me and somehow managed to communicate how to get to the nearby Dentetsu line station. It only ended up a ten-minute walk and I got there just as the train to Unazuki Onsen was arriving. I really liked the train - it was just a small old model travelling slowly on a little back route. Too slowly though - I was busting to relieve myself and these sort of old relics didn't even consider toilets when they were built, or maybe they used potties in the corner to start with. Fortunately I lasted, but it doesn't help having a bladder the size of a pea.

Upon arrival at Unazuki Onsen I put my pack into a locker at the station - at a cost of ¥400. Lockers cost an absolute bomb in Japan and certainly extracted a fair ransom this particular weekend. Unazuki Onsen is a very popular spot and obviously expensive too. As I experienced more of Japan I realised that this was a fairly atypical resort town that the Japanese flock to in their frantically short pleasure excursions.

Onsen are of course natural hot springs, and once used to all the formalities required, a very relaxing and pleasurable aspect of Japanese society. They are another thing that I miss greatly about Japan, particularly in winter.

There are two types of bathing in Japan that can be broadly categorized as, *Sento* which are small public baths normally utilising normal hot water, and, *Onsen* that are natural hot springs, generally in unnatural settings - like very expensive hotels.

In many places you can also get *super-sento* that can be several stories high with a vast array of differing pools to bath in. Todd told me of one such establishment in Kyoto where you get to ride naked in lifts between the floors. Public bathing in Japan is almost a religion. It involves carefully showering and scrubbing all nooks, crannies, and orifices, before plunging into water that has a temperature only slightly less hot than that of Mercury (as in the planet). Here you may shout *atsui! yakedo suruya!* - "Owee! Hot as molten lava!"

Before I arrived in Japan I was told that bathing was a very public (and mixed) thing. The former is much truer than the latter, though mixed *onsen* can supposedly be found. I never found one, not for lack of research may I add, but if I did, I think I would be reduced to floating on my back and doing submarine impersonations. If you're lucky enough to stumble across one you should really be armed with some basic phrases so as not to alarm the locals (as quoted in *Wicked Japanese*):

Sumimasen, okina taoru arimasuka?
    Do you have a larger towel?
Hokanohito o odokashi taku nai
    I don't want to frighten anyone.
Anata ga sukidesu
    I like you.
Anata no hiza ni suwattemo yoroshii deshoka?
    Do you mind if I sit on your lap?
Watashi no huto momo o monde kudasai
    Please massage my thighs.

Any of the above phrases will probably ensure a tub to yourself. If this is the case you can reply with an indignant, *Are! Minna doko ittano?* – "Hey! Where's everybody going?"

Although I prefer bathing in winter, other seasons can be just as nice. One hot summer morning in Osaka I was taken by my friend Yoshihiro to a local *sento* that had a large assortment of different style baths. Given the heat I tried the cold plunge pool for the first time ever, which was a refreshing experience. Not quite trusting my luck I decided not to try the 'electric' bath which has a small electrical current running through it. It would be just my luck to have some power surge just after I jumped in and I'd end up looking a dead Charles Manson on a bad day.

From Unazuki I rode on the scenic railway up the gorge which is very famous - but I considered rather boring. That night two people told me that a lot of the line was washed away in the July floods and at its full length is a great trip. The floods were so bad that several workmen had to be lifted off their dormitory rooftop by helicopter. I think I may address the issue of rescue services in another chapter. If I forget please contact my publisher. If I get enough reminders they'll probably ask me to write another book. Win – Win all-round. What a dreadful 1990's saying that is. Doesn't stop one of the management of my former school using it regularly though. But he does still proudly sport a 1980's Tom Selleck-type moustache and calls himself 'Magnum', so that probably explains at least part of it. Upon return from my trip up the gorge I spent a little time looking around, hopeful that I might find a free *onsen*. No such luck - all were firmly inside luxury hotels. Later as I became more experienced I was able to circumvent this problem at times but will not incriminate myself here.

I jumped on the 5.15 train and made it into Toyama around 6.45. I should have changed trains somewhere again as the train takes a very roundabout route to the city. The people who invited me weren't meeting till sometime later so I changed, stuck my pack in a locker (another ¥400), and went for a walk. I really liked Toyama - and liked it more each time I went there.

The night out wasn't late and I decided to catch the last train back to stay with one of my hosts to Takaoka. That's when problems struck. When I got to the *eki* the locker area in the station was closed. Hence I was forced to leave for Takaoka with the others *sans* pack, and relied on my host for sleeping wear and toothbrush. In the morning, with more profuse apologies and thanks, I returned the borrowed t-shirt and toothbrush, and headed off. As life continued for me in Japan this was not to be an unusual theme. On any given weekend morning in the 1990's you may have found me outside a station somewhere in Japan, curled up half asleep in the bushes waiting for the doors to open so that I may retrieve my belongings and some form of normal life may resume once more.

Still it could have been much worse for me. In 2003 it was reported that the "...partially mummified body of an elderly homeless man was found in shrubbery beside a big department store in Osaka after going unnoticed for nearly two months". This is despite the fact that more than a million people pass by the spot each day, just across the street from the main railway station where I had once slumbered, at least for a few minutes. A police spokesperson tried to explain why the body had lain undiscovered for so long because normally people do not enter the stone-walled raised shrub plot. A taxi driver found the body presumably because he wanted to relieve himself in the bushes. The spokesperson added that "…the spot was windy; making it less likely any smell would be noticed."

I had arranged to meet Steve at Toyama *eki*. Steve was the second of only three Aussies in the whole of Niigata prefecture. He had temporarily given up practicing as a lawyer in Sydney to spend a couple of years teaching in Japan. He was one of the beach party survivors who had amused us by spending a good deal of time sitting semi-naked in a cardboard box, then later sleeping in a cupboard. Steve also became 'famous' for inventing the 'Joetsu Dance', which a few devotees always felt compelled to undertake once suitably lubricated. He only lived about an hour away from me in Takada, but after the first few months we saw little of each other. My first priority upon arriving in Toyama was to retrieve my backpack but do so I had to pay another ¥400 for the overnight fee!

We headed to Kanazawa for the day but unfortunately it was raining so we didn't get to see as much as we would've liked. The locker there was a bargain at only ¥300. If you've been counting, that's ¥1500 for the weekend just on locker rental. Back home that would've been the cost of a hostel bed for the night. I was to visit Kanazawa a few more times and it became my favourite Japanese city. I especially recommend the Kenrokuen Gardens there. We thought about staying the night but instead decided to go back to Niigata. I asked Steve if he wanted to stay in Omi but he decided to press on.

That night there was an awesome sea storm, mainly due to a typhoon on the east coast. Sometimes I felt the building move during a large gust. The waves were crunching over the *tetorapoto* (breakwater) in spectacular fashion. The Japan Sea had been quite placid up to this point and missing the surf at home I stupidly thought about going swimming - briefly.

One of the things I looked forward to in Japan before leaving was the thought that I would have more time to myself but it rarely proved to be so. This week after my trip to Toyama and Kanazawa I had something on every night. School had been incredibly busy. I'd been marking, setting lessons, and lots of other peripheral stuff. I even managed to finally finish marking all those essays too. Only took me a month or so.

I could never understand when I heard others saying they had nothing to do. Maybe it was just the teacher in me, whilst for many others it was just a break between university and graduate school. Or some other more seemingly meaningful line of employment. At least I finally felt I was beginning to find what standard the kids were at. In most cases I thought b***** useless and unmotivated. My perception of them was happily to change over time - but I was being paid quite a lot of money to be aggravated.

17: Oh, so THAT was a hostess bar...

Transactions in hell also depend upon money - Japanese Proverb

I finally received a letter of settlement from Ansett Airlines in Australia in regard to my baggage that had been trashed on the sector between Melbourne and Sydney. My trunk, still with the orange airline tape fixed around it, was sitting in the corner and being utilised as a lamp stand and coffee table. Ansett had proposed that I receive ¥15,000 compensation for damages. Not bad - seeing I only paid around ¥500 for them both at a thrift shop. That amount just about covered the amount that had been extorted from me by the PMS-challenged lady at Sydney airport. But that was to come down anyway. Apparently they mucked up my credit card billing and I never had to pay the part I had charged to my card. So I eventually came out in front, and a few years later Ansett went down the gurgler big time. At this point I must note that any number of readers may be former Ansett employees, now living in the remains of a burnt out car, a former shadow of themselves. Obviously you either picked this tome up from the Salvation Army recycle pile, or you sit in the local library all day keeping away the chills of winter. I apologise for any apparent smugness on my behalf. Apart from if you're the aforementioned check-in attendant – you deserve it b****.

The *Idobata* class threw me what I hoped was my last welcome *enkai*. At least I didn't have to give any speeches. The next day was my fun day at *yochien/shogakko* and this time it was the turn of Utatenami (Oyashirazu). I rode my bike the six kilometres which was a very pleasant experience, but which also shocked them as I came cantering through the gate. The coastal road (Highway 8) is fairly narrow and winding and has been rebuilt several times because of the steep cliffs and landslides, as has the rail line. The meaning of *oyashirazu* is 'forget your parents' because in ancient times the road was so dangerous you may easily slip and die. Hence it was no use thinking about your family if you wished to pass that way. Nowadays the truck drivers pose more threat than falling down the cliffs. Utatenami is a rustic village clinging desperately to the cliffs with its many aging wooden houses, seemingly passed by the world long ago, and tumbling down toward the sea.

Both Utatenami and Ichiburi, another seven kilometres further south, were a lot smaller than Tazawa and Omi. This aspect I really enjoyed as I got to see all the kids regularly and even learn some names. What was not so enjoyable at this stage was that at every *yochien* there was some kid obsessed with trying to stick their finger up my bum and yelling at the top their tiny lungs "*kan-cho!!*" The small schools were no different. After fingers some moved onto pencils. It p***** me off to put it bluntly and before I entered the classroom I had to ask the teachers to make sure the students had any loose objects, such as yardsticks, flashlights or traffic cones, safely stowed and locked away from temptation. Generally though, the kids were adorable and did soon learn to keep their digits, and other foreign objects, away from my anal passage.

Tomoe came around to help me pick up the bike that I had ordered from Itoigawa. I had tried to cancel it, even offering the shop owner money for his out of pocket expenses, but apparently it was not honourable to back out of a deal. I was lucky because Joanne had been looking to buy a mountain bike; hence I on-sold it to her with a little bit of discount. Joanne was having a party that Saturday so I said I'd ride it up the eighty kilometres or so to deliver it. Joanne was one of the few teachers who were fortunate enough to have a house, rather than an apartment, and her parties were to become the stuff that legends are made of within the prefecture.

There was a sports meeting on at the *chugakko* sports field for the local elementary schools and Kinokawa, now recovered and back at work, came in to meet me along with several others from the board. He gave me some lunch wrapped in foil as a gift. I thanked him, bowed profusely, then left it on my desk and quite forgot about it. A couple of times during the day a smell wafted around prompting me to think, "Something is off around here!" I drove the other teachers batty as I constantly checked the bin, my drawers and under the desk but couldn't find anything. At lunchtime Kinokawa came back in to see if I was eating. As I unwrapped it in his presence I realised what the smell was - the fish in my lunch. He left after he saw me nibbling at the edges but I was scared he would return and see it uneaten. Eventually after eating mainly the fruit and cheese I discarded the rest in an appropriate receptacle. I felt bad, as I'm sure it was some kind of special delicacy, but what can you do when your olfactory senses revolt?

Between Itoigawa and Naoetsu there is a bike trail that follows the old railway route up the coast for around forty kilometres. The first time I rode this route was for the purpose of delivering the bike to Joanne, but I was to do this ride on a number of occasions. I stopped on the outskirts of Itoigawa to do some shopping and then headed north, unfortunately straight into a head wind. Eighty kilometres to Kakizaki was not going to be easy. The weather wasn't that great and there was spitting rain a lot of the way but not enough to really bother me. It was so nice to just ride, enjoy the scenery, and listen to my Walkman - one of life's warm fuzzy moments. At one stage I listened to Marianne Faithfull sing

'The Ballad of Lucy Jordan'. I felt happy that by age 37 I would not "…have found forever" like the unfortunate Lucy.

I arrived at Joanne's around 6.30 and she was happy to have her new bike. I took a bath to ease out the aches but unfortunately my bliss soon ended when Tim the perverted pom opened the door so that the small crowd gathered could view my butt! The voyeuristic <u>and</u> exhibitionist Tim was a man who could not resist whipping out his tool on every possible occasion. I personally found him quite annoying and was to unintentionally have a hand in assisting him to flash 300+ people at a conference in Nagano the next January. This action almost saw Tim on the next plane home to England, but that did not eventuate. However his board of education did, quite sensibly I think, decline to renew his contract.

The party was huge, with people wall to wall, and most staying the night. A group of Russian women from the local nuclear power plant slept over too and in the morning their makeup and bouffed hair were all still firmly in place. Joanne inquired if I knew anyone who wanted a kitten because her cat was pregnant. When I asked her why she wasn't more responsible in her pet ownership she said, and I quote, "She only got out for ten minutes and came back knocked up". After final clean up and breakfast I lugged home on the train an extra futon that Joanne lent me and used it to make up a larger bed (of sorts). Shanti had been much smaller than I, and the dirty old futon that was left for me was about fifteen centimetres too short.

School was pretty easy at this time because we were just having my first round of speaking tests. The students were to read a prepared piece in class then I would grade them out of ten. By the end of the lesson my concentration tended to be waning though. One day I had to cope with four lessons in a row and by the end they had to poke me with a stick to keep me awake. The one thing that did really attract my attention was the student in Class 1-2 who was attempting his test with a reading sheet that he was holding upside down. Well, if George W. Bush, the most powerful man in the world, can do it, why not?

My *meishi* (business cards) finally arrived - now that I had been here a few weeks and met everyone. They misspelt my name and got the telephone number wrong but still charged me a fortune. After I forked over the cash the talk changed to cable TV for my apartment. I'd asked about cable in the hope of seeing some good movies. They said I couldn't get WOWWOW (the most popular channel) so I told them not to bother. Instead they got on the phone, which made me worry. Every time they got on the phone it seemed to cost me money. Eventually they handed the phone to me. The guy on the other end asked if I wanted a special tuner for WOWWOW,

"How much?"

"ni-man." (¥20,000)

"Sorry, that's too expensive."

A moment's silence.

"Okay I'll give you one."

I handed the phone back to Kinya who confirmed that this guy, whoever he was, was offering to give it to me. Then he told me there was monthly fee plus establishment costs. I had to think about it a bit further but it seemed tempting. There was not too much to watch on Japanese television, apart from the bizarre 'game shows' where the object is to see how much pain and/or embarrassment you can inflict on the participants.

One program I was especially enamoured to was the one where a couple of semi-nude airheads discussed in some depth new cinematic offerings whilst sitting together in a bathtub and soaping each other up. At the same time there was an lobotomized, obnoxious, sunglass-wearing, crap talking TV *tarento* (talent/host) who was surrounded by even more nodding bimbos all attired, at the most, only in underwear. I would just love to have a look inside the deviant mind of whichever TV executive dreamt that that particular concept up. As a single male I could obviously appreciate the subtle visual aspects but not much else.

Variety programs are also very popular in Japan. This generally involves quite a bit of chatting and cutting live to some poor souls in the middle of *inaka* or on a busy street that the hosts then mercilessly embarrass. Not that different from western variety style shows I guess - where a lot of overpaid egos sit around and pontificate on various issues such as, "If I was stranded on a desert island what two items would I most like to have to provide solace." You may notice that few ever exhibit the courage to propose taking a girlie mag and a large supply of baby oil.

A very useful tool was the 'bilingual' buttons that most Japanese TV's have, meaning that if you are watching a foreign program that has been dubbed you can press the button and, hey-ho, it comes on in the original language. Cool! But the ads can be either extremely aggravating or very funny.

Unlike some countries (see Australia) Japan doesn't rely on American imagery to sell its products. Well, as you would know from 'Lost in Translation', they do hire foreign high profile stars (*see:* burnt out has-been looking for cash) by the boatload to actually endorse the products. So if you are wondering why you haven't seen much of people like Martin Sheen, Christian Slater, Peter Falk and the like lately, they are probably in Japan sitting in bathtubs full of yen. One ad showed Rod Stewart stopping at a phone booth, in a rainstorm, in what coincidentally appears desert, to tell his loved one that he is running late. Well, I don't know about you but I can't imagine Rod driving himself anywhere, let alone in a family wagon, or calling his wife.

But I digress somewhat. It must be said the actual advertising is uniquely Japanese. Whatever medium is used it will generally always involve a young Japanese lady with a high pitched voice - unless they are using the abeforementioned 'stars'. Most of these TV ads are fairly incongruous, apart from those used in supermarkets, which are just out and out bloody annoying.

Instead of soothing 'muzak' (muzak would appear soothing compared with what I'm about to describe) supermarket proprietors pump out an endless barrage of inane jingles and shouting on what seems like an thirty second endless loop tape. I think it's designed as a service to get shoppers in and out of the supermarket as quickly as possible. Either that or they're slipping in subliminal messages.

In my early days I often struggled out of bed in the morning and ended up late to school. If a student was still walking up the path to school as I cycled up behind they would begin to run knowing then that they must be late. Why I had to be in for the morning staff meeting was beyond me - I couldn't understand what the hell it was about!

Let me tell you about my mornings. The normal custom when you walked into the staff room was to give a hearty *ohayo gozaimasu* (good morning) - to which you sometimes received a reply in kind by all, a few, or none. At 8.10am the bell would sound, everyone would stand, bow, once again say *ohayo gozaimasu*, and then listen attentively to the announcements that followed. One morning there was a power outage and all the teachers stood around bewildered until one pressed a buzzer to serve as a signal in place of the bell.

The staffroom at Omi *chugakko* was set up in the almost universal style found in Japan. That is, a rectangular style with several 'islands' of desks, surrounded by shelving chock-a-block of files and books, plus a low-slung table and chairs set aside for serving tea and having a smoke. The front row of desks was designated for the administrators and it was from this position that morning announcements were made. *Kubono-san* who was the *kocho-sensei* (principal) also had his desk there but spent most of his time in the adjoining office. Over two years he barely spoke more than a few sentences to me.

At least he just let me get on with my job which is infinitely preferable to some of the more sycophantic administrators I've recently had to suffer.[1] One bloke quite frankly considered it his duty to add to and interfere in everyone else's work just to justify his own position, not to mention undermining others to shore up his own insecurities along with a bald-faced grab for even more power. Sadly and all too often, these types of people - with director's kidneys glued to their silver tongues, rise to the top of corporations and institutions. Their archetypal personality type is of the variety that when in the movies their character gets laser-beamed by an alien, dropped out of a plane by a terrorist, or stomped on by a dinosaur, the whole cinema cheers.

Fortunately, sometimes they're found out. Another misogynistic bully-boy that I had the misfortune to work under only lasted a matter of months in the country before 'resigning for family reasons', and has since continued to move to a new position each year. Maybe he's actually a really nice guy, but just has a great scam going where he gets the balance of his contract paid out by acting

---

[1] Note the subtle use of the word 'administrator' – as opposed to 'manager'.

like a complete Wayne the Wanker. Last I heard of him he was eking out an existence in a former Soviet backwater republic of all places. Maybe it's really a secret *gulag*. Yet peculiarly, in stark contrast, two of the best managers I worked under also only lasted a short time each.

On a less ranting note, do you want to know another of the things that bothered me? It was that there were no vending machines when I was hungry. There were always plenty of drink machines but none near the school and never any with food. Vending machines are one of the basic food groups in Japan, supplying alcohol, 'leisure' magazines, noodles, cigarettes, batteries, and schoolgirl's panties. These machines are conveniently open twenty-four hours a day - unlike automatic tellers. I wondered why couldn't Japan become really civilised and have chocolate vending machines? Maybe it was because that it's unusual for males of the Japanese species to buy chocolate. I didn't find this fact out for years! So, that's why the kiosk and convenience store attendants looked at me as if I was gay, or perhaps just metrosexual.

Mind you, I think chocolate is a not an unreasonable thing to be concerned about. The next year there appeared in our prefecture an obnoxious southerner I shall call 'Ernie'. The first time I met Ernie this is the leading statement he made to me, and I promise I'm not making it up. He posed the rhetorical question,

"Do you wanna know what's wrong with Japan?"

And then quickly taking the liberty to answer his own question replied,

"It ain't got no chewin' tabaca".

I wouldn't call it an epiphany as such, but I knew right there and then, that Ernie and I would never be close. He made few friends in his time there, probably due to the fact that he could not talk about anything apart from sports or his university days. The guy was so empty that if you stood really close you could hear the sea. A conversation with Ernie would generally start off slow, and then go quickly downhill from there. Perhaps that why he allegedly fell into the habit of relating to schoolgirls, in exchange for a certain investment of capital. He stayed three whole years so, if the rumour was true, he was obviously getting good value. Or in advertising-speak, more 'bang for his bucks'.

Late September saw another school *enkai*. I'm not sure of the particular reason for this one. I ran late by a few minutes as usual and the speeches had already started. Maybe to teach me a lesson I was put at a table with all the non-English speakers. But a lot of people moved around and it wasn't a bad night. I handed out a lot of *omiyage* (gifts) which went down well with the recipients. *Enkai* are often followed by *nijikai* (second party) and even *sanjikai* (yes, you guessed it - third party).

I was bundled onto the minibus going to the *nijikai* by some fellow teachers but all the female staff were excluded, which seemed odd to me. The reason would become apparent soon. We arrived at bar in Itoigawa and two barmaids came and sat with us to drink. I figured they must have been coming off shift. Over at the next table there was a group of men in their 30's and 40's who were keeping company with a very delightful looking young lady which I thought odd. She came over and started talking excitedly to one of the teachers. He explained that she was one of his students when he previously taught in Itoigawa, but seemed quite embarrassed about it.

The guys wanted me to sing 'My Way' for *karaoke*, which they assured me, was in English. However as the titles rolled in Japanese they all laughed and I really did end up improvising it my way. They all cheered anyway, but as you quickly discover, alcohol can turn anyone into Elvis or Madonna. Around this time the group next door took me into their company. They all introduced themselves and one revealed that I taught his kid at Tazawa *shogakko*. He tried writing down my address in English and a few tried to communicate in basic English (or Japlish).

Then the strangest thing occurred. The very ugly man in the group said, for want of nothing better to say,

"I like sex."

To which I replied,

"Yeah, I do too."

Suddenly the girl, who was sitting one person away, lunged at me over the top of one of her valued clients and grabbed my arm.

"I do too", she exclaimed.

She grabbed my address that had been written down and brandished it announcing,

"I come to your house yesterday!"

Was this really happening? After trying to get my brain around this statement I replied, "No, you mean tonight".

No sooner it seemed had this escaped my lips than Murayama, my *kyoto-sensei* (deputy principal), trundled up to the table, grabbed my arm, physically whisked me away from her clutches, bundled me down the stairs and into a waiting taxi.

I will never know whether it was just bad timing or an attempt to save my honour. We met up with Inomata and Mizushima from the Board of Education at a local restaurant and they proceeded to drink heavily. Thereafter I was again bundled into a taxi, this time to drink at Inomata's house. I said "enough" and fortunately I was released from their grasp. The *enkai* had cost ¥5,000. On Monday morning I got asked for another ¥3,000 for drinks in Itoigawa even though I had barely sipped on the one whisky and water I had been poured. After converting it in my head to $A I realised it was the most expensive night out I'd ever had. Well, to that point anyway.

I also finally realised that I had had my first visit to a 'hostess' bar - the modern equivalent of a *geisha* house. The job of the ladies in these bars is to pour the gentleman customer drinks, light his cigarettes, laugh at his jokes and listen to his sad stories. These kinds of businesses, quite a good deal of them controlled by the *yakuza*, appear to be the only shining light in Japan's perpetual economic gloom. In the business year to March 2001 the shadow economy, most of it linked to the sex and narcotics trade, was worth an amazing 19.3 trillion yen (about USD$160,000,000). That's roughly double the size of Ireland's GDP - even taking into account all the Guinness they drink. Whilst the whole Japanese economy only grew by 0.6% between 1996 and 2000, illegal income generated by the sex industry grew by 6.1% in itself.

These figures are despite the proliferation of 'discounting' services that currently plague the industry with offers in major cities for 'health services' as low as ¥6,000. By the way I got these figures from a 'respectable' news source. If you can call reporting on these kind of things respectable. It may have involved a whole army of randy or voyeur geeks with clipboards I suppose.

The greatest number of 'hostesses' these days hail from areas of South-East Asia, or occasionally Russia and Latin America. Or so it appears in the very limited research I conducted in Niigata Prefecture. One formal estimate was that as many 150,000 foreign women are involved, many of who are coerced or lured to Japan under false pretences. A fair percentage of those arriving have their passports taken away and are forced to pay off their 'debt' - which can be in the vicinity of ¥4-5 million. With this pool of foreign labour it would be regarded as rather demeaning for a young Japanese lady to be a hostess, hence the embarrassment of my fellow teacher, who probably felt he had failed her in some way.

Anyway, if you're wondering, she never came to see me – yesterday, or tonight….

18: Oops – I think I killed my boss…

The mind of a man and the fall sky - Japanese Proverb

I used to be a great letter writer. I would write up to a couple of dozen in a month. Since the advent of e-mails I would be lucky to have written half a dozen in the last three years. But at this time I was still doing the ole' write, seal and stick. A couple of months in and I'd finally completed all my letters to family and friends and I took them down in a large bundle to the post office to post. The staff at the local post office were a jovial lot, and loved taking the p*** out of me every time I ventured in. They would talk and laugh with others when serving me, obviously at the expense of the dumb *gaijin* whom could not speak Japanese. I would do my servile guest role by just nodding, bowing, smiling and graciously responding with comments like,

"Thank you so much for helping me today. I also hope a huge goat services you up your private passages on the way home tonight." So all round it was a win-win…

I made my first foray up to Nagano City around this time. Nagano is a very groovy town, but the foreign population at that time tended not to be an exciting lot. In Niigata if we were sitting around thinking, "Who are some funky party people to go hang out with?" the *gaijin* in Nagano was not a thought that immediately popped into our heads. There were exceptions of course, but not too many.

This night I was met by Sue who I had met on the plane from Australia, and we headed out with some others to a club called 'Kings and Queens'. The girls were able to get in free before 10pm but males paid a substantial admission. However as compensation, it was all you can drink before midnight so I tried to make damn sure I got my money's worth. This involved getting a drink and then heading straight to the back of the line to get another. That way I was getting to the front of the line just as I was finishing off my previous beverage. As you can probably surmise we were fairly intoxicated by the time we caught a taxi home about 1.30 (I think). As usual my pack got locked inside the station and I had to again rely on the hospitality of my host.

Saturday morning neither of us was feeling terribly chipper so we had a slow start to the day. About 1pm we headed out to get my pack and then visited Zenkoji temple. This ancient edifice is just incredible. It was packed to the gills with tourists but would be still highly recommended for anyone passing through that part of Japan. There is a main temple and lots of other 'minor' ones. The highlight, which we decided against doing, was to go into the dark vaults underneath to grope around for the 'key of happiness'. Sue, who is rather a buxom young lass, had already had her fill of groping in Japan and hence was not terribly keen to wander around in a very dark passage with a lot of unsatiated male tourists.

As my tenure continued I came to realise that Japan is an international hotbed of pornography, lust and bizarre sexual mores. Female English teachers in Japan would find themselves the target of unwanted attention, especially if you were 'well-built' or blonde. Sue had been asking a man for directions one day when he just suddenly reached out and grabbed her on the breast. When she complained loudly about the inappropriateness of this behaviour he issued a rushed *gomen nasai* (very sorry), bowed deeply and wandered off into the sunset. Wendy and Rananda both had tales of men knocking on their door late at night, either asking them out or wanting to come in. Maria did too. But she was so desperate she didn't mind. Another teacher received several phone calls late at night from strange Japanese men whose vocabulary was limited to "You. Me. Sex. Yes?" I told her to give them Maria's number.

Women also had to make sure they didn't hang their lingerie out in places where it could be seen and/or souvenired. Panties fetish seems to be a fairly common theme. Not that it's restricted in any way to the Japanese, Homer Simpson once declaring it as, "….purely an issue of comfort". In Tokyo you can even buy schoolgirls' saliva and panties from vending machines[2]. There was a proprietor of a shop in the city (Final Fantasia) who was arrested for selling used female underwear. Apparently females would come into his shop and sell their undies direct to waiting men. The owner had built up a database of 1,800 schoolgirls willing to sell their panties. Why was he arrested? Because he didn't have a licence to peddle second-hand goods.

I know that's strange but I think the most bizarre story was from a teacher up north in Niigata. It started out that there had been a workman around earlier in the day with her supervisor installing something for her. Late that night there was a knock on the door and it was the same guy again. He was prattling on loudly and waving a product brochure above his head. She looked at him, looked at the brochure and wondered what on earth it was about. <u>Then</u> she looked down. He was masturbating. I would've kicked the guy in the cods but she just slammed the door in his face.

---

[2] Though by early 2004 there was a bill working its way through the diet, albeit an excruciatingly slow pace, to outlaw this practice. One presumes a number of Diet members are giving themselves enough time to stock up before it passes.

It wasn't just the women. One male teacher recounted the following,

"Oddly enough some of the younger boys in my Karate class seem strangely interested in whether I am wearing briefs or boxers. They wait in the change room for me to change and then proudly announce to the rest of the class 'the choice of the day'. I guess I shouldn't complain, at least they have learned how to say black, blue, and white briefs. Just making my little contribution to the improvement of English education in Japan."

But at least the Japanese were trying to deal with all this *seku hara* (sexual harassment). They started by inventing a word for it in 1989 after the first sexual harassment case came to court. By 1997, according to the 'Financial Times', the Japanese subsidiary of an American insurance company was to start selling insurance for Japanese expatriate managers and companies. This would protect against damages and other financial liabilities incurred due to sexual harassment suits abroad. It would also cover liabilities due to discriminatory employment practices and unfair dismissal. That was certainly an innovative way of dealing with the problem. So from then on I guess Japanese businessmen could behave abroad like they did at home.

To the uninitiated, Japan is a home of genuine sleaze - lingerie bars to peep shows to *omiai* (matchmaking) pubs where women from across the social spectrum receive a free opportunity to perform karaoke and a platform to "sell it", as they flippantly say. Even the *manga* (comics) so avidly read by males of all ages can contain graphic scenes of under-age sex, paedophilia, homosexuality, rape and incest. Early readers can learn language such as,

"*Katakute atsukute*"
– "Hard and hot"
"*Ne…Motto motto hayaku ugokashite!!*"
– "Come on…move it faster, faster!!"
"*O-shiri no ho de sasete ageru no*"
– "Let him do it in your ass"
"*Oppai wo sawatte kudasaimashi*"
– "Please feel my breasts"

Even their run of the mill crime can have fetish overtones. During 2003 in Aichi Prefecture the police arrested a man who robbed a woman of ¥15,000 while 'disguised' in a schoolgirl's uniform. Dressed in a typical female uniform, a navy blue miniskirt and a white top with a sailor's collar, as well as a shoulder-length brown-coloured wig, Yoshifumi Moriwaki, 24, admitted snatching the handbag of a 19-year old student from her bicycle basket as she was riding home. The local police had been on alert for a few months after five reported purse snatchings by robbers dressed in schoolgirl uniforms. Officers questioned Moriwaki late that night after they spotted him in a miniskirt and a navy blue cardigan near a local train station.

But wait, it can get even worse than that! How's this for entrapment? Later that same year in Ube City, Yamaguchi Prefecture, a 21-year-old policeman dressed as a high-school girl in uniform including a miniskirt trapped a flasher. The policeman had been operating undercover as a woman for some time after more than twenty young girls were molested or encountered a flasher in the city, located 800 kilometres southwest of Tokyo. An Ube police spokesman stated that, "As our enhanced patrolling failed to catch the culprit, we decided to arrest him red-handed by disguising a policeman as a woman."

The young policeman chosen for the task reportedly, "…looked good in the borrowed school uniform without a wig or make-up". He was wearing, "…a floral-pattern cravat bow, navy-blue jacket and miniskirt with a hemline ten centimetres above the knee", when a middle-aged man decided to whip out his gearstick in front of him. The disguised policeman's legs were unshaven but the flasher, identified as Isamu Nakashima, 50, did not seem to notice this in the dark. Despite the fact the policeman was 165 centimetres tall and weighed sixty kilograms Nakashima was quoted as saying after being arrested on obscenity charges that he "…was stunned as I believed he was a girl."

I could continue down this path on the more bizarre sexual proclivities of the Japanese, but maybe I'll save it for later. It would be a big chapter let me tell you, if this one is not long enough already.

Returning from Nagano on the Sunday there was a man sitting next to me on the train who had obviously only just taken his suit out of mothballs. I stopped in Naoetsu to meet up with Steve who I was going to an opening ceremony with. Naoetsu City had built a memorial peace park on the site of the old Naoetsu POW camp and it was to be inaugurated that afternoon with much pomp and ceremony. In attendance would be some of the former prisoners and guards, the Australian ambassador, a number of high officials and a plethora of news crews, including one from Australia. The unveiling ceremony was quite moving. Australians are not generally a patriotic lot, except maybe when it comes to sport. Did you see how many medals we won at the Sydney Olympics? But that day when they raised our flag and the band played 'Advance Australia Fair' I felt a mixture of nationalism, pride, and homesickness - all in one fell swoop.

After all the formalities had concluded we spoke for awhile to John Shovelan - the ABC Radio correspondent in Tokyo at that time, plus an old digger who regaled us with his yarns about all the happenings in the camp. It was really interesting. They had to work in a local iron factory and often would undertake dodgy workmanship such as leaving air bubbles inside the metal. When it was used in ships or the like it would apparently corrode or collapse quite easily. The camp comprised nearly all Australians, and six old POW's plus many relatives had made the trip. At the following *enkai* we were stuck at the back with all the locals, but I guess for the moment that's what we were. Later we got to meet the ambassador, his deputy, plus a couple of more old 'diggers' - as Australian soldiers are known. Steve was madly networking and largely left me to wine and dine with his colleagues from the education office in Takada.

I'd really been hoping for a sleep in the next weekend but I had to go to the Kinokawa's house at 9am. It was National Sports Day and they were escorting me to a local 'sports festival' held nearby to their house on a little piece of gravel and moss covered dirt. This had to be one of the most bizarre cultural events I've ever attended. First we did warm ups and stretches to some scratchy music which was amplified via a megaphone from a very small tape player. At the end I still didn't feel any better. Then the events began; frivolous picnic/party type games many of which I just can't begin to explain and seemed to have little relation my western notion of 'sports'. When we arrived I was left in the marquee under the care some *oba-chan* (old ladies) who were trying to pour me shots from enormous bottles of sake. And it was not yet even 10.00 in the morning.

Despite the entreaties of many assembled I refused to take part in the drinking race. This entailed one running up to a chair, blowing up a balloon, sitting on it till it bursts, <u>then</u> running to the bar for a beer, after downing that running back to the finish line, <u>and then</u> (as most competitors did) sit down and have a smoke. This did not seem to be promoting a healthy lifestyle, which I must have mistakenly thought might be the actual theme of a National Sports Day

Lunchtime came and most people appeared to be leaving. Mrs. Kinokawa handed me the lunch and I made the presumption I was to follow Mr. Kinokawa who had just wandered out the gate with many others. So I took off down the road after him. Eventually a guy came after me on a bike and breathlessly indicated with a strong pointing of his thumb to go back. So we were having lunch at the park and I was found standing fruitlessly in the middle of the road with some form of casserole in my hands.

At the end of the day we ventured back to their house. First, Kinokawa gave me a grand tour of his house. Well, I thought it was to be the grand tour. Rather, he led me up the hall to a bedroom. Inside he pointed to the bed and enacted what I could best describe as a 'jiggy-jig' type action. Obviously this had been the previous teachers' 'action room' and Kinokawa was intimating I could follow suit. After returning to the sitting room he asked me to massage his shoulders and neck. It seemed a somewhat strange request but I complied. He closed his eyes and then indicated I should tweak a bit more firmly. As I did so his head started to loll forward and his head drooped. Shortly thereafter he started to slump to one side and I really thought he was 'dropping off the twig', as I always feared he would while in my presence. How good would that look on my C.V.?

Recent employment: Omi-machi Board of Education, Japan
Referee: None. I killed my boss.

Fortunately Mrs. Kinokawa came in and indicated that he had merely fallen asleep and maybe it would be best if I went home now.

The Sunday brought a nice sunny day, maybe the last for awhile, and I decided to see if I could go to Oyashirazu or Ichiburi via the mountain road. I was not disappointed. The scenery was incredible and for at least an hour I didn't see a car. At the top of the mountains I found a lookout and further down a lake with tepees for accommodation. There's one I would not have expected. When I asked friends if they wanted to come up to the mountains with me and stay in some tepees they really decided that I had obviously had been too long on my own down there. It was getting a bit late to go to Ichiburi so I finished with a spectacular 8km downhill run to Oyashirazu.

That same evening my relationship was finally laid to rest and I was a single man again. Now, how to break the news to my employer, especially Kinokawa?

19: Gifts from the Omi gomi guy and a flying 'W'

Fortunes exist among leftovers - Japanese Proverb

Needing some recharging for my soul, or perhaps just needing a weekend free of alcohol poisoning, I headed up to Karuizawa for a spiritual retreat. We had a laid-back Friday evening, and then on the Saturday afternoon some of us went for a ride around Karuizawa, which is completely different to anywhere else I'd encountered in Japan. It's very rich, very western, and is full of beautiful homes in many styles, trendy cafes, and expensive shops.

My research tells me that the area was 'discovered' by Christian missionaries early in the century. To escape the hot summers of the Kanto plains many would retire to the coolness of the North Alps. These summer escapes for those of European blood were a common story across the colonised world, particularly with the British in Asia. Once up safely tucked away from the heat they could continue to operate in their own surreal, and quite often peculiar, world. Then again, one has only to research British colonialism to discover such affectations were lubricants that made the 'machine' work, and sprang from the confidence of the colonisers and their chosen elites. Eccentricity and other such behaviours could be afforded if one knew that they could be gotten away with. In Karuizawa they constructed their retreat homes, and still do in typical Western styles – from Bavarian to Cape Cod to Cotswolds, all on huge allotments. And so as one wanders along the leafy avenues traditional Japanese style homes are few and far between.

We took the opportunity to wander around some of the homes, which were obviously vacant at this time of year, waiting for the summer tenants from Tokyo and surrounds. Some had servants quarters attached that appeared as quite substantial lodgings in themselves. One had a huge dining room, and although it was obvious there was no owner *in situ* at that time, the dining table was fully set for sixteen people. After we took the bikes back we walked through a Japanese graveyard discussing the meaning of the wooden grave markers, then around a lake. With the autumn leaves out it was a wonderful afternoon. But maybe not for the girl in another group who fell off her bike and broke her leg. There were more meetings on the Sunday and then the fifty or so of sidled away back to our various postings.

Coming in from my experience of heaven the next day was hell as Setsuko worked me over on every point from lesson plans to an upcoming seminar, even the dates for the birthday party I was planning. At lunchtime I changed and was going to the gym to play basketball with the students when I was told there was a staff photo session in five minutes. I went back and changed again rapidly, and because I wasn't prior informed was the only male staff member without a jacket on. I also probably had my worst 'best' clothes on. Thanks for telling me everyone! After school I had to endure Setsuko's agonising at English staff meeting, as well as the silence of Fukushima and Matsuki. Then before I left I was told that I would be involved the next day with a student bike ride that would be about seventy kilometres in length with the last stretch being all uphill.

I called Jeet that night and it seemed that she, along with Wendy and Rananda, all had bad days. When I spoke to Rananda afterwards we decided that Monday must have been the national 'Give *gaijin* a hard time' day. Well, why not? The Japanese appear to have national days for everything else.

It must be noted that the bike ride the next day followed the old rail line track up the coast and turned out to be a lot of fun. The kids rode slowly and orderly - sometimes too slowly, but that didn't stop them from getting into trouble. As I was following a couple of boys one of them was watching some motorcyclists passing by on the adjoining road. I could see some poles looming up on the path, which acted as a sort of chicane, so I yelled loudly to them "Look out!" I know it may have maybe been more helpful if I had actually learnt some Japanese and used it in a form that a young testosterone-charged Japanese boy could understand. However I hadn't. At this point the one who had been watching the motorcycles turned back toward me, presumably to query what exactly I was telling him to watch out for. However the words had not yet crossed his lips before he was flying through the air in a classic 'Flying W' manoeuvre. Fortunately it didn't cause much damage - apart from a bruised ego.

Halloween came and the Catholic Church in Takada was throwing a fancy dress party. I realise the concept of a group of Scottish Catholics throwing a satanic celebration championed by God-fearing Americans is somewhat unusual. However there was free booze and maybe the chance of some pretty ladies so I was prepared to toss aside any philosophical resentment for the night. I caught the train up then got changed into my Fijian *sulu* in the station toilets. I'm really not sure why I had taken a *sulu* to Japan with me. But damn it, cometh the hour, and I had an opportunity to wear it. Hence I sallied from the station toilets looking like I was wearing a tailored dress. However I was not completely sure of the directions and spent an hour or so fruitlessly wandering around attired like an idiot, and a cross-dressing one at that. I decided that I was just not fated to get to this Halloween party. I removed my costume in a darkened alley and caught the last train home.

The next day was my birthday and it would have to be one of the most memorable I've ever had. I was visiting Omi *yochien* that day and once they heard it was my birthday the teachers and kids went into full celebration mode. I had to emerge from a big gift box then the kids presented me with gifts, and sang me a very cute Japanese birthday song with actions and lots of hand clapping. Then it was the photo session with a couple of kids sliding into the shot 'dancing variety' style that would have done Fred Astaire proud. The teachers also gave me a very *oishi* (delicious) birthday cake. It was all so extraordinary and I sat there thinking there was no other place I would want to be in the world than where I was right then.

It was getting incredibly colder and darker very quickly. The onset of the cold weather brought about my first serious cold and I had to take some time off. I ventured into a local 'chemist' and managed to convey to him my suffering via a phrasebook. Sympathetically this grey-haired old man sat me down on a stool and proceeded to cluck over me and ask a number of questions that I had no hope of answering. As I fumbled through my phrasebook he brought me some sweet gingery thing to drink that I think might have been ginseng. Eventually he weaselled out from under the counter a large bottle of tablets and putting them in my hand indicated that I should take four of them every few hours. Then he relieved me of ¥4,300. I couldn't believe it – but I could hardly say no given that I had been sitting on his stool for the last forty minutes or so. When I got back to school Setsuko informed me that the pills were a Chinese medicine. Somehow I had managed to stumble into the only herbalist place in town. Not that I thought I would ever find such a thing there. Two weeks later I finished the bottle but was still sniffing. So I located a <u>real</u> chemist on Highway 8, bought myself some 'Bufferin' as recommended by Setsuko, and two days later was back to full health. I put the thick quilt on my bed, and started wearing my thick pyjamas. I couldn't believe that just three months before I was sweltering in the heat!

Soon it was time for the tri-monthly recycle day so I grabbed the bike and went 'shopping'. There were so many bikes left out that day. I figured the *gomi* guys would have to sort the rubbish into 'burnable', 'non-burnable' and 'bikes'. This would actually be easier then in some other municipalities where they have to sort garbage into <u>44 different categories.</u> They would have to take time off work just to sort their rubbish out.

I had picked up and was mulling over a gas heater when the recycle truck turned up. The drivers took that away from me and put it in the back of the truck. Then they wanted me to follow them and were talking about '*prezento*'. When I got back to the apartment I took the heater off the back off the truck but they kept saying '*dame*' (no good) and '*prezento*', took it off me yet again and told me to wait in my apartment.

A little while later they arrived back with a working gas heater and a ten-speed racer! I didn't know how to thank them. As they moved off they stopped and picked up my *mama chari* bike. In a panic I thought they were taking it, not that it didn't deserve to be thrown out, but they were only moving it to get by in the truck. After they left I continued my shopping, and with winter coming up was looking particularly for skis. I found six good pairs bundled together - apart from the fact that the previous owner had sawn them in half to make it easier to dispose of. I couldn't find any others but along the way did pick myself up a VCR and TV for the bedroom in the hope that they would work. Which they did.

20: Junkie jellybeans and dancing Elvises

You can tell a lot about a fellow's character by the way he eats jelly beans.
- Ronald Reagan

I love jellybeans. Yes, I know they're bad for me, but I can't help it. My obsession started when I was fifteen years old. I was wearing braces at the time, that strange ritual of adolescence inflicted upon us by parents, mostly designed to stop us fornicating regularly with members of the opposite sex because they will no longer find us attractive. Naturally I was told by the orthodontist that I was not to have any sweets of any kind for the two years or so they were to keep all that metal in my mouth. I figured that this was just a conspiracy between my mother and the orthodontist. So in a spat of teenage rebelliousness I sought out all the sticky type lollies that I could and that's where the jellybeans came in. Eons later and living in Japan I stumbled across a shop selling jellybeans. Cool. For the next couple of nights I didn't sleep that well because of the utterly weird dreams that plagued me. None of them involving nudity or small furry animals however. There must have been some bizarre additives in those things! I told Rananda, who promptly sought out the shop and bought some too, but was disappointed when they didn't have the same effect. With a name like Rananda it was obvious that she had old hippies for parents.

It took me several months but I finally rented my first video in Japan. There was one video store in Omi but because there was not much choice I also joined up later at the video shop in Itoigawa. They had a lot more choice there - especially in the extremely large pornography section. Who needs jellybeans with bizarre additives when you can pick up a Japanese porn video? Unfortunately one of my Idobata students, Ken, worked there so it would be a bit embarrassing if I was to bang down 'Kyoko does Kyoto' and my rental card on the counter.

Until a few years ago any display of pubic hair was not allowed to shown in any kind of Japanese media. This law was relaxed for the print media, as exemplified by any magazine display in any convenience store. These also double as libraries as it's perfectly okay to go into a store and spend up to half a day reading all the magazines, or at least looking at the pictures, but never buying anyway[3]. To ascertain if the ban still existed in the film industry, and purely for research reasons only, I managed to get hold of a couple of these films. I waited until the night Ken was off shift and told the attendant I had forgotten my card. He being the trusting type, as most Japanese are, I told him my name was Maria along with Maria's phone number. This did not seem unusual to him. I thought about not returning them just to see how she would react, but given her volatile nature thought better of it.

The upshot was I discovered that to get around the ban Japanese filmmakers blur out the offending bits, although it doesn't take much to imagine. What about the story lines? To fill in the gaps between the 'naughty bits' they often have the filmmaker and/or lead actor ramble on incessantly or have a Q & A with the main actress about their hopes, desires and fantasies. In the one I watched, and you must remember my Japanese was not that good, she was saying something about snails and windsocks. I think. At this juncture I began to formulate the theory that Japanese porn is much akin to Japanese bureaucracy. As a westerner you just want them to get quickly to the important bits, whereas they believe in talking around the whole issue before they start getting anywhere. I got to bed late that night and slept pretty well - without the influence of jellybeans.

With winter closing in I decided to take the opportunity of a nice day for a bike ride. I rode up past the school and toward some of the snow-covered mountains in the distance. As seems to always be the case I rarely saw anyone else and these mountains had become my own personal domain. The road rose steeply above the valley and I began to admire the bewitching autumn hues of gold, green, brown and orange on the mountainsides. The white snow laden mountain tops drew closer and I felt encouraged to push on. I came to a clearing and beheld a view that took away the breath. In the distance past the rolling colours was the Japan Sea that seemed to go on forever. In another direction were majestic snow topped mountains of the North Alps glinting in the late afternoon sun. Below me lay Omi, Itoigawa, and far away Nou. I could have stopped and gazed at that view forever. When I left Albury I knew I would miss the countryside, but now Omi has subsumed that love. In my ears the soundtrack from 'Until the End of the World' rang out from my Walkman. It was then that I realised again how happy I was to be here and that I would indeed love this place '...until the end of the world'.

As I pushed on I chanced upon a tunnel. As I came out of the other side I found that I had made it up above the snowline and pressed on as far as I could. Soon after darkness was setting in so I considered it was time to turn back. I took another road and began to worry because it appeared to be going nowhere.

---

[3] Yes, you guessed it. As of early 2004 there was another bill slowly winding its way through the Diet - this one to make booksellers make certain materials unavailable for general reading by minors. It seemed to have come into force by 2005.

It was also very steep and dangerous, and because of the failing light I began to worry. Eventually it did turn out to be the right course. The only thing I had to worry about then was freezing fingers and face. The road down was steep and fast, and the temperature had dropped quickly. Eventually home, I thawed out in my small furo (bath).

Getting out of Omi a few days later found me aboard a very modern Limited Express heading for Nagoya. I had to change trains in Toyama and the lady in the information booth there spoke reasonable English and gave me all the advice I needed. I could have caught the Hokiriku Line train down the coast but decided to take the later Takayama Line train over the mountains. I bought myself some snacks for the train at the adjoining C.I.C. department store where the Christmas music was blaring, and all the paraphernalia on show. At first I considered this a little strange for a Buddhist country, but then dismissed as nothing more than just one more example of the juggernaut of global capitalism.

The trip over the mountains was quite spectacular with the mountains, rivers, gorges, and autumn colours. It would be even more amazing in mid-winter I think. In Nagoya I stopped for awhile to watch the twenty or so Japanese 'dancing Elvises' in Central Park. I later saw the same kind of thing in Tokyo's Harajuku. The whole activity involves a large number of men, dressed uniformly in black with pointy shoes, dark glasses and slicked back hair, sitting in a circle with a 'boom box' in the middle. There appears to be a leader who designates who should get up and perform a hip-thrusting 1950's style dance at any particular time. He may also deem that everyone should cavort at the same juncture in which case all will rise and twist away in a circle. And they don't do it for money – it just seems like their bizarre weekend hobby.

On the train back toward Niigata I was surrounded by smokers, and the guy next to me (until Takayama) loved hacking up phlegm and sniffing loudly, as many Japanese are wont to do. I thought it couldn't be any worse until I went to live in Shanghai where the Chinese have this behaviour down to an art form. Even Mao and his Cultural Revolution couldn't wipe out this habit. There was another guy on the train wearing the ugliest plaid jacket you would ever clap eyes on. I guess the scary thing was that somewhere out there were pants to match.

As I rode to school the next morning I noticed that the autumn leaves had turned to brown or disappeared - old man winter was now firmly ensconced. I was a few minutes late again that morning as usual making me consider the need to build a tunnel that came up underneath my desk. Later that week I went to an English seminar where all the Japanese teachers refused to speak in English. No wonder few people in Japan feel confident to speak English if even the teachers decline to do so. I had coffee with the girls afterwards and left just as Jeet and Rananda were getting stuck into another of their serious altercations.

21: Bōnenkai, plus wielding the mochi mallet

The merry year is born. Like the bright berry from the naked thorn.
- Hartley Coleridge

Oshōgatsu (New Year) was advancing toward us rapidly. Traditionally people eat *mochi* rice cakes at New Year made from pounded rice. This is a sticky glutinous mass that is usually filled with bean paste and is meant to be a symbol of happiness. I can't say I cared too much for it, but neither was it anything too awful, unlike *natto* – the cursed and smelly fermented beans that my wife loves to have for breakfast.

Beans are another of the basic Japanese food groups. Beans are found inside just about every possible food, and some not quite so possible. Before you buy any baked goods in Japan you must prod and prick it carefully to see if cohabited by any beans - which it generally will be. The Japanese have also invented one of the most evil tasting foods in the universe made from fermented beans. This awful concoction is the aforementioned *natto* - which means, I think, 'Nasty Awful Terrible Tasting Offal'. When you lift it out of the bowl it brings with it a long stringy residue, not unlike your snot after a three-week head cold. Some westerners have sung the praises of *natto*, but these personality types did the same about opium in China too. I'm assured the end results of ingesting both substances are very different.

You have to be very careful to chew properly on *mochi* though. In my experience this can take sometimes up to half an hour for a piece about the size of a large pea. Paradoxically, quite a number of Japanese die over the New Year period due to choking on this symbol of happiness. The award for lateral thinking must go to the woman I read about in a news article around this time, who saved her elderly mother by sticking a vacuum cleaner in her mouth and turning it on reverse.

Mochitsuki happens in late December to make *mochi* to eat at *Oshōgatsu* so it can be dedicated to the gods. One day at Tazawa *yochien* the kids were holding *mochitsuki* with their teachers and parents, and I was asked to join in too. This process involves pounding special soft rice in an *usu* (wooden tub) with *kine* (large wooden mallets) until it morphs into the previously mentioned sticky mess, er, mass. Most mothers turned up to help in their aprons along with cloth head coverings. There were also two fathers in the same attire looking decidedly uncomfortable and embarrassed. Just like I was when I had to put on that stuff too. I resembled Enid Sharples out of 'Coronation Street'. But we laid all others to shame when the three of started swinging those mallets in synchronised fashion. I even got to share the fruits of our labour with my two fellow males in a kind of bonding experience afterwards. Instead of "Hey, how about them Lakers?" we could do stuff like compare the size of our mallets.

Enid and 'her' mallet

The *chugakko* students had been practicing for the choral competition for what seemed months. Any kind of competition at a Japanese school is treated with the utmost dedication and seriousness. All of the groups did really well and I was stunned when the most difficult class in the school sang 'Swing Low Sweet Chariot'. A song in English from a group who generally refused to speak any! At the end the winners were announced and lots of the losing girls were crying bitterly. I felt so sad for them because there was so much pressure to do well, especially after so much effort had been expended. A couple of *san-nensei* (Year Three) girls in front of me were really letting the tears flow. I waited for other teachers to say something comforting to them but no-one reacted. Then an insensitive photographer took a close-up photo of them and that made me pretty b***** angry. Finally, I leant forward and tried to encourage them, but it only seemed to make it worse. Oh well, live and learn. Another cultural *faux pas*.

Every year before the New Year there are always lots of *bōnenkai*. The meaning of this means something like, 'forget your worries'. In other words, this year is over and next year will be better. At school we put in quite a bit of money in every month to pay for any *enkai* but I always seemed to have to pay an extra amount every time we actually went anywhere. This time I got slugged ¥7,600 for the *bōnenkai* despite figuring I'd had at least ¥15,000 already in the 'kitty'.

Nonetheless it was fun – not that I really understood any of it. The food was just okay, even though the restaurant was very highly rated. It was funny because even with all the food laid out in front of me I found myself craving for a steak and chips. Soon after what appeared? Steak! But, it was like much Japanese cuisine I had come to expect at these dinners - cold and almost raw!

Oh, for a hot plate. Chips turned up later too, even crinkle cut, but they too were cold and soggy.

Afterwards we went to a bar in Itoigawa for the *nijikai* where as usual we all proceeded to get very inebriated. Some of the teachers wanted to kick on so I invited them back to my place. Part of the reason was to entice Matsuki, the very good looking, and very drunk, computer teacher back as well. She is what is referred to in my culture as a 'two-pot screamer'. It basically means that with two drinks someone is pretty well on their ear. Unfortunately for me our colleagues stopped the taxi on the way to take her upstairs to her apartment and put her to bed. Nonetheless the five of us remaining had a fine time, and I introduced them to strange new intoxicants such as Tequila, Kahlua, and Southern Comfort.

They all left about midnight and it was then that I realised how very drunk I was as I kept tripping between the toilet and bedroom. Finally I got to sleep, or I passed out – I'm not sure which! I woke face-up at 4.00am with all the lights still on (in the apartment – definitely not me that's for sure), and still in my dressing gown and slippers. I rearranged myself as best as I could in my condition then crashed until about 8.30.

I awoke decidedly seedy. With various forms of Japanese alcoholic substances still secreting themselves from my body I found it even more disturbing to realise that a monkey had attacked me. The cheeky bugger was banging on my head and had s*** in my mouth. Or so it seemed anyway. If this was a New Year hangover then *bōnenkai* was not worth it! I managed to put down some cereal for breakfast but couldn't take anymore than a couple of mouthfuls of coffee. I threw some things into a suitcase, plus my passport, and somehow managed to get myself onto a train heading for Tokyo and Narita Airport. Christmas vacation was calling me.

Somehow I managed to navigate my thick-headed way to Narita Airport. In my blurry state before check-in I line up to buy a newspaper only to find that the fat European tourist at the front has forgotten that he's in an airport shop, not at b***** Woolworths. So there I stand and fume as he checks out newspapers, magazines, enough souvenirs and fluffy toys to distribute to half of Frankfurt's children, plus a weeks supply of food - just in case his Lufthansa crashes in Siberia, and then he won't have to eat his fellow passengers.

But wait it gets worse - I then have to check-in. One of his friends is trying to carry on some huge apparatus that he's obviously just purchased in duty free. What is it about some people that makes them think that if they fasten some tape and strings around a huge box it won't be recognised as a 600kg refrigerator? Then when you get on the plane they are, of course, not going to find room near their seat. No, they will be waving their smelly Teutonic crotch in your face and still be struggling to put it in the locker above you as the plane taxis for take-off. I lay back, think of warmer climes, and soon am snoozing deeply in alliance with my fellow Japanese passengers.

22: The Yakuza Ramen Bar

Obviously crime pays, or there'd be no crime - G. Gordon Liddy

I spent the Christmas break back with old college friends in California and hadn't experienced the whole Japanese New Year thing. Flying into Narita Airport my body clock was on 4.30 Friday morning, but according to the Japanese clock it was 9.30 Friday night. Do you want to know about one of the <u>really</u> great things about living in Japan? When you come back from overseas you can get in the Japanese passport line. This is <u>so</u> cool. You're just standing nonchalantly amongst the Japanese returnees and when you look over to the foreigner line, which is really easy because you're always the tallest, you see this long queue of white tourist faces staring back at you. And they're just thinking, "What the hell is this guy trying to pull? He can't be Japanese. Maybe he got his eyes done, no?" and similar conjecture. So you skip through in about five minutes, compared to their often one hour plus. You look back at them as you skip through, flash that mischievous grin, and think, "Suckers, eat my dust!" I must mention at this point that if you are <u>not</u> a resident <u>but</u> you are merely married to a Japanese citizen they will still make you serve your dues in the *gaijin* line – even if there is <u>no-one</u> in the Japanese section.

All my baggage made it in one piece this time, unlike my last trip to Tokyo. I sorted out my train schedules and figured I could get home just after 1.00am so I decided it just wasn't worth staying in Tokyo. Lugging all the extra stuff I had bought was too atrocious a chore to be navigating my way around the subway. I had to stop every twenty metres it was so heavy! I had just over an hour to wait at Ueno Station then I struggled with everything down to the platform, finding I had to walk to the furthest carriage. I had a fifteen-minute break in Nagaoka, just enough time for hauling all my stuff from one platform to another, and then I got the express to Itoigawa.

It was almost impossible keeping my eyes open. Unlike the Japanese who seem to wake up three minutes before their destination, I was afraid I'd miss my stop(s) but eventually made it okay. Taking the late trains worked well because there weren't many people on them, hence no hassles with baggage. What really p***** me off were two similar incidents. Let me elucidate,

1) I was coming in on the Skyliner train from Narita and one lady was obviously upset that she and her husband had to sit next to me. She was chattering away to all in the near vicinity and was actively looking for another seat, her head craning back and forth - somewhat like an owl on smack. I smiled at her in a knowing way and she quieted down, almost certainly worried that I understood what she was talking about. I didn't, but it was a bit b***** obvious.

2) After I switched from the *shinkansen* to the express at Nagaoka a family of three went and asked to be moved as soon as they saw they had to sit next to me. The younger son, obviously not yet aware of the concept of xenophobia, or perhaps even having a foreign teacher at his school, seemed disappointed. What was I likely to do to these people? Or had twelve hours on a plane made my body odour repulsive within a five-metre radius?

Yet the Japanese people will need to quickly come to grips with what appears to often be a collective national paranoia. With the rapidly changing demographics of Japan, a national discussion has begun about opening the country to more overseas immigration. A prime ministerial commission concluded, that Japan must, "encourage foreigners who can be expected to contribute to the development of Japanese society to move in and possibly take up permanent residence here."

At the same time resident *gaijin*, some having lived in the country all their life, must run campaigns against the once mandatory fingerprinting of foreign residents in Japan, and to end discrimination against them in public places in the country - especially *onsen*, where a Japanese-only policy remains in some places.

The likelihood of greater immigration to a nation that in 2003 granted asylum to only ten refugees seems slim. In the last decade Japan has issued about 50,000 work visas a year – a veritable drop in the ocean of the 640,000 immigrants a year that demographers say are necessary to prevent Japan's population from shrinking. The New York Times reported that, "…building on such xenophobia, Japan's nurses' unions successfully lobbied lawmakers of the governing Liberal Democratic Party to block the admission of foreign doctors and nurses. Caught between Japan's high labour costs and anti-immigrant sentiment, some mainstream politicians have even suggested exporting some of Japan's elderly to Thailand and the Philippines, but that has never won much popular support." The next few years will be interesting in this regard indeed.

The first Monday night back was <u>another</u> school *enkai*. This is the *shin-nenkai* 'welcome the year' party. The usual frivolity however was just a mere kid show compared to the upcoming conference in Nagano where I was not to sober up for five whole days. The Ministry of Education had designated the town of Togura in Nagano Prefecture as the conference site for English teachers and the main hotel in town had been booked.

However our pre-conference material warned that it would not be a wise idea to wander away from the hotel as most businesses were *yakuza* (Japanese 'mafia') owned or controlled. Presumably that meant that the hotel we were staying in was probably likewise. We were warned again on the opening night that venturing into the wrong bar may cost us a substantial loss of 'the readies', or maybe even some digits. The latter was not specified actually, but could be easily speculated. Why were we staying there if it was so dangerous? Obviously someone in the government owed someone in the *yakuza* a favour.

You see, to maintain *wa* Japanese society must work together. So government, big business and even the police will all somehow manage to get on with the local crime bosses. Crime gangs are so open in Japan they hand out business cards for goodness sakes. The relevant authorities even possess industry employment statistics - 84,000 at the last count in 2001. For the 2003 Japan Almanac the National Police Agency had kindly broken the numbers down into percentages on a pie-chart with the notorious *Yamaguchi-gumi* topping the list with 43%.

However as Japan moves into the 21st Century the *yakuza* have begun to fall on hard times. It is not only the recession, nor a harsher a legal environment, but more from increased 'foreign competition', such as the Chinese *Triads*, and even a labour shortage. Apparently the soft Japanese youth of today do not find the lure of the underworld as appealing as it once was and look upon mob work as *kitsui, kitanai* and *kiken* (arduous, dirty and dangerous) – more commonly simply referred to as *san-kei* or 3K. The lack of recruits beating a path to their door has even forced some gangs to advertise in newspapers and employment magazines!

While we're on the subject of crime I must say that generally the Japanese police are a charming and efficient lot, and most times don't shoot or beat people, particularly minorities. They also don't seem to make many arrests but that can be attributed to, a) there's not a lot of crime, b) what crime there is can generally be attributed to the *yakuza* anyway, and, c) it's hard to find a suspect.

Here's a hypothetical example. A foreigner walks into a police station,

"Officer I have just been mugged and had my wallet stolen."

"Ah thank you. Yes, please sit down. Did you see this person?"

"Yes, quite clearly."

"And what did this Korean look like?"

"He wasn't Korean, he was Japanese."

"Are you sure? How about Chinese? Apart from the *yakuza* crime is very un-Japanese."

"Yes, I'm sure he was Japanese."

"Okay if you insist. What did he look like?"

"Short, with dark hair, and brown eyes."

At this stage you realise what a very foolish thing you have just said. The policeman also points out that you were a very bad person for allowing yourself to be robbed. To avoid losing face you decide to kill yourself, bowing politely as you hurriedly leave.

Another thing about Japanese police is their cars. In America the cops drive big cars, and wear leather jackets and mirror sunglasses. You're not going to do diddly if they are nearby. In my part of Japan they all seemed to drive 'K' cars. What the 'K' stands for I'm not exactly sure, but these cars are so small (*see: ashtray*) that the drivers have to get out to change gears. As you sweep past them at 240km/h are you going to think, "Oh no, there's a cop!" Of course not.

Unlike every other country in the world the police in Japan still possess good manners. The best example of this inherent politeness was described to me by Joanne. At every train station there is always a cache of abandoned bikes. At one particular station I had 'borrowed' one of these bikes and rode it to a nearby stop in an effort to avoid an otherwise lengthy connection. A few weeks later Joanne had decided at the same station to also 'borrow' one for an errand and return it in a few minutes. Within thirty seconds the police had swooped in an unmarked car. She was riding a 'stolen bicycle'. How they worked this out she never knew.

Jake, another friend, just happened past and stopped to see what was happening. So they were <u>both</u> taken to the *koban* (station) for questioning. After the initial interview the policemen pulled out world maps and wanted to know where in Canada she came from, what Toronto and her family were like, and other such relevant questions. Eventually after a couple of hours she had to sign a statement and then the police drove her home to Kakizaki - about forty minutes away, because they had kept her so long. They stopped at McDonalds to buy her food because they were worried she was hungry. A pity she was vegetarian. As they left they assured her it would not get back to her school - probably because they wouldn't want the town to look bad by having employed a criminal.

And so, having been graciously granted half a day by my school to travel there, I headed off for the conference and got into Togura about 4pm the following day (Tuesday). Most others had not and so I was forced to wait a substantial amount of time for a shuttle bus to come. I guess I could've wandered out looking for a taxi but feared I might get lost, get my dick lopped off, get all my cash taken, or a combination of all three.

Accommodation was typical Japanese style with six people assigned to each room. This number remained in flux somewhat over the next three nights. I only remember spending the first night in my room, and that according to my hazy alcohol-impaired recollection was with something like about twelve to fifteen individuals of both genders – all in a similar or worse state than me. The first night it was obvious who the 'party' prefecture were. Many of us from Niigata turned up in our guest *yukata* for dinner, much to the astonishment of others, including most of the hotel staff. When dinner was complete and most teachers had left there was a remaining core of Niigata-ites laying siege to the beer supplies, and after being moved on from there proceeded on to the bar.

After the bar closed we drank in a room for quite awhile then decided, "Hey, let's head out for *ramen*!" We considered whether this was wise given the warnings but the demon drink had us in its hold and foolishness was the order being served. We eventually ended up in a small *ramen* bar where the dragon lady proprietor was obviously quite displeased to have our custom. She kept serving up beer for ¥1,000 each, even when we didn't want it. What appeared to be her evil henchman with a 'barcode' hairstyle lurked in the corner eyeing our digits so we just coughed up the dough without complaint. However once outside Peters produced a plethora of goods from inside his jacket and explained that he felt it his duty, as at least some form of passive resistance, to relieve her of some chattels from her bar. Until very recent times I always believed, obviously derived from a beverage-related misassumption, that Ian the Kiwi was the culprit. Hard to believe seeing Ian always seemed a respectable sort of chap. He has become even more respectable of recent times, first by marrying Yukiko, next finally finishing his doctorate, and then becoming a respectable university lecturer, of sorts, in Nagoya.

The morning wake up call was delivered by the cleaning ladies at some obscene hour. Breakfast was distinctly un-*oishi* - as were, well, all the meals. The seminars were also quite uninteresting and unfortunately tended to get in the way of the partying. Wednesday night there was a disco where I got charged ¥700 for my first drink so I spent the rest of the night with a large bottle of Coke and Southern Comfort that I had salvaged from the suitcase in my room and shoved down the front of my pants. Apart from lowering my drinks bill by a wide margin it also caught the attention of a number of females. Rob confided to me later he was talking to a girl who had promptly abandoned him when I walked into the room. Her excuse? "I've heard he's got a huge ****", she had said. It would've been nicer if she appreciated my personality.

Thursday night was the Talent Night where I crashed and burned with my stand-up routine, then got thrown off stage when Tim the perverted pom came on and showed his very small genitalia to the gathered throng numbering several hundred. Months, even years later I would be recognised with, "That's the guy who did the really bad stand up in Togura while another flashed his knob." Friday we all split and many of us went to Hakuba to ski, and drink. We finally all went home on Sunday, mostly to join detoxification and AA programs.

That evening I was writing a letter when some emergency vehicles rushed by. Looking out the window I noticed flames down behind the town hall. Wandering down to observe I found the sight of one house and two sheds well alight, and several others looking seriously threatened. The owners were madly throwing belongings out the windows to bystanders who were stacking them up and covering them with tarpaulins that had appeared from out of nowhere.

The whole exercise impressed two things upon me. One is the very temporal nature of material possessions, indeed even life itself, which can be so quickly snatched away. All is but dust to the wind. Should I say 'dude' at the end of that last sentence? Second impression was the community resolve of the town. The vast majority of people were there to help out, not gawk at the misfortune of their neighbour. This must be the very essence of community. Neither did anyone have to watch over the possessions stacked out on the road. No one would have dreamed of taking anything. I realised again that, despite the frustrations and misunderstandings one must bear, that opportunities like this to be with people at their natural best made it all worth it.

23: *O yuki*, or the fine art of coping with cold Niigata weather

Ambitious of blue sky - Japanese Proverb

The weather became even colder and more unbearable. December had brought the disconcerting sight of new red and white marker poles on the road to school. I guessed that they were snow poles and the full white winter experience would not be too far away now. And then one Saturday morning in January, there it was – the first heavy snowfall. I was excited, but it was soon to wear off. I thought I was living in Japan but it sometimes felt more like Siberia. Just call me 'Scott of the Antarctic'. Well, that's how I felt walking to school most mornings through freezing blasts of *yuki*.

One of the first words you learnt when you came to my part of Japan was *yuki* (snow). After that you quickly also learnt the meaning of *o yuki*, which roughly translates as 'big snow'. I'm still looking for a Japanese word that translates from the English, "Bugger me! I can't believe how much bloody snow there is!" You see, as you probably realise by now, I come from Australia. Australia is the driest continent in the world and my state just happens to be the driest state. Our local newspaper will stop the presses if the temperature drops below zero overnight. And just occasionally every twenty years or so, about three centimetres of snow will fall on nearby Mt. Lofty.

At this stage please note that Mt. Lofty is not actually tall enough to be a mountain, nor is it particularly lofty. The only reason why it could be accredited as such is maybe that early English explorer who named it (Matthew Flinders) might have had a particularly big *enkai* the night before. Anyway this fall of definitely un-*o yuki* is a cause of celebration, not to mention traffic jams, car accidents and the odd fatality as roughly half of the one million or so population rush up a tiny one-laned road to the summit for snow play. The other half either don't own cars, watch the special live broadcasts, or have real lives to live.

Anyway, what I'm trying to say is that winters are not that tough in my hometown. After being rejected to teach in Japan for the first time I took a job in Albury, New South Wales. Albury is not far from what we Aussies jokingly refer to as the Australian Alps, probably named so by another white explorer after a quite savage *enkai*. It still didn't snow in that town but during winter it dropped below zero overnight quite often. This is what Australians refer to as 'brass monkey' weather, ergo it could be said, "Geez mate, it's cold enough to freeze the balls off a brass monkey". Living in an unheated timber house did not help, and this one-year sojourn was enough to solidify my disdain for cold weather, and of course unheated homes.

When filling out the J.E.T. employment application for a second time I was at pains to ask for a posting as far south as possible for the very obvious reason that, "I do not enjoy living in cold weather climates". The big day came and my acceptance letter duly arrived. It read 'Niigata-ken'. I checked every prefecture on Kyushu in the south, but no not there. As my finger moved further and further north up the map my palms began to sweat and my temples throbbed. Just before I hit Hokkaido there it was. With typical bureaucratic aplomb I had been placed in one of the wettest, coldest, and snowiest prefectures. In fact I have been assured that, for its latitude, it's the snowiest place on earth! Did they bother to read what I said, or was I just the unfortunate loser in a shady game of *janken*?

During my first ultra *o yuki* winter I was told, "You are very lucky. This is most snow in ten years". Obviously this was a new concept of 'lucky' I had not encountered before. Later I realised it might have been worse as I could have been placed in nearby Nagano-ken. But then again Nagano had actually found a semi-useful purpose for all of its snow by holding something called a Winter Olympics. This sort of festival is akin to having a hundred strangers around to your bed-sit for dinner, whilst flushing your life savings, and a few of your neighbour's life savings, down the toilet. Nagano busily constructed lots of shiny new infrastructure that will be useful for years to come. It's just that the people who it would be useful to are not there anymore. Neither is any of the government documentation - which somehow was all burnt by local bureaucrats before the auditors could get to it and jail anyone for graft and corruption.

Anyway let's stop digressing and look at the problem itself. First of all the people there obviously are a hardy bunch. They refuse to concede that winter is any different from summer - the hot sweaty season that starts two weeks after snow stops falling in April. "No", they cry, "we can go on exactly the same as we always do. We have no need for central heating because we like sleeping with the rest of our family under a coffee table. We are one of the most technologically advanced nations in the world; we just don't want to flaunt it!"

And I ask you - what compels old people in weak states to act like lemmings and fall off roofs or into rivers while trying to clear large piles snow by hand? Is this some sociological form of acceptable matricide/patricide? Honestly, every time the prefecture had a dump of snow another few pensioners dropped off the twig shovelling snow. Why can't Japan have a marginalised class of people that will do this simple job for food like any other civilised country? Fortunately I have a simple answer. At the time of writing the American president (*motto:* have guns, will travel) had just announced that the U.S. would move toward having 60% of the global arms trade. Yes attentive followers of world affairs may note - the very same global arms trade that the very same American president was trying to actually stop.

Well Mr. Prez, and his successors, you can get off to a flying start by throwing a few thousand flame throwers into crates and addressing them to 'Niigata-ken, Japan'. This will not only reduce snow drifts and promote goodwill, but will also take the focus off Okinawan objections to all your military bases down there and their occupants transgressions with local twelve year old girls. It will also mean the redeployment of medical personnel, because so many old people won't die, to the role of fire fighters - because we all know that many of the sturdy and well designed wood and paper Japanese houses might stand in the way of a really good snowdrift. And if any more of those pesky North Korean boats land? Well, they will all be roasty-toasty won't they? Of course, all those people who wish to thank me can send me cash. I'd accept credit cards or cheques but maybe that's a point of discussion best left for later – if I remember.

While we discuss the concept of 'cold' did I mention that around this time I had been seeing someone that I'd met in the conference in Togura? Well, it was all wine and roses for the first month or so, and then it became patently obvious that it wasn't going anywhere. You would think I would learn from experience by now. My last three 'partners', to use one of their PC terms, had all been from the land of the free and home of the insecure. The first one I had dated in America at college but after I went back to Australia she got sick of me waiting for my green card and took off with someone else. The first I knew about that scenario was the day her answering machine message chirped, "Mike and I aren't in at the moment…"

Number Two was the insecure clinging vine from Louisiana on a Rotary scholarship who had tried to build me into the perfect man, and whom I'd been forced to pry off like a mollusc before I'd left for Japan. Number Three was the self-described misanthrope that I met at the conference. There were a number of warning signs, but the most obvious was when, feeling a little romance might help, I turned up on a surprise visit on a roundabout trip home from Tokyo - one that we originally had meant to be going on together. She freaked out, said I couldn't stay more than a few minutes, and by the time I got home had taken the opportunity to dump me by e-mail. I was going to include the full text here as a final ultimate act of retribution. However, as is the case, I could not under legal advice. I can nonetheless reveal that it did fall into the one of the 'usual excuse' categories – this one being of the "It's me, not you" variety, with just a hint of the "I still want to be friends".

So that was that. I was supposed to take the hint and slide away under a rock somewhere. I don't know where she is now. Probably head of a witch's coven somewhere is my guess, or maybe locked away in some kind of cult with herself as the solitary member.

I must give her one thing - at least she was being honest, apparently, even if it wasn't to my face. And that was true to form in at least one way in Japan. When it comes to lost and found Japan must contain the most honest people in the world. This is one marvellous trait that I so love about the Japanese. Stories abound of full wallets being returned with apologies for it being returned so late, even non-descript items such as cheap umbrellas or spare keys. In Tokyo, with a larger population of something like 33 million in the metropolitan area, thousands of lost items more usually find their way to the Tokyo Metropolitan Police Lost and Found Centre. In a warehouse that is four stories high, hundreds of thousands of lost objects groan on the shelves - meticulously catalogued according to the date and location of discovery, the information put in a database and then able to be searched via the internet.

In fact smaller versions of this exist all over Japan, based on a 1,300-year-old system dating back to a code written in the year 718, long preceding Japan's unification as a nation and its urbanisation. At that time, lost goods, animals and, even more mysteriously, servants had to be handed over to a government official within five days of being found. After a year, the government took possession of the property, although the owner could still reclaim them at a later date. The code was both very strict in its definitions (it stipulated that people had no right to keep lumber found adrift in a flood) and any subsequent punishment (in 1733 two officials who kept a parcel of clothing were led around town and executed).

Strangely, to western eyes, it has even apparently survived the economic slump that has contributed to a general rise in crime. In 2002 people found and brought to the Tokyo centre US$23 million alone in cash, 72 percent of which was returned to the owners, once they had persuaded the police it was theirs. About 19 percent of it went to the finders after no one had claimed the money during a statutory six-month period. If the original owner is not found after half a year, the finder can claim the object or money. But most of them don't bother making any claims, and the objects and proceeds usually end up going into government coffers. Children are taught from an early age to hand in anything they find to the police in their neighbourhoods. So most of the 200 to 300 people who come to the centre every day looking for their lost items take the system for granted. I wish that this may not only continue forever in Japan but that other nations may learn from it as well.

24: *Matsuri* month madness

A bad day skiing is better then a good day at work – Bumper sticker

I entered a month that seemed to be chock-full of *matsuri*. I was invited one Sunday afternoon to an international folk dancing festival in Toyama that sounded like fun. I had visions of fully regaled *cossacks* and *campesino* in a truly exhilarating performance – live and direct from the Edinburgh Festival. Well, maybe that was a bit optimistic. I ended up watching mostly middle-aged ladies twirl around on stage in folk costumes. I'm sure they'd practiced a lot and indeed were putting in their best effort. It was also a huge step of internationalisation for the locals. As for me, well at least I scored a neat poster from the foyer.

I slept very well but woke up the following morning feeling like crap, which continued through the day. I finally asked Setsuko if she could help book me in for a doctor's appointment. The doctor spoke a bit of English and sent me on my way with some ointment for a rash and packets of variously coloured powders to swallow for my cold. It seems that whatever may ail you in Japan your local doctor will always have a packet of coloured powder to fix you right up.

"A broken leg you say? Well here, take one packet of this blue powder every three hours." "A brain haemorrhage? Ah, two packets of white powder will have you up and about in no time".

The sad part is that after you've been in Japan for awhile you don't even ask what it is or why he or she's giving it to you. In fact, if you don't get any you might come away feeling a little uncomfortable, thinking that maybe whatever you have is terminal.

At least, 1) the stuff the doctor gave me seemed to work, 2) I got some value out of my extravagant national health insurance plan, and 3) everybody in town knew I had a cold. I found out later though that I had to take *nenkyu* (paid holiday) because I didn't get a doctor's certificate – even though my supervisor had booked the appointment for me. Ah, bureaucracy!

The next two *matsuri*, back to back, were the Koide Snowball Fight Festival, and the Tōkomachi Snow Festival. One of the local English teachers had scammed some free tickets from the town for the Snow Festival and we had a really great view. The ice castle that had been built was incredible, the fireworks brilliant, and the sculptures fantastic. However the acts put on were mostly, let's say, very mediocre. The local *shogakko* students had a choir that sang a few songs then the ridiculously attired hosts spent the best part of thirty minutes having an in-depth interview with one of the kids while we all froze our asses off. Most of the students grew restless, as did the crowd. Perhaps the next act was running late. Another student, who definitely looked like a troublemaker, had been sat next to a teacher at the back. As he started to get a bit edgy I noticed that the teacher, in a fine example of behaviour management, was holding him in an arm lock behind his back. Presumably they did not wanting him spoiling the occasion, or maybe the teacher is just a sadistic bully.

The next day was the Snowball Fight Festival in Koide. The town had set out an area that was the size of about half a football field and constructed a few barriers in which team participants could hide behind. The object was to make snowballs, naturally enough, and then try to inflict as much damage as possible on the opposing team. The first few rounds went well until as such time as the snow in the allotted area began to suffer from being trampled underfoot. By lunchtime there had been no replenishment of snow and competitors were suffering from bleeding fingers as they attempted to extract small shards of crushed ice to throw at their competitors. So one must probably pronounce the whole exercise somewhat a waste of time - unless you were going to the *enkai* afterwards. The most fun our group had was sledding out the back - particularly when we had a chain of eight go over a jump and wipe out a bunch of passing pedestrians. But they saw the humour in it as well, fortunately. In another particular nation they would have sued our asses off.

Another festival on was the Tochio Fox Festival. I didn't make it to this one but apparently it entails the local residents dressing up as foxes. Okay, I follow that part. The next connection is a little tougher. After dressing as foxes (see Part One), the males then go out into a parade and pinch the females. Then, and I'm not making this up, the female response is to slap the male back. What happens after that I don't know, apart from there has to an *enkai* in there somewhere. There is also fertility festival in Niigata somewhere up north where, if you have the right connections, you can ride the large wooden phallus float through town.

In the same month I attended not yet another festival, but the staff ski trip to Akakura. I never thought skiing could be a chore until then. Once again the group mentality of the Japanese meant we had to all ski together and do the same things, including ski lessons which I hadn't had for fifteen years. But it was all meant to be part of *wa* and the bonding exercise. I spent most of the weekend waiting around for others and God forbid that we may do anything individually. If anyone got separated they had walkie-talkies so that they could find the main group. It went something like this.

11.05am: You'd be skiing along nicely, trying not to get too far ahead or too far behind. Suddenly they realise, someone's missing! A teacher reaches into his pocket and produces a walkie-talkie.

"SCHHH. Matsuba-sensei, where are you?"

"SCHHH. I'm skiing the bottom run with Kiyomura-sensei. SCHHH Where are you?"

"SCHHH. We are up the top run near the restaurant. SCHHH We will all wait three hours here for you to come."

"SCHHH Okay – see you soon!"

11.30pm: "SCHHH. Matsuba-sensei, where are you?"

"SCHHH. We are in the gondola. SCHHH We saw Wada-sensei at the back of the queue as we were leaving. SCHHH Please wait for him too."

11.55pm: "SCHHH. Wada-sensei, where are you?"

"SCHHH. I am nearly to the front of the line. I will be there in twenty five minutes."

12.30pm: Finally we are all together, after freezing our asses off for ninety minutes, but then we have to have lunch.

I was not that bad really, but you kind of get the feel. Fortunately they decided to be culturally sensitive in the afternoon and allow me to go off and ski at my own pace. Or maybe it was just because I'm such a grumpy bastard.

25: A Tale of Two Capitals

Like all great travellers, I have seen more than I remember, and remember more than I have seen. - Benjamin Disraeli

There was a conference in Kobe followed by a long school break and I decided to go travelling. The alternative was to look at postcards stuck on my apartment window whilst tearing up a large quantity of ¥1,000 notes. Much the same effect and I wouldn't even have to leave home.

My work colleagues in Omi were always surprised at the number of trips I took. In fact I was much better travelled in Japan than probably about half the staff. I guess it doesn't help when the average Japanese worker takes less than ten days off during the year. Three days off in a row was deemed an unusual bonus for many of my co-workers. Plus I explained to them that I only had two years to see Japan. They had their whole lives.

The conference was in Kobe, so I settled on the following itinerary. I would catch the train to Kyoto, the ancient capital of Japan, then to Kobe with a side trip to Himeji to see the famous castle. After that I would head up to Tokyo (formerly known as Edo, or Eastern Capital when it took over from Kyoto under the military 'shogunate'), further to Nikko, then complete the circle to home.

In Kyoto I stayed with a friend I had met in Karuizawa, along with several other of her acquaintances who had much the same idea. Kyoto is a beautiful old city and fortunately escaped the ravages of American bombers in WWII. I believe it was one of the cities that were considered possible targets for the A-Bomb. The decision was finally nailed down to four possibilities - Niigata City, along with Kokura, Hiroshima and Nagasaki. The planes were actually on their way to Niigata but they had to turn back because, due to the usual s***** weather they have, the 'Enola Gay' would not have been able to see anything to bomb. There's nothing worth bombing there still.

There is an amazing amount to see in Kyoto that can take several days. Like Tokyo you have to prioritise what you really want to see. If you don't you can get 'templed' out rather quickly. First stop on my list was Kiyomizu temple, which was just packed. I didn't bother to go in as I was really only using it as the starting point for the Heritage Walk, which I highly recommend. I figured that the biggest crowds are generally at the places where you have to pay. So extrapolating that theory out one perhaps could be so bold as to come to conclusion that there must be kickbacks paid to the tourist companies whose buses hog the majority of adjoining car park space.

I walked along to Maruyama *Koen* (park) stopping to look at some sights on the way. As I sat in the park eating a morning snack a guy wandered over to talk to me. There was something about his face that I couldn't work out to start with. Then I realised - he shouldn't really use so much foundation in hiding his bad acne. He had been getting his make-up tips from Bette Midler and really had laid it on thick! From the park I walked to the art galleries but they are closed on Mondays. Always seems to be my luck. I did the walk along the Path of Philosophy before going to get some lunch. I didn't feel enlightened afterwards but it was quite pleasant. I was into meditation at this time, which had been good for the soul. Despite its Buddhist traditions meditation is more popular in other parts of Asia than Japan. It's not everyone's idea of a good time but at least it's better than sitting around doing nothing.

The rest of the day was a bit wasted. It started to rain but I managed to find an umbrella at a bank before it got serious. You don't have to be worried about taking umbrellas – they are forsaken by the thousands in Japan. I was a little circumspect in this regard. If it started to rain and I didn't have one I would look outside nearby convenience stores, restaurants, etc. If there was one in the rack outside that was not wet, and maybe a little dusty, I figured it had been abandoned and nobody would be bothered if I took it.

Conversely my N.Y. friend Alan had come up with a groundbreaking 'Social umbrella fund' theory. This theory went along the lines of – you buy one umbrella when you first came to Japan. If you ever lost it there was no need to worry because you could just take another. Then the person's you took takes someone else's. And so on, until someone circumvents the cycle by either picking up a truly lost umbrella, thereby breaking the chain, or taking Alan's again. Then you can work out what happens from there. A sort of karmic chaos theory of umbrellas where nobody is really inconvenienced. Later I walked down and caught the train to the *geisha* district in Gion. I had a bit of a walk through the back streets and along the riverside, but didn't spy any *geisha* or *maiko* (apprentice *geisha*) making their rounds, but did notice lots of what I presume are hostess bars/brothels.

The next day I was off to Himeji and ran into Alan, he of the umbrella theory, and Aaron, another friend from N.Y., at the castle. Aaron was definitely a 'party hard' type guy but with a quite funny acerbic wit about him. Peters, as he was more commonly referred to, would send bizarre e-mails without any context, such as,

"This is the root from the oolaponga tree. Today we'll cook it up with some beer and Vegemite. . ."

When I informed him a couple of years later that I was at last getting married his encouraging reply was,

"It looks like I lost a bet to someone on whether you'd one day become a useful member of society…"

I'm unsure whether he ever actually became a useful part of society as he now refuses to answer any e-mails. Even the ones offering free beer. While Peters was in Japan he dated a road worker for most of his tenure, who also moonlighted as a hostess at night. Alan became the thorough capitalist, first working for a multinational in Tokyo and then later moving into a position based in the Wall Street precinct. On that fateful September day in 2001 he left the World Trade Center just a few minutes before the first plane hit.

The castle is really worth seeing but this day it closed early so we had to hurry through the last section. A pity as a local group had adopted us and was showing us some of the design subtleties that would never have noticed. We caught the train back to Kobe and lobbed into the hotel at about 6.30. That evening a group of Niigata-ites ended up in a Mexican restaurant harassing the waiters and also any passing Nagano-ites. The food was lousy, even though Todd assures me we tried everything on the menu just to make sure, and the bill was expensive but was still outrageous fun. Afterwards we went to an Irish pub, then to a crowded *gaijin* bar, and to finish went looking for a reggae bar. Along the way we were tempted to go into a bar called the 'Little Bastard'. (as pictured left) What a marketing tool. I thought of opening up a bar in Japan and calling it 'Bar Garee'. The advertising for it would go something like, "Where can you go? You can go to Bar Garee!" I'm sorry if the subtle play on words is not appreciated from those outside the Commonwealth.

What a great name

That's me in the centre of the picture above and flanking me on the right is British James - he of the fellow nervous *shinkansen* rider fame. Somewhere, sometime, amongst his primary pursuits of snowboarding and drinking, along with a little bit of English teaching, he managed to find the time to meet, woo and marry Leta, a fellow JET. The remarkable coincidence was that they both shared the same family name, thereby saving a bucket-load of paperwork.

On the left apparently ordering two beers is Kiwi Jake, or *hebi* (snake) as he was more popularly known. Jake brought his Japanese girlfriend 'Mig' from New Zealand along on the JET Program with him. She acquired a great job with a famous corporation and amassed a small fortune in savings, while Jake generally p***** all of his money away on drinking and travel. When they returned home to the Land of the Long White Cloud the amazing differential in currency rates meant they could pay cash for their new home, a not insubstantial dwelling I'm informed. They have now started a family and Jake, who has long possessed excellent Japanese skills, apparently is settling down and head of a large Japanese language faculty in a well known school.

The opening ceremony in the morning was the bore that could be expected. Most people were more interested in the nightlife than workshops, a position not entirely without a good deal of justification. The second morning I arrived just a few minutes late to the morning lectures. The conference organisers were indeed taking attendance checks, as had been rumoured. After 10.00am anyone late got marked as a non-attendee. I think quite a number of Niigata people would have fallen into this category. A few would have only been getting back to their rooms at that time.

The last evening I spent rummaging through the shelves of the wonderful Wantage Bookshop, and Tower Records, before heading to the *eki*. The overnight train was good and very cheap too. I arrived just after 6.00am and headed to McDonalds for breakfast. McDonalds didn't open till 7.00am so I went for a walk through Ueno Park where all the 'bums' were just waking up in their cardboard castles, as was Tokyo in general. Ueno Park is very pleasant at that time of the morning and after breakfast I went back there again. I found that at 7.30am there was a baseball game going on with the homeless acting as spectators and loudly offering advice. I guess they didn't have that much to do, especially as the day-labour market had dried right up with the bursting of the economic bubble. I listened to some traditional singers for awhile, then sat down and just watched humanity pass by. It was not yet 9.00am, and I was waiting for the National Museum to open.

It was quite interesting, as was the architecture. Interestingly there were no exhibits from Niigata. Niigata is very *inaka* (rural) and not thought of as terribly exciting, apart from its excellent sake, skiing and rice. I think that's three excellent points in its favour - but it seems many Japanese would think of it in rather the same manner as maybe, South Dakota in the U.S., the U.K. Midlands, or similar places. I went to the Metropolitan Museum of Art, but to see all the exhibits it would have cost a substantial sum so I just didn't bother. The Museum of Western Art was closed (my usual luck) so my time in Ueno finished quickly. I went to the electronics district in Akihabara, which was incredibly busy. I didn't stay long because the only thing there was shopping, but very interesting nonetheless. You can stumble across all manner of must-buy things that you had never previously even realised you needed. Next stop was Tokyo Central that was by comparison extraordinarily quiet - due to the holiday one would guess.

From near there one can spy the Imperial Palace from outside, because nobody is allowed inside unless you are <u>really</u> important, and I also just chanced upon the changing of the guard. The changing used to just be the two guys walking out from inside and saying to the others, "Oi, it's time to knock off!", or something along those lines. So the two outside would stub out their cigarettes, express thanks, and then drop off their guns at the armoury before heading for the pub. But the powers that be didn't deem that formal enough, so now they have to go through all the salutes, marching, twirling of guns, adjusting of crotches, and so on. The hardy few assembled seemed to appreciate it as some form of spectacle at least.

Like Akihabara the nearby Ginza was packed with shoppers. I went to Akasaka to see the famous temple, but upon arriving realised it was at Asakusa. Potential travellers please note the subtle difference. I saw the Diet building (I think); the PM's residence (maybe) - but then decided I was lost. By this time it was getting late and thought it was time to find digs. I ended up in the Tokyo International YH that was very nice, cheap, and the views were terrific from it's location on the 18th floor.

I bought a subway day ticket the next morning, then, getting right this time, headed for Asakusa. The temple there was really nice and not too crowded. I walked through some of the back streets and arcades, and then jumped back on the subway to Ueno. There I found that the Museum of Western Art was still closed, and also that my ticket was not valid on the JR Yamanoate Line. It meant a bit of diverting but remember, 'getting there is all part of the fun'. On the same line I chuckled over the railway attendants whose uniforms made them look just like Japanese versions of Mussolini, the Il Duce himself.

I went to Ikebukuro and promptly got lost again looking for a post office. When I sorted myself out I looked through the Seibu department store which is just huge. Afterwards I went to the Sunshine Building, which was unimpressive, but inside there I passed a home centre called 'Tokyu Hands' that included a 'sales and counselling centre'. I guess that's useful if you have a nervous breakdown while purchasing home wares! Also nearby I found a shop called 'Mens Biggi' - the mind boggles with connotations. By this time it was after 5pm again so I decided to scrub the rest of my plans and head back to the hostel.

Later that night after much procrastinating I went out to Shibuya with three guys from my room - Milan (American originally from India), and Jim and Dave (two Brits). We missed our stop and ended out in the suburbs somewhere, so we didn't end up getting to Shibuya until after 9pm. Once there we decided on an Italian restaurant and ordered pizza.

Before the meal arrived we were viewing the condiments on the table when Dave spontaneously asked how much we would give him if he drank the server full of chilli. Milan, Jim and I discussed this deeply and decided that ample recompense would be to pay for his pizza. Importantly Jim insisted that, to collect, Dave also had to eat the chilli pepper in the bottom of the bowl as well. Promptly Dave picks up the bowl, fingers properly askew, and without fuss downs the contents. His immediate expression was hilarious, even while he tried to put on a brave face. As he pursed his lips and tried to appear cool his complexion turned bright red. We all laughed naturally enough, and make jokes about hot glowing rings. When we asked the waitress for some more she brought it, but then kept on eye on us to see what we actually did with the stuff.

I was a bit late waking up in the morning and by the time I stopped for breakfast at McDonalds I didn't get to Kamakura till after 10. It was a nice place for a day visit but I didn't get to see all of it. The more popular sights, such as the big Buddha, were quite crazy with the hordes of tourist buses pulling in and out. After a great deal of tramping I eventually came to the famous Shonan beach which is really pleasant - with actual sand and waves! Shonan is to Japan is what Bondi is to Australia or Malibu to Hawaii. It was more of a beach culture that I recognised too - as in lots of people surfing, sitting around on beach towels, wearing bathers, etc. This was as opposed to what I had grown accustomed to in Niigata – with those present generally fully clothed, with a tent, and eating at least three courses from full catering equipment.

The following day I headed for Nikko, which I had been informed was quite an agreeable place. I blundered through the busy subway back to Asakusa, and then somehow managed to find the cheap train to Nikko, which was just over two hours away. It was only 11.30 so I decided to have lunch before I went sightseeing but while I was doing that it started to rain. Guess who'd left his umbrella in the locker? I couldn't find any spares outside shops (first time I'd experienced that), but eventually found some back near the *eki*. Before I set out I noticed a girl with a top which read 'feel of the bigi'. Two days in a road - was this telling me something?

The huge cedars in Nikko really reminded me of my old haunts amongst the towering redwoods of Northern California, particularly in the rain. However after a couple of hours of tramping around I started to call it the 'ABT', short for 'Another Bloody Temple' tour. It was really picturesque, but with all the rain I decided I'd had enough of temples, and shrines as well I guess. Just in case you're confused 'temples' are Buddhist and 'shrines' are Shinto. I think. I'm always just a little confused on this. Well, not just this but I won't elaborate here. At a small Christian chapel I would have liked to stop for a moment of meditation, but I was heading up into the hills to see the Kegon waterfall, and the bus was almost there.

The rain had not let up by the time I got to Kegon about an hour later. It was also quite cold and I was wishing I had a coat with me. I had left Tokyo that morning wearing shorts and t-shirt, but had emptied out my backpack in Nikko with as many clothes as possible. I met a couple of other *gaijin* who were wearing very warm tops, but that were also a bit short in length. They explained that they were so cold they had popped into the nearest tourist shop and bought the largest sweaters they could find, which were still about three sizes too small. They were also expensive. But they figured it would get them through the day, and then they could offload them to nieces or nephews as gifts when they got home.

The waterfall was very average to say the least; despite the fact it's meant to be one of Japan's most famous. But everywhere you go in Japan you stumble upon things that are amongst '…Japan's three most famous…'. Doesn't necessarily mean they're any b***** good. On a later trip I travelled to the three most famous sites in Japan. These are, in no particular order, the sand spit at Amanohashidate (where the best view is apparently looking at it through your legs), the islands of Matsushima (where the tourists appear more interested in feeding the seagulls than viewing the scenery) and the floating *torii* at Miyajima. I would say they're all good, but not great. In Japan they are famous because, well, they're famous. Plus they are a long way away for most Japanese. People didn't seem to know much about their own area. I was told that when one did take a break it was expected that you would go far away. To go to anywhere close-by was no good.

It was far too cold for a lake cruise so I jumped on the bus and headed back to Nikko. I thought it easier to stay in the town, and ended up in a dirty little hostel. In many Japanese hostels they provide meals as well, but as I didn't fancy what was on offer I bought a frozen pizza at the supermarket. The lady in attendance, and I use the term 'lady' loosely here, had an absolute spaz when I tried to cook it in the mini-oven. Probably some cultural thing about men, women and kitchens – or maybe she was just a fat annoying bitch. Every time I went near to check it she would go right off. Eventually after twenty minutes I managed to get close enough to see that it was still frozen. The old battleaxe was even more p***** off when I pointed out that it would probably help if she plugged the oven in. Wonders of electricity, heat and all that. The other people staying there were friendly, but I was glad to leave the next morning and finally head home to Omi.

On the way back from the station I went into the bank and withdrew the last dregs of my remaining cash. I was pleasantly surprised to find they had put English instructions on the teller machine, which was a nice thought - particularly as I was the only one in town who needed them. Then, as usual, I stopped at the vending machine nearby to buy a can of 'American 350 Coffee'. I didn't like it that much but it was, a) a bigger can than the usual size, and b) I loved to hear the vending machine play 'I'm a Yankee Doodle Dandy' every time I bought one.

26: That's…ummm…shampoo

Beautiful lotus flowers are born from mud - Japanese Proverb

The school year ends in Japan in March. Before then was the graduation ceremony which is always an emotional time for the students and there are many tears and solemn speeches. I think these times are much more difficult for Japanese students as there is much more of community / group ethic than in the west.

With the start of the new school year in April I arrived at the *chugakko* to find out that all the desks had been moved into new positions. I walked around confusedly for a few minutes studying all the clean desktops then gave up and had to ask where mine was.

Later that same day my FBC order arrived which I had had trouble getting delivered. FBC are a Kansai based company that specialise in foreign foods and send orders out all over Japan. I asked Fukushima to call the company and he, without consulting me, told them to deliver it to the school. Matsumoto-san, one of the OL's, came upstairs to tell me that several boxes had arrived. Just as I was trying to figure out how to get them home on my bike, all three OL's flocked around and asked me to open them up and show them what I had got. I went through each box explaining the contents. Suddenly at the bottom of the third package I reached the forgotten condom box and dismissed it hesitantly, without opening it, as 'shampoo'.

Why was I buying condoms via postal order anyway? Without having done much research I admit, the general assumption is that Asian males are not as generously sized as their western counterparts. The only time I could do a direct comparison was in the toilets at Ueno McDonalds one day when I decided I had a quarter-pounder, but the guy next to me only had a junior burger, or maybe fillet-o-fish.

At the end of the day I had to rush home to change then bolt to the welcome *enkai* for the new school year. In front of each diner at the restaurant there was placed a small ceramic-cooking bowl under which a flame was lit. You then placed a few small delicacies inside to slowly cook. However tonight *moi* was playing the philistine. I seized this as an excellent opportunity for a fully cooked meal and dumped just about my whole meal inside. Let me reveal at this stage that I am quite a fan of *sashimi* and other such Japanese specialties. However, tonight I was just not in the mood for raw beef and things that had only been half cooked. The waitress came around checking all bowls and the look on her face when she took the lid off mine was just precious. The teacher next to me politely explained to her that I was, I presume, "…a stupid asshole who has no appreciation for much of anything", which she accepted with grace and moved on. At the close of the evening I was elected to lead the final banzai which was a great honour. But which I also did a great job of stuffing up.

All the new *ichi-nensei* (first year students) at the school seemed a *genki* (lively) and happy lot and I recognised a few faces from my visits to the elementary schools. On the day of staff photos I had received more than a few minutes warning so at least this year I was dressed in reasonable clothes and a jacket. Although I taught all years equally I was somehow designated a Year One teacher and had to be in all the *ichi-nensei* class photos as well.

At my desk in the staffroom

Four of the best English students at the school (as well as best friends), Rie, Tomomi, Yumiko and Mai were standing behind the camera and trying to make me laugh during the shot. The photographer kept on taking the same photo and wondered why. Then it dawned on me. You're not meant to smile. I kept a straight face for the next shot and the photographer finally proclaimed, "OK!" When I viewed the class photographs later I was happy to see the rebel in one class. Amongst the sea of straight faces there was a lone student sprouting an oversized grin and obviously happy with his lot in life at that time.

Rie often brought me more food and I was never sure if it was extra or if she was trying to lose weight. Not that she needed to. She complained that she was fat but was actually wafer thin. Rie incidentally graduated from one of the best high schools in the prefecture, from where she went on to study nursing in Niigata City. She grew into a fine young lady and I was a little disappointed as, whilst nursing is an extremely worthy profession, she had the ability to follow even higher paths in life. Then to top things off she met a Russian 'businessman' in Niigata, got herself knocked up, and ended up with an older foreign husband and very cute baby *babushka* by the age of 21. Until recently, Tomomi and Mai never kept in touch and so their post-*chugakko* lives were a mystery to me, but after meeting them at a reunion discovered that they were now in university in Tokyo and Kanazawa respectively.

The school population in Omi was very stable and there was little turnover in students. In fact it was not unusual to have more teachers leaving than kids. Generally it was only when Denka might transfer a family away somewhere. The next year Yumiko left with her family for Kanagawa where her father had been transferred. Yumiko was a tall girl, shy at first, but had blossomed with self-confidence in the preceding months. She was very proficient in the art of *kendo* and had won several tournaments. *Kendo* is an ancient Japanese martial art that is becoming more popular with westerners. To the untrained eye it appears as a sport where one can dress up in ridiculous and expensive *samurai* style clothes, slide round in very small steps, and beat some poor innocent around the head and in the genitalia area with a large bamboo pole. However it requires great depth of concentration and commitment.

Soon after Yumiko departed a letter postmarked Kanagawa arrived for me. There was a cute little illustration on the front of the envelope. The back of the letter said, "I give you my gold medal as a present. Thank you for teaching me English. Please make it your treasure". In the envelope was the gold medal she had won at the last *kendo* championships. It must have been, it was, one the most touching moments for me in Japan. These are the things that make teaching so worthwhile. She finished the note entreating me to never forget her. Don't worry Yumiko, I never have. It's moments like this that reminds one that teaching is one of the most worthwhile professions in the world. But sometimes, at junctures such as that, also one of the saddest.

I always wondered what happened to Kato, a *genki* short young lad in the same grade with glasses, and two brothers who were all like peas in a pod. He declared one day in a speaking test that his career ambition was to be a taxi driver. I imagined one day coming out of the *eki* on a visit and there would be Kato sitting smiling in the driver's seat of his taxi. And just maybe his two brothers would be seated in the two cabs following. But the script ended differently with Kato going on to work at the great Omi behemoth that is the Denka Corporation.

With the changing of the school year there were new teachers at the *chugakko*, plus also at the various *yochien* and *shogakko*. I was hoping one teacher at Utatenami *shogakko* might be replaced but he was still there. The elementary teachers had to send in their lesson plans to me a couple of days at least before I visited so I could do some extra preparation. This fellow was always leaving it to the last minute and it was usually bloody woeful. The first one he sent in for the year was on 'kitchen appliances'. The basic plan was the names 'oven', 'fridge', 'mixer', 'microwave' and 'toaster'. That was as far as his planning got and after that I was on my own. I made up my own and Setsuko let them know. The next time I had his class he sent in one for 'tools' – 'hammer', 'screwdriver', 'chisel', 'spanner' and 'drill'. I sensed that could be a bit easier as I could teach the kids actions and sentences along the lines of, "Hit your teacher with the hammer, gouge his eyes with the chisel…." <u>Parental Warning</u>: I'm joking – I'm such a wimp and pacifist that I won my last fight by fifty metres.

April is also the most beautiful time of year in Japan - *o hanami* (cherry blossom festival). The *sakura* (cherry blossom) bloom each year around March and April, and last from a few days to a couple of weeks. The blooming of the *sakura* provides yet another excuse for the local inhabitants to go and get substantially inebriated. Takada *koen* (park) was famous in Japan for its thousands of *sakura* trees and the hordes would descend on the park each season from a substantial distance to celebrate. On the nightly national TV news, charts are provided showing the progress of the blossoms north, which is watched with great interest. *O hanami* is a time of great happiness and warmth - especially if you own a liquor store.

At Ichiburi *yochien* we went for a walk to see some of the blooming *sakura*. Most of the kids were being cuddly and friendly, and would fight over who would hold my hand until we struck a deal with time-sharing. They were all so sweet and one of my all-time favourite photos is of the Ichiburi kids standing in front of the *sakura* wearing their yellow sun hats. As we walked I saw a bottle of Coke left on a gravesite, which rather struck me as strange - the old meets the new. Ichiburi is a quaint little fishing village with still many signs of old Japan. Down by the harbour, where I would usually have lunch, I would often find some old fisher folk sorting their catch, and mending their nets. Evidently it was a tight-knit community. When I first came and the kids introduced themselves they nearly all had Tatebe for a family name.

In the afternoon at the *shogakko* the Grade 1/2 class lesson was sumo wrestling. I never worked out how this fit into the English curriculum but often you just had to go with the flow. I would generally grapple with the kids a little bit. Let them win sometimes, and lose at others. There was one exception and that was with one of the smelliest little girls I've ever encountered. The bouts with her lasted about three to five seconds on average so as I wouldn't gag on the overpowering putridity and throw up on their pristine P.E. mats. Another young boy was a fairly solid little character. When you picked him up it was like lifting a wombat.

There were a couple of new female teachers at the *shogakko* and another one, heavily pregnant, was just getting ready to finish up her duties there. After lessons I stood talking to the three of them for awhile. Toward the end of the conversation the pregnant one surprisingly declared that all of them were 'free'. They also suggested they might like to take me for pizza in Asahi on my next visit. Things progressed a little from there. The pregnant one went off to be a

Cherry blossom time at Ichiburi *yochien*

single mum, and the remaining two, 'Ma-chan' and 'Ta-chan', went out several times with Todd and myself. Despite both of them being attractive and fun ladies, nothing ever came of it. Their English was only very basic, and Todd and I could never get our heads around the whole Japanese dating dynamic that they were into. They were both quite sad to find out some time later that we had both found Japanese girlfriends. The same ones we were later to marry.

I had picked up a short wave radio on one of my *gomi* shopping days and so it was one Saturday afternoon that I finally picked up 'Radio Australia'. They used to have a very good service into Asia and the Pacific before the new economic rationalist policies of the Howard government stuck the knives into it. Over a short period they cut huge swathes from foreign language programs, incarcerated refugees in off-shore camps, labelled themselves as America's deputy sheriff in Asia, went to war in far off Iraq, and generally moved away from the previous positive engagements with Asian nations. Then to top it all they reserved the right to strike militarily on a pre-emptive basis against any country in the region. They later wondered aloud why nobody liked Australians anymore. D'uh! Not that it seemed to matter as long as we were chums with the

Americans. Naturally there were the bluff denials that followed regarding any fault on their behalf, and that it of course didn't mean "…any bellicosity toward our friends."

On this day anyway, I listened to the Australian Football League broadcast, but unfortunately my team (the Adelaide Crows) lost. I discovered that for the best reception I had to have the radio on the open window ledge in the kitchen, so all the neighbours heard the broadcast as well. What a long suffering and kind bunch they had been.

27: The Five Levels of Drinking

First the man takes a drink, then the drink takes a drink, then the drink takes the man
- Japanese Proverb

A few days later I was heading north for the annual 'cabin' party at Osake Dam outside of Urasa. The town of Urasa has a lovely fully imported Norwegian log cabin that it has placed at the foot of Mount Hakkai outside of town next to a lake. Hakkai-san is famous throughout Japan, not because of being a mountain of any significance, but because its name adorns the best known *sake* in the land. The town rents the cabin out cheap to local residents and the town English teacher always made a regular booking. The gathering was nothing more than an excuse for a large number of the local *gaijin*, as in any foreigner within 200 kilometres, to have a sociable barbeque plus, you guessed it, to drink very heavily. The invite from Kevin did say that one could, "....spend eight hours the following day, climbing to the top of Hakkai-san", but that kind of effort was unlikely.

Things can get wild and some people, like Jack, uncontrollable. Did you know that in Mongolia uncontrollably drunken people are often wrapped up in a blanket and tied with rope so that only their heads stick out? A little bit like an adult papoose I guess. One presumes that this still allows them to sing and/or vomit in the corner of their yurt and hence still be part of all the action.

Being a frog may help. It was discovered on a NASA mission that a frog can throw up. This is not so strange in itself but the method certainly is. The frog throws up its stomach first, so the stomach is dangling out of its mouth. Then the frog uses its forearms to dig out all of the stomach's contents and then swallows the stomach back down again. I'm positive the frog's partner would insist it washes its hands thoroughly afterwards. And why they chose to do this experiment in space I have no idea.

Maybe we should, at this juncture, pause to consider this phenomenon of drunkenness in a holistic sense. I was e-mailed a theory, originally devised I believe by comedian Larry Miller, about the joys of drinking to excess. I worked on it somewhat to come up with an adapted 'Five Levels of Drinking in Japan'. Apologies for any possible copyright infringement.

LEVEL 1:
It's 11:00 on a weeknight, and you're sitting in your local bar ('The Happy Kitchin' or 'L'il Bastard'). You've had a few Kirin, plus some *sake* that the group next door insists you drink. You get up to leave because you have to teach Period One the next day, and one of your friends buys another round. The friend with *nenkyu* (the day off) tomorrow. Here at Level One you think to yourself, "Oh come on, this is silly, why as long as I get seven hours of sleep (snapping your fingers), I'm cool."

LEVEL 2:
It's midnight. You've had a few more beers. You've just spent twenty minutes arguing against *natto*. You get up to leave again, but at Level Two, a little devil appears on your shoulder. And now you're thinking, "Hey! I'm out with my friends! What am I in Japan for anyway? These are the good times! Besides, as long as I get five hours sleep (snapping your fingers) I'm cool."

LEVEL 3:
One in the morning. You've abandoned beer for Suntory whisky. You've just spent twenty minutes arguing <u>for</u> *natto*. And now you're thinking, "Our waitress is the most beautiful woman I've ever seen!" At Level Three, you love Japan, you love the world. On the way to the *toire* you buy a drink for the *salaryman* at the end of the bar just because you like his face. You get drinking fantasies, like "Hey fellas, if we bought our own bar, we could live together in Japan forever. We could do it. James, you could cook." But at Level Three, that devil is a little bit bigger....and he's buying. And you're thinking, "Oh, come on, come on now. As long as I get three hours sleep...and a complete change of blood (snapping your fingers), I'm cool."

LEVEL 4:
Two in the morning. And the devil is bartending. For last call, you ordered the extra large bottle of *sake* and a Pocari Sweat. You ARE *natto!* And now you're thinking, "Our barman is the best looking man I've ever seen." You and your friends decide to leave, right after you get thrown out, and one of you knows a...hostess bar. And here, at Level Four, you actually think to yourself, "Well....as long as I'm only going to get a few hours sleep anyway, I may as well....<u>stay up all night</u>!!!! Yeah! That'd be good for me. I don't mind going to that staff meeting looking like Shoko Asahara. Yeah, I'll turn that around, make it work for me. And besides, as long as I get nineteen hours sleep tomorrow (trying to snap your fingers),..........cool."

LEVEL 5:
Five in the morning. You unsuccessfully try to get your money back at the tattoo parlour ("But I don't even know anybody named Emi!!!"). You and your friends have jumped on the *shinkansen* to Tokyo and wind up in a bar with American sailors and guys who have been in prison as recently as...that morning. It's the kind of place where even the devil is going, "Uh, I gotta turn in. I gotta be in Hell at nine. I've got that brunch with Hitler, can't miss that."

At this point, you're all drinking some kind of thick blue stuff, like something from a weird Japanese animation feature – at roughly ¥800 a pop.

A waitress with nose rings and orange hair comes over, and you think to yourself, "Someday I'm gonna marry that girl!!" One of your friends stands up and screams, "LET'S GO TO A KARAOKE BAR!!!!!" - and passes out. You crawl outside for air, and that's when you hit the worst part of Level Five - the sun. You weren't expecting that were you? You never do. You walk out of a bar in daylight, and you see people on their way to work, or jogging. And they look at you in that strange way, as if to say..."Who's Emi?"

Let's be honest, if you're 19 and you stay up all night, it's like a victory because you've beaten the night. But if you're a bit older, then that sun is like God's flashlight. We all say the same prayer, usually kneeling at the porcelain shrine, "I swear, I will never do this again (how long?) as long as I live!" And some of us always have that little addition..."and this time, I mean it!"

Unfortunately the mad Canadian Jack had not yet been through this epiphany of regret. He and some others borrowed a friend's car to do a beer run and had a slight 'accident' on the return leg. With the amount of blood alcohol for Jack probably approaching double digits he decided not to hang around to face the music. The next day we received a visit from the local constabulary and Jack was now contemplating his future in those parts.

This however didn't stop in the indomitable Jack. Just a couple of months later he fell out the third floor toilet window of a *karaoke* bar. He apparently had wanted to make a surprise entrance back through the front door, then on to the nearby drum kit which the proprietor had forbidden him to play. Unfortunately he forgot that he had climbed up three flights of stairs on the way in. Friends wondered why he was taking so long in the toilet and when they went in to search for him heard a wee voice beckoning from outside, "I'm down here!" In between the buildings they found Jack prostrate in the snow with his leg broken in two places. When he had to fill out the medical insurance form for his employer, the local board of education, he claimed that he had, "…tripped over a gutter." Unimpressed, they refused to renew his contract. Nevertheless he effortlessly found another position somewhere in Shizuoka and over the years somehow paradoxically worked his way into a position of authority. Maybe it's because he's so good at *enkai*. Now back in North America he apparently is president of the local JET alumni chapter.

28: Marching to a different beat

Drunkenness does not create vice; it merely brings it into view
- Seneca, Native American

As the weather started to warm up, people started to think, 'beach'. And when they thought 'beach' the word association often came out as 'Nic'. Then followed some other words like 'party', 'good time', and naturally 'drinking'. And so it was that fourteen hardy souls came down one weekend to drink copiously, trash my apartment, keep my neighbours up, and block my toilet. The latter is definitely an inconvenience, particularly when some present cannot hold down the evening's repast. In the morning we had to wend our way down to the public toilet block by the beach, only to find it closed. Fortunately the kindly caretaker came along shortly thereafter to the relief of all assembled.

As most were still sleeping off the night before I had to struggle over to the 'Sports Festival' at the field down by the *eki*. Kenichi Igawa (my Idobata supervisor) had asked me, and I presumed this was very much an honour, to carry the banner at the front of the opening parade. So there I waited and sat nursing my awful hangover as the school band warmed up nearby. I think it would have been better to tie me down and make me listen to Barry Manilow at full volume. I don't think I stuffed up my duties too badly, apart from not giving the 'Heil Hitler' salute to the mayor. Everyone else did it, but because I was in front I didn't realise I had to. Also I must have just wanted to get out of there quickly because *kyoto-sensei* told me to 'slow down'. After an indeterminable time of marching on the spot and the inevitable listening to speeches I was finally able to escape. Everyone had left by the time I got home, except for Kevin and Anne who had attempted something resembling a clean up of my sorry digs. Shortly afterwards they roller-bladed off toward Itoigawa to catch the train from there but ran late when Anne couldn't stop and went over a guard railing.

In Japan there is a time for everything. The air-conditioners go on and off by certain days of the calendar, and the same with heaters, regardless of the weather. On 30th September the students are still wearing their summer uniform but on October 1st they must arrive fully kitted out in their winter uniform. The morning assembly of the changeover day provided a strange sight. About half way through one of the teachers got down on his hands and knees and crawled around checking the level of the girl's skirts, making sure they came below the knee. He then proceeded to inspect more closely, and berated strongly those infringing. I could just envisage all of the male teachers in the change-rooms beforehand doing *janken* to decide who would get that job!

After many warnings from Kinya-san and others I had finally got the message and was no longer riding my bike to Ichiburi or Oyashirazu. Usually at both those places we would go for a short walk with the kids. These would be a delight as the kids would be always their *genki* little selves and fight over who would get to hold my hand, or being extremely lucky, get the piggyback ride. Sometimes in the morning they would see me coming and run out to gang hug me. A highly recommended way to start a morning's work. One particular day we had an early lunch at Ichiburi and after that we ambled down to see some men standing on the roof of a partially built house. I'm not sure whether they were priests, owners, builders or any combination of those, but they were wearing *yukata* and holding banners. They conducted some sort of traditional ceremony then poured *sake* on the roof. A little bit like champagne and boats in the west I guess, then they threw out gifts of sweets, *mochi*, and coins as the kids (yes, and me) scrambled to collect.

After *shogakko* that day I waited around till 5.20pm and went for pizza in Asahi with Ma-chan and Ta-chan. Miyazaki-*sensei* (the pregnant one) was sick so she couldn't come. It was a pleasant evening, but difficult communicating in lots of Japlish. A friend of theirs, a former Idobata student, turned up later. I didn't know at that time if it was coincidence or arranged but as I became aware of these strange dynamics I realised it must've been. They also invited themselves to dinner next week as well.

One of the things that we were warned about early in our tenure by old hands was not to be too forward. If someone asked you out to dinner, particularly to their home, you should merely thank them, not ask "When?" To do otherwise would be crass and presumptuous. They may only be being friendly. However when I sounded out the ladies, rather tentatively, in regards to dinner Ma-chan came straight out and asked "When?" So much for cultural sensitivity. After I got home I called Todd and invited him along. It was a nice dinner anyway, despite the language barrier, and they flattered me when they couldn't decide whether I looked like Harrison Ford, Mel Gibson, or Kevin Costner.

Knowing more *nihongo* (Japanese) may have helped. Many *gaijin* come to Japan just to improve their *nihongo*. Some actually even learn some. They proceed to labour heavily over ten thousand or so *kanji* characters, learn the correct conjunctive use of *wa*, *ne*, and *no*, and maybe begin to communicate with the locals - who generally hate *gaijin* that can speak good Japanese. A collection of hardy souls even attempt the hell called the 'Japanese Proficiency Test'. A few pass it as well. And when their time in Japan is done they can place their hard won skill prominently on their resumes. Not that many will use it after then - and others wish they'd learnt Chinese.

However a minority of these *gaijin* prefer to get by during their time in Japan using phrase books and hand signals, along with lots of *wakarimasen* (I don't understand) and occasional profanities. No mindless tedium for these vapid souls. To them there are better pursuits than the conquest of a strange language - like drinking, staying in your room, cleaning the toilet, or even writing a useless 'Life in Japan' type book. I couldn't see the sense in learning the complexities of a language that, I was positive, would no longer be required after my departure. A serious miscalculation on my behalf – as you will later find. Strangely, most of my Japanese was learnt in *enkai* as locals are even more reluctant to speak English at that time. Hence, these days, the drunker I get, the more Japanese I remember…

The rainy season had begun and one afternoon a couple of agitated staff members came in late in the day and turned on the TV in the staff room. The news was on and showed pictures of a very swollen *Himegawa* (Hime River). Apparently some of Highway 148 had got washed away and those nearby began to speculate if the floods would be as bad as those in the previous year. After school I rode down to where they had closed the span bridge near the port. The surging river beat hard against its pylons and looked soon to maybe begin washing over the top. The authorities closed Highway 8 at Oyashirazu, which meant that night the road out front of the apartment was nice and quiet for once - as opposed to the constant racing of trucks whose drivers were too tight-assed to pay the expressway fee but still intent on getting to their destination in the same time.

I felt really upset around this time because there were school events going on that I was not invited to - a concert and a school trip to Tateyama. It p***** me off that I only seemed to be included when there was a need, otherwise forget it. However this did seem to be a similar theme with most other English teachers I talked to, so I was no orphan. On the bright side, at least I got that day off…

29: Are we there yet? The pilgrimage to Fuji-san

You are wise to climb Mt. Fuji, but a fool to do it twice
- Japanese Proverb

In Japan Mt. Fuji (or Fuji-san) is regarded with spiritual reverence. Most *gaijin* staying for any reasonable amount of time aspire to climb it. Mount Fuji is probably Japan's most recognisable symbol and captures the paradoxical mix of spirituality and consumerism that is at the very heart of its modern identity. There are roughly two thousand registered religious organisations based around Mount Fuji along with 117 golf courses. Complimenting this, on Mount Fuji's eastern flank, is a 55-square-kilometre area used by both the Japanese and American militaries for live-fire exercises.

Every day during the summer climbing season over five thousand tourists / pilgrims make their way up the mountain. As opposed to the traditional saying I hereby wish to coin a new *gaijin* phrase – "You're a fool to climb Mt. Fuji, you'll have a better time in Roppongi". Rather than tell you the deep meanings of Fuji-san, which can be found in any other proper travel book, I will just tell you about my pilgrimage.

In May I received a call from Rananda. As she was only staying the one year, her sister was coming for a visit before she left and did I want to climb Fuji-san with them next month? Why not? It was on my 'to do' list, and I would be in the area that weekend for a retreat anyway. As the day approached Rananda decided to switch the dates so I was left hanging. Determined still to go I called Todd. Now, anyone that has spent time backpacking or in international company will know that Canadians and Australians tend to bond. If we knew what was in front of us we might have chosen not to stretch those bonds.

We were going to be climbing in June, two weeks before the official start of the climbing season. The Japanese social orientation precludes them from climbing anytime between September 1st and June 30th, so we were assured of no crowds. Little did we know that it would also assure us of absolutely bugger all else. The national tourist office had advised us that only 'experienced mountaineers' should attempt the climb outside the regular season but we regarded this as mere folly. We started our journey from Niigata-ken at lunchtime. On the way we met Jennifer a fellow English teacher from Nagano who asked if we had the right gear for climbing.

"Yes", we claimed, "we've got rain gear and warm clothes."

She replied, "Oh, I meant ice picks and crampons."

The furrowed brows of insecurity began to crease.

After a succession of trains and bus we arrived in Kawaguchiko at 9pm. Being outside of the climbing season there were no buses to the fifth station, the usual starting point, so we approached some drivers at the taxi stand. According to the guidebook a taxi ride would cost about ¥7,000. The first driver said, "No - too dangerous". The second said, "¥12,000 - yen, not dollars", to which we replied something along of the lines of, "Thank you, but your price is a little expensive. Besides, we live in your fine country and teach English to your wonderful children." Actually it may have been something rather more curt, but I can't remember. The third driver told us ¥10,000, the fourth ¥8,000. The price was falling so constantly we thought of staying all night and by morning we'd make a profit.

However we didn't have that much time, so we decided to go for option four. The driver took us as far as the road would allow. In other words, as soon as it turned to dirt we were turfed out, relieved of our hard earned cash, left on a dark road with no idea where we were and nary a tourist centre in sight. We shrugged, and started to walk. It was 10.30pm, with a supposed four and a half-hour journey in front of us.

We discovered later in the harsh light of day that we had been deposited somewhere near the fourth station. It was at this stage that Todd admitted that he'd forgotten a flashlight. Gradually as the trip wore on he would also admit to forgetting food, a map, and sunglasses in the bright morning that was to follow. He was also only wearing his sturdy track shoes, backed up with rubber boots - standard Japanese baby blue and yellow issue. I was over prepared, having to cart my huge backpack because there were no lockers to be found, and unfortunately no *sherpas* either. I carried to the top, well almost, of Mt. Fuji about ten kilograms of such useful items as two novels, a walkman and tapes, sandals, spare underwear and socks, my toiletries bag, and a bible to be used on the retreat.

Actually as the night wore on the bible did prove useful. I was continually dipping into it for verses of encouragement like, "In despair I look to the mountains for God...", and "Yea, though I walk through the valley of the shadow of death..." In my state I was positive I would meet God sooner than originally envisaged. A few years ago I climbed the tallest mountain in Australia - Mt. Kosciusko. This involved a ride on a chairlift and a casual, only slightly strenuous, three-hour walk to the summit. I knew Fuji-san would be tougher, but never in my wildest imagination imagined I would wish to be reborn as Sir Edmund Hillary. Or maybe not born at all - just stay as a twinkle in my father's eye.

Altitude, dehydration, a heavy pack, and lack of sleep soon all began to take their toll. I was sometimes stopping every twenty metres or so to get my breath. Todd - much more young and sprightly than me - was forever prodding me as I lay gasping on the path with encouraging comments like, "Wake up!", "Get going you lazy bastard" and, "I'm glad I revived you, your heart stopped beating". The sunrise that was meant to be so spectacular, happened behind a bank of cloud at 4.15am. By this point we had already gone well past the expected four and a half-hour journey time and seemed no closer to the top.

By 6am we reached what we presumed was the 9th station, or was it the 8th? We had hit the snowline, and I had hit a brick wall. At least with the snow we get some moisture back into our system, even if it did include some grit. I decided the view was good enough for me right there. The view being some fields, towns, and lakes in the distance, mainly obscured by cloud. I found a nice piece of dirt outside a closed hut, as they all were, and settled down for a kip. These mountain huts are rest stops that are usually operated by local families. Many climbers (well, those actually climbing at the right time of year) mark their feat by having attendants brand the name of a particular hut and its elevation on their walking sticks. I didn't particular care for any branding or for what elevation I may be at. I just wanted to sleep. Todd pressed on to the top and returned two and a half hours later with pieces of volcanic rock, plus stories of fog and hyperventilation. We could now start down, but the journey was far from over.

The supposed two and a half hour trip down ended up more like four. We finally started seeing other people on their way up, some of whom were wearing ski boots and carrying their skis. There was snow - but not quite that much snow! We asked some of them for directions to the fifth station and ended up in a workman's camp where we managed to purchase a few expensive small cans of 'Pocari Sweat' – a drink that could be loosely described as a Japanese alternative to Gatorade. Mr. Pocari must obviously sweat quite a bit, or maybe it's the whole family. Anyway, from the camp we were redirected to the fifth station which meant we had to trudge back <u>up</u> for awhile.

While waiting for the bus we stashed away some of the obligatory *omiyage* (gifts) which is a useful, almost obligatory, tool for sucking up to your 'higher ups'. We had lunch back in Kawaguchiko and parted ways at the *eki*. The next day it took ten hours for me to get home, but Todd fared worse. He slept the night in the Minamiotari *eki* after taking the wrong train. At least the station attendant felt sorry for him, lent him some blankets and a heater, and let him sleep inside what would normally be a locked station. At a later date, when our wives were both expecting at the same time, he sent me an email expressing his first piece of sound parental advice, "Looks like our kids will graduate together. When they're old enough to understand we can warn them about the dangers of climbing Mt. Fuji and ordering the entire menu at Mexican restaurants in Kobe."

Later that weekend as I related my experience most people said, "Well, if you'd asked me first..." As for Rananda, she and her sister abandoned the idea of climbing and just ended up taking photos from the base. Smart ladies. My recommendation is that unless you have a masochistic streak you do exactly that. And while you're there nearby Fujiyoshida has one of the biggest and fastest rollercoasters in the world...

30: Those awful five letters

To praise one's own work, maybe shamelessly - Japanese Proverb

An acquaintance e-mailed me about his experience with some 'pyramid sellers', or 'multi-level marketers' as they prefer to be known, which paralleled something that happened to me. Some of these operations had begun to appear in Japan during my time there and their methods were no different whatsoever from the place of origin, apart maybe from the language. When I went to live in Shanghai I was pleased to see that these breed of corporations, all usually emanating out of North America, were forced by law to operate out of shops and actually sell something.

The cults are all there too, including many of the home-grown variety (See Chapter 37). Though weaning the Japanese off Shintoism and Buddhism is no easy task, apart from weddings where they all go crazy for the 'white' Christian version. I was harassed several times by the Jehovah's Witnesses and had a close call with a Moonie who stumbled through town one time. One pair of JW's were particularly persistent. The first time they knocked on my door they were confused by the 'Casá del Klar' sign and thought I spoke Spanish. They prattled on for sometime in Japanese and the only thing I think I understood was that they had a missionary friend in the Philippines who spoke Spanish. I kept on trying to explain that I didn't understand but it didn't deter them. They offered to bring back some material for me and asked whether I wanted it in English or Spanish. I tried to communicate that, in fact, I wasn't interested and didn't want any material at all. I didn't have the heart to tell them that if I were going to join someone it would be the Mormons. That way I could have as many wives, and hence as much boofing, as I wanted.

There was another knock on the door about three weeks later and the same pair of ladies were standing there on the landing outside. Hesitantly one began to speak, in English, "Hello, we are from Jehovah Witnesses…" Amazing. They had gone away and studied some English, obviously not in my class, in an attempt to come back and convert me. I smiled as nicely as I could, informed them, "I'm still not interested" - then closed the door in their faces. But that's okay. I'm assured by those in the know that every rejection earns them some extra frequent flyer points in the great beyond.

But I digress, as usual. The story about the pyramid sellers went something like this.

One night there was a call from one of the local kindergarten teachers who said she wanted to discuss something. She came soon after and I was instantly worried because she had her husband in tow and he was carrying a brief case. Brief cases, especially after hours, are not a good sign for me.

He began the evening by asking us questions about goals. S***. He asked me what I would do if money was no object and I told him I would become a crack addict and die in three weeks. He didn't laugh. S***. He opened his brief case and pulled out a pad of paper. He had a pen and provided me with some goals because I having so much trouble with Step A. He passed a few uncomfortable moments with light banter about the place being 'cosy'. Before I dozed off into a fitful slumber and dreamt of chartered accountants copulating with their accounts he thought he should obviously up the ante.

He said, "You want to know what?"

"What??" I asked, at least getting this step right.

Home sales are expanding at a rate much faster than retail. Growth rates that would make a marketer go hard. It just takes a little effort he said. And then he told me that I wouldn't be able to retire at the rate I'm going and that I've got to want something more.

"Like what?" I thought. I already had satellite TV, mountain bike and even an answering machine.

Then he set out his pad of paper before his beaming wife, who looked to the unfolding (and soon to be aborted) deal with the pride a woman who thinks her man is soon to morph into Bill Gates - or some other stupendously rich bod. On the pad he wrote five letters and handed it to me.

AMWAY, it said.

I asked them to leave and told them that Amway was a cult. I felt dirty and had to take a bath.

Stories like this were always coming up, and I mean not necessarily on that topic. One couldn't help but notice the large number of contributions by people from Niigata to various publications such as the 'JET Journal'. Barry Humphries, the famed Australian entertainer better known overseas as his alter ego - Dame Edna Everage, once stated that Melbourne produced the most and best performers and writers in Australia. This, he claimed, could be readily attributed to the atrocious weather that Melburnians have to suffer. Many people have nothing better to do than stay inside and write jokes about the weather - and obviously other things as well. I can assure you that I would far rather endure a Melbourne winter[4] than one of the Niigata variety. Maybe this in part explained the Niigata propensity toward the written word.

---

[4] At least you can go to the football in Melbourne on a weekend... and get a decent cappuccino

31: Sleeping on concrete – no more ferries tonight

Autumn to winter, winter into spring, Spring into summer, summer into fall,
- So rolls the changing year, and so we change; Motion so swift,
we know not that we move - Dinah Maria Mulock

On Sado Island there lived an American-Japanese guy who was universally lusted over by the majority of western female teachers. The ones who didn't were lesbians, but even they seemed to be equivocating whenever he came within a certain radius – like ten kilometres. It was just as well there was a reasonable body of water between him and his plethora of admirers. One weekend he arranged a dance party in Sawata and a large crowd was making their way over for it. The weather was a bit threatening but I decided about 11am on Saturday morning to go. I rode up the bike trail to Naoetsu and fortunately just made it to the ferry with ten minutes to spare. I left straight for Sawata from the port at Ogi, a distance of about another thirty kilometres, and made it bang on the rather early starting time of 6pm.

The only problem was that the party was not at the place where it was meant to be. I rode around looking, then when I couldn't find anything gave up and grabbed something to eat. I sat around the campground chewing on cold chicken wings and hoping someone might show. Finally around 7.30 I found a small note attached to a tent and rode to where it had been moved a couple of kilometres away. It was not a bad evening, but pretty poorly organised, and it finished before 10am - what must have been a world record. Most dance parties I've ever been to are only just getting in the groove around that time. Afterwards we went back to the campsite and I crashed at goodness knows what time on the rooftop of the nearby surf club. I woke up severely sore which by now I was painfully aware of the fact that sleeping on concrete will do to you.

Sunday morning we had to rescue the tents from the wind and drenching rain that had sprung up after breakfast. Many of us headed off for an *onsen*, then when the others left for Ryotsu to catch the Niigata City ferry I departed for Ogi about thirty kilometres away. The wonderful *onsen* staff saw me going out the gate on my bike and ran after me to give me a map. The weather had fined up by this time and it was a perfectly pleasant time and place to be out for a ride. Some difficult uphill section parts, but not too many, and they were balanced out by the downward runs.

Then difficulties struck. I took a wrong turn and ended way up a mountain somewhere. I asked for directions and the two *oji-san* (old men) looked at my map, scratched their heads and jabbered to each other before finally pointing uphill – which actually catapulted me further in the wrong direction. I was thinking I'd still just make it to Ogi when I realised I had made another wrong turn. I stopped on the main road and my look of mad desperation must have caused a couple of cars stop and check on me.

One contained a young English speaker who was part of the famous 'Kodo' *taiko* drumming group based on Sado. The ones Rananda and I had seen for free, but I didn't mention that. He wasn't going toward Ogi but he explained the situation to the family in the other van. They quite happily put my bike in the back and we made off toward Ogi. Lamentably my English-speaking friend must not have expressed the urgency of my situation to them. They bounded down the road in a tortoise like fashion taking the lengthy opportunity to explain that they were (gulp, not again) Jehovah Witnesses.

"Yes", I agreed as they went through their spiel, "it must be pleasant to be a member of such a well-known cult".

But my thoughts, by now increasingly agitated, were more focused on getting to the port on time. As Ogi hoved into view I could see the boat reversing out – I was a mere three minutes late. "No more ferries till tomorrow", informed the harbourmaster, and so there I was stuck.

I went for a ride around the sleepy town, and decided a meal was in order. I stopped at a *ramen* place run by a kind *oba-chan* who felt sorry for me and was very keen to hear about where I was from and what I was doing in Japan. Well, at this point, bugger all. I was stuck on an island with no way home for at least twelve hours. I went back to the terminal and found a nice area of tiles by the ticket office doors that would serve as my bed for the evening. I called around and left a message with Steve, asking him to contact Setsuko in the morning and let her know I'd be running late.

I was so tired by 8pm I couldn't stay awake. Who could blame me? I had ridden eighty kilometres the previous day, gone to a dance party, stayed up carousing, slept little on a rooftop, then ridden another forty kilometres or so up and down dale back to Ogi. So I laid out my sleeping bag and slept fitfully until 4.00am. This was accompanied by the distance sound of *muzak*, which they had obviously forgotten to turn off for the night. I realised that I'd spent four nights on Sado up to this point and they had all been outside! Well, this night was sort of inside - but I was still sleeping on concrete.

Before leaving I cleaned myself up as best one could, sparked myself with some cold coffee from the vending machine, and then boarded the 6.00am ferry. There were very few people aboard, maybe six in total, and I was the only one with any form of transport. It must have appeared somewhat surreal when we docked at Naoetsu Port. Outside men in safety overalls and hard hats were waiting with lit batons to guide the traffic coming out from the hold. Then the bow ramp noisily ratcheted down and one lone *gaijin* cyclist came riding out on his bike. They all laughed as they pointed me in the right direction and I rode past giving them my best royal wave. With time being of the essence I went straight to the *eki*, pulled my bike apart and caught the 9.10am train. I eventually got to school by 10.45 to fortunately discover that they had cancelled all my lessons. God bless 'em. I was so knackered, but that night I had to be out again for Jeet's farewell in Itoigawa.

There were so many meetings one had to attend. Many I was shoe-horned into I had absolutely no idea of why I was there and/or what they were about. That week we had a meeting in between lessons with some men who had travelled down from Joetsu City. All the staff introduced themselves, and then the two gentlemen made long speeches. When I broached the subject with Fukushima afterwards he was surprisingly candid but brief. He said that it was a 'stupid' meeting, and it was only something about everyone having to drive carefully.

I had been teaching the Idobata class now for almost a whole year, and so I asked them to undertake a speaking test for me. Some were a little reluctant but most seemed to do well. The choice of subjects they chose were quite diverse, and in some cases eclectic. Ken (he of video store fame) spoke about Ravi Shankar, and had trouble getting his tongue around all the Indian words, whilst the very bright and lovely Kaori Nishiyama spoke on psychoanalysis and Freud's theory. By the time she was fifteen minutes into the speech and elucidating something about the balance of the cerebellum, or maybe it was Oedipus theory, I had to ask her to stop and let the others have a turn.

By now the rainy season was finally over. Most days were generally sunny, and not as humid. Those not renewing their contracts, and in my area that meant everyone except me, were busily packing up and counting down the days. Maria had been offered a job at an English language school in Myoko-kogen and came around to ask if she could dump her things in my basement storeroom. After she'd left to go back to America the owner of the school changed his mind so Maria sent a message through her friend Nicola asking me then to sell it all off. I managed to offload most of it and passed the proceeds onto Nicola. Apparently she was not happy with the amount raised, but seeing she never bothered to contact me directly, or even pass on a word of thanks I frankly didn't give a s***.

All of the other *ichi-nensei* teachers and students disappeared to Tateyama on the Tuesday before the end of term, and I was left twiddling my thumbs all day in the staff room. No matter how much I tried to adapt I was aware that I would always be an outsider. Everything else was falling into place or winding down. I'd managed to do most of my planning for next term, my air fare for summer break was fixed, I had the final Idobata *enkai* and fireworks, I'd said my final good-byes to the girls and cleaned out their books and plants. My friend Laura came up from Uozu for a farewell dinner and we walked home via the beach where we were spotted by a group of *ichi-nensei* who could not resist crying *'girl-furendo!'* We insisted that we were merely *otomodachi* (friends), but that was plainly not an acceptable explanation to them.

So my first year of school in Omi was over. The *cicada* were chirping maniacally once again, meaning the seasons have come full circle. I sat down and reflected on the past year while I watched the sunset. There had been up and downs, but it had been a good year. I would miss the people leaving, but looked forward to those arriving. I hoped the next year in Japan would every bit as good.

"It had better be", I wrote in my diary, "or I'm not renewing..."

32: A cow fell from where!?

Some mornings, it's just not worth chewing through the leather straps
                                                            - Emo Philips.

I spent the summer in Thailand trekking around the jungle areas adjoining the northern Burma border with Betty, a friend who had not renewed her contract and was heading back to California via South-East Asia to study Law. On my second to last day I ate some dodgy chicken and spent a week recovering from the 'Thai Trots'. The doctor in Bangkok recommended I stay at a five-star hotel near his clinic rather than a local hospital. Tough choice. Who would mind as my national insurance was going to foot the bill anyway? So instead of a sterile hospital room I could either sit by the pool and read a book, or stay in my room and watch lots Indian warrior movies. These movies, commonly known as 'Bollywood', are certainly unique in the celluloid world. I imagine a typical screenplay may go something like this,

Scene: Two large mean looking males, bare-chested, walk toward each other. Woman cowers behind one.

"Raja, you scum, I will kill you for insulting my woman"

"Ha Baja! You cannot scare me you dog. It is because you have a very small penis!"

"My sword is much bigger than yours. But before I send you off to meet the gods - I will go through my song and dance routine…"

Scene: Baja and Raja, with gangs, do 6.3 minutes of song and dance. Afterward both fight and die.

-- Roll titles --

I would've been stuck at least another two weeks if I'd waited for North-West to give me the next available seat after I'd missed my flight. Finally I got sick of the Bangkok office 'waiting for approval from the Tokyo office'. I went into the United Airlines office, banged down my credit card and was on a plane the next day.

Shortly after my return I went out for dinner with the four replacement teachers in the area and who seemed keen to milk the 'old hand' (with all one-year of experience) for all the good oil. These four new chums all seemed to have varying experiences and backgrounds. Charles was an older fellow who had come to Japan after just missing out on a parliamentary seat in the recent Canadian elections. He had put his law career and radio talk show on ice while he sorted out his future. It seemed most weeks Charles was always ready to pack up and leave yet he still managed to stay three whole years. He was also a very big man and one of his reasons for coming to Japan was to thin down. He wasn't starting on this first night however as he kept on asking, "Where's the steak?" Charles did achieve his objective by the end of his tenure and a year or two later was fit, healthy, enjoying his engagement to a fellow Canadian he met in Japan, albeit only temporarily, and working in the New Brunswick Legislature, though not as a member.

The lady downstairs from him in Itoigawa was Hang, a Vietnamese-American fresh out of college, who used to be mistaken by some of the locals for a hostess bar girl. She was to fall madly in love with one local Itoigawa gentlemen and for some time after she left they were both shuttling back and forth wondering what to do with the relationship.

Tom was an Englishman who graduated early out of Oxbridge at the tender age of twenty-one. He was teaching in the high school and with little age difference between him and the student body he had to carefully watch for every nuance from the female division.

Rounding out the collection was Dwayne, a cigar-chompin' Kansas City boy, who used his three years to write a doctoral thesis and also marry a local girl from Nou, the fishing village he was based in. Last I spoke with Dwayne he was teaching at a very exclusive high school in Tokyo, attached to a very exclusive university, where he thought most of the male students needed a good "whuppin'". He was also the webmaster of a highly regarded internet site extolling the many foibles of his now adopted country.

On the way home that evening I fell off my bike which left several holes where once there was flesh. With hands, knees and a variety other important body joints bandaged and/or painted with antiseptic solution I went the following morning to see off the students on their exchange to Portland. Before getting on the train I ran them through some important last minute basic, but important, tips with them:

Beware of guns, gangs and the women,
Don't open your wallet to let the friendly shopkeeper take your money out,
Don't speak to men in suits with badges that say 'elder',
Try to fake that you're not a Japanese tourist
Look left first, not right, when crossing the road,
Don't eat the hotdogs in 7-11 stores
Portland is not as bad as it looks in 'My Own Private Idaho'
And most importantly, don't let any of the girls near Bill Clinton or boys near Michael Jackson

The town let it be known they had not been impressed with my getting sick in Thailand. As if I really had any choice? Did they imagine me looking up brochures and thinking, "Oh yes, I think I'll round out my week by getting a huge case of the runs and spending several days flat on my back, all the while losing eight kilograms in weight. That would be good thing to do instead of visiting the Golden Palace." Not only that, but they also warned the other local boards of education about the *gaijin* predilection for diarrhoea in South-East Asia.

Tom went to Thailand the following Christmas. On his first day back he was meant to go to one of his 'visit' schools but missed the train by a couple of minutes. He didn't know how to contact the school so he pulled out a book and prepared to wait the hour or so for the next train. When he didn't turn up the school contacted the Board of Education who went into a flat panic and imagined Tom lying somewhere in the Thai jungle in a pool of his own excreta. Several employees circled the town for some time before finally locating him at the *eki*, followed by a stern talking to.

The weather turned very rough one afternoon that week, but it was still warm and I was intent on having my usual dip. I'd been down swimming every day and improving my tan since I got back. One of my neighbours saw me on the way down and was telling me not to do it - it was *dame* (no good). Further up the beach I noticed emergency services doing what I thought was a drill. I went in and swam around for awhile, then discovered getting back into shore was not an easy thing with the undertow, which I had not experienced before. I was not panicking, but it wasn't easy. I swam strongly with each swell and tried to maintain my position in between. One guy on the beach appeared worried when he noticed me and started walking towards me, but stopped when I finally made it out. Though very tired, my ego would not let me collapse, so I just stood and dried myself as if nothing in particular had occurred.

Afterwards I walked further down the beach and realised that it wasn't a drill and somebody had drowned. All the emergency rescue services could (would?) do is stand on the beach in their overalls and look out forlornly. I almost felt like plunging in again for them, but thought,

    a) it wouldn't be appreciated,
    b) the poor unfortunate was already a goner, and
    c) I did not want to join him at the great Japanese snack bar in the sky.

Maybe none of them did because of the same reasons, or maybe because they had forgotten their Speedos. Beer bottles, a blanket and discarded snack containers on the rocks nearby were the sad reminder of a small gathering gone very wrong.

First light Friday there were search flights zooming up and down past my window. Out to sea a naval patrol vessel plied the waters. Had anybody heard of rubber dinghies and scuba divers in this country? It turned into a circus. A marquee was set up where about fifteen to twenty 'rescue' workers sat and drank *o-cha* while they plotted their next move. Three or four vehicles stood by, including one with a rubber dinghy on the back. Nobody was yet walking along the top of the breakwater, but occasionally a couple of them would walk up and down the beach. Obviously the body just floated out from under the breakwater by Friday night because by Saturday morning everybody had gone home and had to stop claiming overtime.

I think the word 'rescue' here is a little bit of a misnomer. More appropriate would be; "Let's get a huge amount of men wearing overalls and helmets to erect a marquee, sit around together, scratch their heads, drink *o-cha*, try to form some consensus, and wait hopefully for the bodies to emerge." Unfortunately this is too tragically true to be funny. Large-scale disasters in 1996 in Hokkaido (a road tunnel collapse) and Nagano (mudslide) - not forgetting Kobe in 1995 - only confirm this. The drowning on the beach was a prime example. Two people in wetsuits, with a rubber 'duckie' and safety-winch would have perhaps been a little more economical, and maybe even quicker.

After the mudslide in Nagano, the government boasted that it had 1,870 people involved in the rescue effort (*see:* search for bodies). Every other day rescue workers would turn up, and I'm not joking here, a leg, shoe, or piece of head, before the newspapers got sick of the lack of body count and stopped reporting on it. In efforts to correct this shortfall in disaster preparedness, the government started to specially train fire fighters to deal with emergency situations. In the Nagano mudslide the excellent job they were doing in watching the situation from a nearby vantage-point was noted with satisfaction by the media. Hence, what is the bottom line here? One supposes that it's don't ever get into an accident in Japan - or at least hope for a very big air pocket!

Before we sadly depart the theme of 'rescue', hopefully to something more meaningful - however unlikely that is, I will pass on a story that came to me via email around this time and supposedly originating from a reputable news organisation. More likely urban myth, but humorous nonetheless. Apparently the dazed crew of a Japanese trawler was plucked out of the Sea of Japan clinging to the wreckage of their sunken craft. Their rescue was followed by immediate imprisonment after authorities questioned the sailors about the loss of their ship. To a man they all claimed that a cow, falling out of a clear blue sky, had struck the trawler amidships, shattering its hull and sinking the vessel within minutes. They remained in prison for several weeks, until the Russian Air Force reluctantly reported to Japanese authorities that the crew of one of its cargo planes had allegedly stolen a cow wandering at the edge of a Siberian airfield. Apparently the crew had forced the cow into the plane's hold and hastily taken off for home. Unprepared for live cargo, the Russian crew was ill equipped to manage a frightened cow rampaging within the plane's hold. To save the aircraft and themselves, they shoved the animal out of the hold as they crossed the Sea of Japan at an altitude of 30,000 feet, and it somehow managed to pinpoint a lone boat in a large sea. So if you were ever wondering if cows could fly, they can. Just not for very long…

33: Japanese Dead Heads

We're fools whether we dance or not, so we might as well dance
— Japanese Proverb

Being summer the Sado Earth Festival was on again. There was also a blues and jazz festival starting a couple of days earlier on Mt. Donden so I decided to take in both of them, plus see a bit more on the bike. The ferry from Naoetsu was packed, unlike my last trip back. If one thinks that Japan is purely a uniform society, a trip on this ferry would have quickly dispelled that notion. There were Japanese Rastafarians, Japanese punks, even some Japanese 'Dead Heads' that drove Kombi-vans with Grateful Dead stickers plastered on the back windows.

I got off the ferry at lunchtime, grabbed a bite to eat, and then headed up the coast past the point where I last encountered the friendly JW's and their snail-paced van. There was a head wind, and it took me nearly five hours to cover the sixty odd kilometres to Ryotsu. I stopped for something to eat at a supermarket, before starting on towards Donden. By now it was after 6.00pm and the light was starting to fade. I climbed for awhile, but eventually decided the task was useless. A couple of cars zipped by as I sat by the road contemplating my options. As a third car approached I tentatively stuck out my thumb and the driver kindly stopped and offered to take me up the next nineteen kilometres of steep winding road. As you know this was not the first offer of help I had received on Sado and was certainly not my last. Japanese people are incredibly generous by nature, and this was more than exemplified by the fine souls who inhabit Sado Island.

The concert and camping fee was minimal and there was a succession of excellent bands, mostly blues and reggae, with some other stuff mixed in between. The crowd was generally the alternative type that I had encountered on the ferry, with a few other *gaijin* thrown in for good measure. The concert started at 7.30 and didn't finish till the wee hours under a gorgeous full Sado moon – 2.00 or 3.00 am I think. I sat on the grass watching until tiredness overwhelmed me and I just crashed out there on the spot in my sleeping bag about 1.00am. I woke at first light to find much of the site being blown away by the wind with tired roadies attempting to pull the stage apart before it was picked up by the vicious gale and carried away into the Sea of Japan. In my experience storms seem to be a popular occurrence on Sado. Whilst everyone else battened down or had their tents dismantled and/or blown away I snuggled down inside my sleeping bag. One Japanese guy remarked as he walked past, "MMM. Sleeping outside is better - no tent". After packing up (1-get out of sleeping bag, 2-put on backpack, and 3-get on bike) and leaving I had a short hard ride uphill before I came to a lodge where I slipped in for a bath and clean up.

By 7.00am I was on my way down the other side of the mountain, but by the time I got to the coast the weather was turning foul. I was riding into a headwind, which was blowing in the opposite direction from yesterday and soon accompanied by harder rain than Bob Dylan or Bryan Ferry ever imagined. After about twenty kilometres of sloshing on I was sheltering as a temporary respite behind a house garage. The *oba-chan* in residence had just came out and kindly opened the door for me to come inside when a driver pulled up and offered me a lift. He was from Kanagawa and was just driving around for something to do. He would have taken me all the way to Ogi I think, because he was obviously bored shitless driving around in the rain, but I felt bad and got him to drop me off in Sawata. I bought some breakfast, stopped at a laundromat to dry out some clothes, and it was just drizzling occasionally when I set off again.

It was a pretty slow ride with the wind a definite impediment. When I was nearly to Soboma it started to come down again so I forced to take shelter once more – this time in a sand hill. A few others were arriving just as I got to the camping area at the beach. That night we went to an Irish concert in Shiroyama Park. Yes, this time I paid. I think it will always be one of my most fragrant memories of Japan. As we set off up the hill the rain came down, but had stopped by the time we got to the top. Then the band came on and the heavens opened again, at first light but gradually getting heavier.

Before the interval, when the rain stopped briefly, most of us were up dancing anyway. We gave up trying to shelter under the tarpaulins and felt they better served just trying to keep our packs dry. We danced the night away and got thoroughly soaked. It never mattered - we were all happy, warm, and of course a little drunk. I found myself lying face down in the mud after trying at one stage to slam dance to the music. The rain had stopped by the encore, and the venue had turned into a steam bath. In a state of drying out we all went our separate ways. Because of the rain, and still lacking a tent, I went to sleep by the shop and shower block at the beach.

Just as I got off my bike and was unpacking my things a very nice looking young lass from the shop was just locking up. She asked about what I was doing and I told her I intended to sleep there. She giggled over this and told me that she considered it a wee bit silly. After we chatted for awhile she indicated it would be good if I could come back to her place. Her parents were away and she was a little scared to be by herself. At her place she gave me a *yukata* to wear and slipped into one herself. After a couple of *sake* she asked,

"Do you think I am attractive?"

"Yes, of course", was my somewhat startled reply.

"I am so lonely here. All I do is work in my parent's shop", she bemoaned.

"Look" I said, not sure where this was going, "Sado is a beautiful place. You are very pretty and friendly young lady. Surely you must have many men who want to be with you."

"No" she replied sadly, "None I have met, until tonight…"

She reached over slowly and tenderly kissed my cheek. Then she took my hand and led me outside to a natural hot spring behind the house. She removed her robe to reveal her lithe young body before we descended into the steaming waters together and bathed for some time. Afterwards followed a passionate night of lovemaking in her upstairs bedroom and when we woke in each other's arms the sun was glowing through the window as we looked out over a glimmering Sea of Japan.

Well, that's what I <u>would have liked</u> to have happened. Instead I just found myself bunking down under an awning to protect myself from the rain. And on concrete - naturally. Later I was rudely woken by two obnoxious *gaijin* in a van who had decided to also camp there at some wee hour. But they had to completely unpack their van first. They took so long I figured they must have left their sleeping gear stashed in a secret compartment they couldn't find or had lost the combination for. Or maybe the guy was giving his engine a whole tune-up and oil change because he might just b***** forget in the morning. I thought about waiting till they finished their complete reconditioning and preparation for a rummage sale. Then, when they actually went to sleep, I'd stick a hot crankshaft from their very own van up their orifices and make off with their last can of baked beans.

The next day the weather had picked up a bit, though it was still nowhere as good as the previous year. I rode into Ogi and just hung out near the fringe events and market-place before I went down to meet the ferry about 4.30 to meet the Itoigawa crew. A *gaijin* from Kyoto saw me and started asking me some questions. Then we were joined by Charles, Hang, and Tom, along with some Nagano and Toyama people who were coming off the boat. In the end I was giving a travel guide spiel to the assembled throng, and having a Q & A session. Eventually I led them, minus flag and loudspeaker, to the ticket office. There was another concert that night but lots of people decided to give it a miss. Hearing the reports I was glad I did too.

I got lost heading back from Ogi to the beach. It was a nice ride along the coast until it got dark. Eventually I got back about 7.30 to find not one, but two bonfires going. For some reason there were two lit, and there was a competition between them. The other fire was heavily patronised but ran out of both fire and alcohol by midnight. I had managed to find extra wood, and ours went much later, helped along by bottles of rum and gin. I slept on the beach without the threat of rain or concrete. It was still remarkably chilly though, especially for late August. I must make an apology at this stage to the poor farmer who would have came along some months later and found that somebody had stolen his bamboo ladder and burnt in on a fire. I thought it was abandoned – honestly. I realised much later as I became attuned to the seasons in Japan that, even though it was rickety and entangled with weeds, it was probably a ladder that has served a local farmer faithfully every harvest time for many years. Or maybe it <u>was</u> just thrown out into an old rice paddy and I'm on a complete guilt trip for absolutely no reason at all.

On Sunday evening we all went to see 'Kodo' at Shiroyama Park. It was a fantastic concert but a very different experience from Friday night. One of the things that struck me was that the local mayor gave a speech first. It's probably just as well Eminem or U2 aren't Japanese. Otherwise they would need their local mayor to go on the road with them, and warm up the crowd with a half-hour speech beforehand.

Most people left straight after the concert on the special midnight ferry, including myself. There were so many people on board that sleeping space was at a premium. At least it wasn't concrete. I lay down and just crashed until the bells rang about two hours later.

After disembarking I headed to the *eki* in Naoetsu. I had about forty-five minutes to wait for the last train. Just before it left the students from the Portland trip got on the train, fresh from Narita Airport in Tokyo and all jetlagged and tired. I felt the same but didn't have to go a few thousand kilometres to suffer the same condition. All the kids seemed to have enjoyed themselves. However being on the same train meant that when we reached Omi I had to endure the speeches and boredom of the welcoming crowd when all I wanted to do was go home and sleep - and so did the kids I'm sure.

After everything was said and done, all assembled got into their varying forms of transportation and left, all forgetting to ask if I perhaps would like a lift. Mizushima did hang around just to make sure I was okay but after I had put my bike back together he bid me *ki o tsukete* (be careful) and left as well. I guess it was not that far. I passed the lady out late walking her cat on my way home and was very glad to sleep in an actual bed that night.

34: It's English Jim, but not as we know it…

The only English words I saw in Japan were Sony and Mitsubishi.
- Bill Gullickson

The Japanese have been keen to learn English for a number of years. There was a large upswing in this interest post WWII with a particular emphasis on phrases like "Hello GI Joe, you want girl?" and, "I am not a war criminal". So was born the start of true Japanese internationalisation, and a new brand of English. So what? Everybody has his or her own particular brand of English. When I went to live in California I had to adopt a whole new vocabulary because each culture has their own particular slang. A Canadian friend once gave me directions to their place in Shanghai and said it was 'kitty-corner' from the supermarket. What the hell did that mean? Do I find a cat on the corner by the supermarket and follow it home?

However, Japanese English (or 'Japlish') is a breed apart. I'm informed that Japanese advertising executives don't care if it's not grammatically correct. It just has to <u>look</u> (or <u>sound</u>) good. Conversely, this confirms the suspicion that around the world advertising executives are culturally no different.

Anytime I travelled in Japan, in so many things I read or watched - examples of 'Japlish' could be seen everywhere. Therefore I have put some of these real, honest to goodness, written as seen, examples together below. Many were discovered by me, but a quite a few were passed on, and others via various publications.

Train + ing = Traing (Japan Rail ad)

Let's make it ready in your home. This bread presents you with a kind consideration in the morning and afternoon, or the dinner at home. (*Your Queen* bread wrapper)

These drawings in this exhibition are the best selection of many kind drinks in these days. You would be given the happy and tasty time by drinking one of them. (vending machine)

Bomb kuchen is dangerous cake. When this cake will spoil, it have to bumb. So, please help yourself to the cake, while it keeping fresh. Nobody stop it to bumb (*Bombe Kuchen* bakery box)

Konnyaku is well-known for refreshing your stomach and intestines. (*Konnyakubatake* jelly shots)

Ski feel is a concept like balance, which is instinctual to individuals who are athletic, but which can also be developed by others who approach skiing more socially than athletically. (Milk cookie wrapper)

Live Asahi for live people (*Asahi* beer)

Let's try homeparty fashionbly and have joyful chat with nice fellow (packet of straws)

Confidence of creating deliciousness. This tastiness can not be carried even by both hands (Wrapper on a chocolate dessert)

Dear Everybody, A hamburger, eaten when you're feeling blue, isn't very tasty. But when you're feeling energetic, with a smile on your face, and in love...that's when hamburgers really taste delicious (coffee cup at *Mos Burger*)

Our little friend 'TOMTE' use magical secret powder for delicious BREAD that. Well enjoy in next morning. Children who living in NORTHERN EUROPE tell us secret that just baken BREAD. Yes-TOMTE's secret. HOKUO as. BREAD country SAPPORO is very similar with TOMTE's land (*Tomte* bread wrapper)

FAMILY What is valuable thing to you? Are you happy now? Please value the valuable things to you (Seen on a backpack)

A lovely and tiny twig 'KOEDA.' A heroine's treasured chocolate in the forest. The sentimental taste is cozy for the heroine's in the town (box of chocolate covered pretzels)

You bask sunshine in the fresh morning. You breath fresh air and listen to birds singing. Lying down on the broad grass, you see a cloud in the blue sky changing its shape, look like a bread, and sometimes to cake,etc. (pastry wrapper)

Counselling and Order Centre (*Tokyu Hands* store - just in case you have a breakdown while buying hardware)

Men's Biggi (Menswear shop in Tokyo)

When passenger on foot heave in sight, tootle the horn. Trumpet him melodiously at first, but if he still obstacles your passage, then tootle him with vigor. (Brochure of a car rental firm in Tokyo - courtesy of *Far Eastern Economic Review*)

Wonders of electricity are displayed for children to be easily digested (sign-*Electric Science Museum*)

Magic House where anyone will be quite surprised and utter "S.O.S." 100 percent thrill. (sign - *Children's Sportsland*)

The efficacy of this beer is to give the health and especially the strength for Stomach. The flovour is so sweet and simple that not injure for much drink. (label - *Fuji Beer*)

mecca of dude, dundy, or fop (Shop sign - Harajuku, Tokyo)

When a guy is in love, it's a lot like being right in the middle of a banana jungle no matter where you look there are big bananas everywhere! (Advertisement - *Banana Daisuki*)

BABY SHITTER - I take care of your children. Please call up me. (Sign in Tokyo)

'Don't shit down here' (Warning sign - *Kyoto*)

Hi - I'm Nudy (advertisement for aftershave)

Mind Altering Drugs Store - Punk, death, and visual sounds (Music store - Niigata City)

With fried chicken you give taste and smell and also communicate your thankfulness (packaging from an Osaka fast food store - which sold probably the worst chicken I've ever tasted)

The following courtesy of 'Niigata JOHO'

Trade Mark K - Showvels Scoops and Spades which are exhibited of the above trade mark is very cheap in the pice and it is bonvenient bor Use. There is neceity exclain ally aeknorulebqe by thebll customers.

Return to nature only three hour ride away from Tokyo! - In snowy hills hares and foxes hop around and in streams trouts and chars swim about. Also you will enjoy the glare of sunbeams and freash ozone. Down at the foot of the 4200 feet over sea-leveled hotel, there are factories of cameras, watches, and music boxes.

Please use your foot to handle the cock.

The perfect goods to climax a happy occasion....to make any occasion happy. BITS GOODS goes along.

Butchering is our specialty Glue no extra charge!

Wel come to Japan the sea men you gentlemen drop in the bar king at girst: Ladies are ready. In boxes and stands

Your charm and dandyism is began from feet. All time all seasons, KAMIKURI's moody up your dream wear.

Vertical parking only

Don't urine water

But wait there's more! Here is a collection of some true, verifiable, honest to goodness, motor vehicle names in Japan....

Verbs	*Adjectives*	*Animals*
Works	Windy	Guppy
Inspire	Stormy	Street Racoon Beat
Reflect	Savvy	
	Prominent	

Girls		*Boys*	
Vicky	Cynthia	Rex	Domingo
Carol	Leeza (Cha-Cha)	Cedric	Will
Gloria			

From the shop
Super Potato, Parsley, Lime, Carrot, Cappucino

Appealing to the younger female
Cutie, Rouge, Perky, Femina

Miscellaneous (see: Unexplainable)
Joypop Landventure, Rex Combi La La, Sunny Super Saloon, We've, Midget II, Bongo Friendee, Elf, Master Ace Surf, Today Humming, Today Pochette

There you have it. I feel better now and normal programming can resume….

35: Oh my God! It's an eyeball!

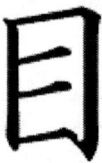

There's a fine line between fishing and just standing on the shore like an idiot
- Steven Wright

As with my first summer I had returned to a desk full of essays and was marking a lot of papers. The work was inconsistent, as could be expected, but there were no wild claims this time around. Actually there was some brilliant stuff written and it was probably the best assignment work I had seen so far. I felt bad because the kids who had handed in their work late, even one day, got no marks. I guess they were told, but it seemed sad that a few of them were not being lazy. Just forgetful or trying to do a better job. If I did that at my current school I'd have to fail a fair percentage of my students.

Just after summer break Todd and I were invited to go fishing with Ma-chan and Ta-chan. Let me say right here and now that fishing has never been my forte. I would be lucky to have caught more than half a dozen fish in my life. One of those only because it got hopelessly entwined on my line whilst swimming past minding his own business – as opposed to actually taking what was on the hook. Even though my desire to go fishing is, on a social scale, just below that of attending a Leonardo di Caprio film festival some aspects are not too bad. I heard it once said,

"Give a man a fish and he will eat for a day. Teach him how to fish, and he will sit in a boat and drink beer all day."

They conveyed us to the Himegawa Port and we slotted into a position just by a coal ship that was being loaded. Of course not an insubstantial amount of the said coal was landing not in the hold of the ship, but in the surrounding waters – right where we were fishing. So before I had even begun to bait my hook I was a bit worried about all the carcinogens any fish we caught may contain. The first fish I landed was probably about 5-6 centimetres. This was actually pretty good for me but I unhooked it and was just preparing to throw it back when Ma-chan grabbed it from me and put it in the bucket. How the hell we were going to scale and fillet it was beyond me but all the fish caught that day were of a similar size. My best catch was a Quentin Tarantino cardboard cut-out left in a nearby *gomi* pile which was stuck up in the *genkan* (entrance hall) when we returned.

Back at the apartment Todd and myself, later joined by Tom, were hustled out of the kitchen while the girls and their friend Muki cooked us dinner. All we could hear was the sizzle of deep-frying and the loud banter of the cooks. Shortly thereafter they sallied out with a plate of dishes including the fish that had been battered and deep fried whole. They waited while we cast an eye over the food. Todd picked up a fish, and urged me to do the same, saying,

"Well, we don't have any choice. You just have to eat it."

So we popped one each in our mouths and smiled as we crunched down, head, bones and all. Our fine cooks and fishing companions, now satisfied, retreated once again to the kitchen. Whereupon I retreated to the study and hacked out the remnants into an old envelope and deposited it in the bin.

However I was still bothered by something stuck between my teeth. A bone presumably. But I couldn't go to the bathroom to check in the mirror, as I would need to go past the kitchen. I did the normal thing of prying away with a fingernail until finally it came loose. I stared at the remnant that had been part of a fish swimming happily in the Himegawa Port until just a couple of hours ago.

"Oh my God!" I thought, "It's an eyeball!"

Another month came and I took another short trip to California as autumn began with a full display of its brilliant colours. I found myself wearing warmer clothes at night and by morning sleeping under a thin blanket. A new *kyoiku-cho* (Head of the Board of Education) was appointed as Kinokawa finally retired to write his memoirs and presumably focus on his other business interests. Mr. Yamagishi, a former *kocho* (principal) at Itoigawa *shogakko*, was his replacement. Not that I was to have too much to do with him. In a way it was sad that Kinokawa was finally gone. Despite his failing health he was obviously a man who had taken great pride in his work and was concerned for the welfare of the resident foreign English teacher. Apart from me naturally. I was far too badly behaved.

One Sunday night I wasn't feeling well so I decided to ask Yuko to take me to the hospital. Since my return from America a large lump had come up on my chest just above my heart. I could not recall having knocked or bumped that area in any kind of traumatic fashion so it was somewhat of a worry. Yuko called Kinya, who freaked out, and so it ended up that all five of us (Yuko and husband, Kinya and wife) went to the emergency section at Itoigawa *Byoin*. After the nurse helped pull my trousers down low for the doctor ("…but the bruise at the top of my chest – not down there!") he had a look at my bruise and referred me to a dermatologist (huh?) the next day. They obviously thought it was a rash while I was imagining it was a blood clot about to bring all of my internal organs to a shuddering and final halt. I went back the next afternoon and the doctor informed me it was a 'tumour with bleeding'. I was hoping that the translation given was no more than just bad English. He gave me some medicine and told me to come back the next week.

The weather turned nasty, autumn seemed to disappear almost as soon as it arrived and winter now seemed not too far away. Almost like a metaphor, the lump in my chest did not get any smaller so my Canadian friend Sherilyn offered to take me to a doctor in Toyama near where she lived for a second opinion. However he couldn't say anymore than those in Itoigawa. The lump appeared to be a little smaller, I thought and hoped, but when I went back to Itoigawa *byoin* the doctor was still unsure. I was told to come back in a month and if it was still there I would have to go under the knife. My insecurity was not helped when I realised the next day that I was wearing my boxers backwards. Bad *juju* dude....

Things did not seem to get any better so a couple of weeks later I went back down to Toyama and spent the night at Sherilyn's before going to nearby Chuo *byoin* in the morning – probably the most modern hospital in the area. That ended up a complete waste of time. There was a huge line up, then I got bounced around a couple of departments. Unfortunately for me nobody spoke a scrap of English and my Japanese was so woeful I was eventually got sent back to the dermatology department. I just gave up and threw the folder I had been given onto the front desk as I left. Just as the bus to the city arrived the parking attendant came over and waved his nightstick at me, all the while yelling "money, money". Two nurses were standing at the front door shouting at him to chase me so I had to go back and pay my small gap contribution above and beyond my health insurance. Eventually after some weeks the lump and bruise disappeared and I could stop getting my affairs together with some urgency.

It was around this time that there was an election. To ensure fairness every candidate gets to put up the same size poster on a billboard constructed by the local authorities in every town. To capture the voter's imagination it appears the standard action is to drive around in a van between defined hours with very loud speakers on top containing people with white gloves waving out the windows. I was always worried about how the Japanese talked about elections. Fukushima once asked me how often Australians have elections, and misunderstanding his pronunciation I declared,

"I don't have any firm statistics, but in my own experience I usually have one in the morning when I wake up."

This mispronunciation of the 'L' and 'R' can also lead to many misunderstandings. Up north there lived a lanky African-American named Rob. Rob was an extremely funny guy who had ended up on the program on very short notice – just three days in fact. He had been selected as an 'alternate' and when a person assigned to Niigata-ken had dropped out just before leaving Rob was asked to take their place. He was given those days to get his life together and get on a Japan-bound plane from Chicago where he lived. He accomplished this fairly well. So well, that by late afternoon on the day before he was due to leave he had everything packed up in his car ready to go. Then his car caught fire and he had to start all over again with less then twenty-four hours remaining.

Anyway, why I mention Rob is that he once told me about a speaking test that he had. The students had to introduce themselves and talk about their lives. One rather amply endowed young student started by discussing her name and what it meant in English. She stated quite distinctly,

"My name is Chieko and it means 'a thousand bless'".

But she was mispronouncing the 'l' and had dropped off the '-ings'. Rob said he asked her to repeat as his "…eyes lit up like a Christmas tree." I'm not sure what score he gave her but I'm positive it rated highly.

Though from some of the stories Rob told me it was easy to be confused. Another tale he passed on was how he was on his way to *karate* practice when he saw a big group of students, mostly girls, sitting in front of the building. They were there with fireworks, music, food and laughter practicing their dance routine for the upcoming sports day. They saw him and screamed with delight. One girl asked him if he had a girlfriend and Rob said, "Yes". Another student said that she saw him with her one time and that she was very beautiful. Yet another girl asked him if his girlfriend was prettier than them.

Before he could answer, a fourth student said,

"That's okay if she is prettier. She's probably not bi-sexual like me", and began feeling up one of her friends.

"Rob-*san*, Do you like bi-sexual?" he was asked (in Japanese).

"What?"

"Do YOU like bi-sexual?" This time it was in English – and the girl kept feeling up her friend.

"Whaaaaat!!!? You're bi-sexual!!?"

"No, it's a joke."

But as Rob sighed with relief, she added, "I'm really lesbian".

And she kept feeling up her friend.

At Ichiburi *yochien* we went for a walk one day as the weather become distinctly crisp and 'found' a temple and graveyard. At the *shogakko* I went fishing with one class - we didn't catch anything fortunately - and baked potatoes on the beach with the other. I came home that day smelling like fish and smoke. Ma-chan, who I suspect came up with the fishing idea, seemed a bit off and maybe she was giving up on any ideas of romance. Back at Omi *chugakko* Matsuki had married and become Kuriiwa-*sensei*. Almost just as quickly she was pregnant, which is fairly standard practice in Japan, and away often with morning sickness.

The other *ichi-nensei* teachers arranged a staff function at the Itoigawa Hotel. This was to be a western style meal where, in addition, all the attendees would be taught about western table manners. The problem here was that I was the only *gaijin* present, and I struggled to remember all the manners that my mother had tried to teach me in vain. She did warn, "One day young Nicholas you will need to know these, and if you don't pay attention now you will be very embarrassed when that day comes." Mum, you were so right. I found myself the centre of attention as people leant forward and/or craned their necks to see what I was doing and thus was my example followed - for better or worse.

Later in the month the annual student activity day came around once more and I was roped into the bike ride as usual. I went to the teacher who was doing all the planning and asked him what was happening. The discussion went something like this.

"We are going to Nou-machi" he replied.

"What will we do there?" I asked, remembering that the previous year we had ridden a long way uphill to a park.

"There is a new *onsen* there we will visit." he informed me.

"So, we will bathe there?"

"Yes"

"With the students?"

"Yes"

"Is that actually legal?"

So I was not to be riding up any hills but instead would be bathing naked with some of my eleven and twelve year old male students.

On the day the *onsen* was quite a distance inland from the coast and after lunch we retired to the hot pools. I sat on one side and the majority of boys sat on the other laughing and joking with each other. Eventually Keita Watanabe, obviously elected (correct spelling – with the 'l') by the others, made his way over and sat next to me.

"Nicholas-*sensei*", he said to get my attention.

"Yes?" I replied, not sure whether this was going to be good or bad.

"Look!" he said as he pointed to the top of the bamboo fence that divided the male and female sides of the pool. The divider was probably just over two metres high and they had calculated I had just enough height to reach up and look over.

"No, that's okay", I responded as I waved my hand.

The student sidled back to his friends and they engaged in a very serious group discussion before he returned again after a couple of minutes.

"Nicholas-sensei", he started again.

"Yes Keita", came my standard reply.

He pointed to the top of the divider again and put to me, "Look! Girls!"

So they had figured I just didn't understand what was on the other side, rather than it being a moral dilemma.

I now addressed him in plain English,

"Yes Keita, I'm aware that there are girls on the other side. One of those is even Okimura-*sensei* who I would dearly love to see in an unclothed state. However apart from the ethical considerations I would, as your teacher, be setting a bad moral example for you. So, thanks anyway for the suggestion but I really must decline at this time."

He had sat there nodding and taking this all in. Then he replied, "*Wakatta*" (I understand) in a knowing manner. As he moved back towards his friends I commented,

"No you don't, not at all."

Afterwards we got ourselves dressed and *kocho-sensei* had arrived by this time as well. We all stood outside taking pictures and the female contingent had no idea whatsoever about all the nefarious thoughts that had been considered by the collection of male students just over the bamboo divider in the previous hour or so. The round trip for the day was sixty-five kilometres so I was pretty buggered by the time I got home. Still, it was a beautiful day, and so was the scenery. Even without seeing Okimura naked. I had to have a nap when I got home so I could be refreshed before the *enkai* started.

36: 'Love Select' and 'Memory Notes'

The difference between fiction and reality is that fiction has to make sense
- Tom Clancy

The crew from Itoigawa showed up on the door one night for dinner and in the morning Tom stole my *mama chari* to get home, and that was the last I ever saw of it. Charles and Hang, having heard over and over again the legends of Omi *gomi*, stayed on to go hunting with me upon the first light of morn. Over the next few hours we all scored shopping bikes, plus Hang also found a word processor and a microwave. I rescued an old surfboard, that I would never use for fear of smashing myself to smithereens on the breakwater, and a sixties type radio. I also found one of the old pedal-type sewing machines with the ornate cast iron legs. This thing was so heavy that inevitably I had to ditch the machine and just take home the table. Then I gave myself a triple hernia carting it up the stairs. If you claim that a triple hernia is not possible, well, you've never tried to cart one of these things up four flights of stairs. I would have loved to have taken it back to Australia with me but I didn't think they would it accept it as carry-on. I left it in the apartment upon my departure from whence I'm sure it made its way back to the *gomi* collection.

Later that week I collected a mountain bike, plus another chain and wheel for the previously mentioned shopping bike. One of my neighbours noted that my storage space was rapidly filling with all things bicycular and asked me to quantify "Nic-*san*, just how many bikes do you have?"

I was mighty happy to find that a pizza bar has finally opened up in Itoigawa. I went down to collect a bike to ride there and check it out. I felt like the Donald Trump of bicycles as I vetted my collection.

"I think I feel like the green one with the shopping basket today. No wait. Something with a little more class. No wait. One with brakes that actually work."

I rode along Highway 8 with fantasies of thick crust pizza and lashings of cheese and pepperoni. Imagine my disappointment as I studied the menu (*see: really weird*) and found pizza toppings of pilaf, spaghetti, *miso* and tuna - as in sashimi style. It mattered little in the end, as it was that time of year again. There was major snow on the mountains and some fair hailstorms occurring. I had dragged out the heaters and winter clothing, as well as closing the windows. And the store was not about to institute any deliveries to Omi. Riding my bike five kilometres and back through a snowstorm, while dodging buses and trucks, to pick up a pilaf pizza, was not something to put near the top of my 'To Do' list.

With the snows coming again the school ski days were being planned. Setsuko plainly told me I couldn't go on the *ichi-nensei* ski day because I had to "…teach that day".

"What are the other *ichi-nensei* teachers doing then?" I asked, which was greeted by a stony cold silence. Also with the cold weather setting in we returned to the climate of about fifty degrees in the staff and class rooms, but freezing in every other nook and cranny.

I was able to escape this for a few days up to a conference in Niigata. I was in two minds about going. I wanted to catch up with people, but had become very ambivalent about b***** conferences. At least they provided travel opportunities. I did try to opt out at one stage but was informed, most sternly, that I must attend. As a petulant form of rebellion I was 'late' for the early bus and missed out on all the morning speeches. Over the next couple of days I managed to get my name signed on the attendance sheet for three out of six workshops.

One involved a lot of interaction but which I found incredibly boring. It did actually provide a useful insight into the mind of a student. There were the usual crop of attendees participating enthusiastically, a percentage just going through the motions, and a handful like me who sat down at the back thinking, "What actual use is this to me?" The workshop coordinator used her best teacher's voice to cajole me into action. But I figured I couldn't get the cane or a detention, so when she turned her back I scooted out the door to play truant.

Before returning to Omi I managed to see a number of sights in Niigata City during my 'hooky' times and spent the last night at Kevin's in Nishikawa, just a short train journey outside the city. Kevin was an intelligent and studious young Canadian on a fast track to his goals. That didn't stop him from also being extremely funny, and a person who could let his hair down with the best of them. Last time I saw Kevin in Ottawa he was now also quite fluent in French, as his Japanese disappeared, and one of the rising young stars of the diplomatic service.

In the morning I met up with an old friend of mine from California at the Niigata *eki*. Rod had just finished his Peace Corps service in Fiji and was travelling home the long way. We stopped in Yahiko on the way south and then onto Takada. Rod was trying to save some cash by carting his excess baggage and carry-on three-quarters of the way around the world. The Peace Corps is not the road to material riches – unless you're moonlighting for the C.I.A. So here we were tramping through the heavy snow carting thirty-kilogram duffle bags each that contained most of Rod's earthly possessions. The things were so b***** big that we couldn't even find a locker to accommodate them.

In Takada I was picking up a snowboard from a friend so with the extra load the trip from there back to Omi made me feel the complete *sherpa*. By the time we got to Omi there was no bus for an hour, so we had to walk back home with everything. At least no snow had reached Omi by that time. Rod stayed for a few days before heading onto Hong Kong and ports further west. He later joined the American air force and returned to Japan to crew spy planes flying over Korean and Chinese coasts. Not that he could ever admit as such.

An old friend of Joanne's, Miwa Sato, was now living in Omi and she and her boyfriend took me up one night to Kakizaki for one of Joanne's famous parties. Rather than crush in with the dozing hordes I decided to leave early and slept the night at another teacher's place in Kashiwazaki up the road. Kashiwazaki was regarded by many as a rather peculiar place. Although quite a nice city in itself, it somehow had the knack of regularly attracting a whole host of dysfunctional *gaijin* to lodge within its boundaries. It was almost like the prefecture allocated everyone to different postings, and then any odd sorts left over got dumped in Kashiwazaki.

Not that the resident foreigners had any monopoly on weirdness. It might have had something to do with the fact that Japan's largest nuclear plant was just up the road in Kariwa, but I'm only speculating. I didn't actually see any six-fingered locals there. Though they wouldn't be hard to hide. In the most high profile incident involving the town it was discovered in 1999 that a 40-year-old man had kidnapped a 9-year-old girl in the city in November 1990 at knifepoint and confined her to a second-floor room of his home for that nine years, and two months, if you want to be picky. How nobody woke up to the fact I don't know. His mother had actually been to the police several times to tell them about it, but they seemingly didn't take the reports seriously. When the girl, now eighteen years old, was finally discovered, by accident it must be said, and the story was picked up by the national press the local custodians of the law found themselves with a quite a number of asses left to cover.

And soon I was whiling out the days till Christmas and the winter break. My friend Kiminori sent me a Christmas card. Its inscription read,

"How is it in Oumi? I guess you may be very embarrassed to live there."

I put it up alongside the others and looked forward to my trip to Australia and Malaysia away from the cold.

The Saturday after school broke up I went with Hang and Todd to a mountain town in Toyama for a party. It was a good show, and most partygoers didn't get to sleep till around 4.00am. Most people were sleeping upstairs but it was a real crush in there so Todd and I decided to crash in the party room. After everyone had departed and the heaters were turned off the frigid alpine weather from outside quickly began to make its way inside. Todd and I guessed we must have got only about three or four hours sleep as we piled on curtains, carpets and any other material that could be found handy. I even put the futon mattress and a small table on top in an effort to beat the cold. They were lucky we didn't break the furniture up and start a fire. Todd and Hang left about 9am, then Charles, who had come down by himself and I went with a few others to an *onsen* which had a beautiful view over the valley.

Afterwards our host Anita took us to see the historic and World Heritage listed Taira village, then on to Johana *eki*. I was going to wait in Toyama then head to Osaka via the overnight train to catch my plane out. However, looking at Charles' train schedule I discovered I could catch two local trains that evening all the way through. The theory was that I would arrive at midnight and then I could sleep the night in the *eki*.

Things unravelled quickly from there. I got into Osaka right on time, but when I went to get my fare adjusted they wouldn't believe that I had caught local trains all the way. I tried to explain in my pigeon Japanese but the attendant just kept nodding and saying things like, I presume, "Nobody would be that stupid..." My next discovery was that, unfortunately there's no such thing as a waiting room in Osaka station <u>and</u> that they close the station up at night too. By the time this epiphany had come upon me all the late night trains to the airport had long gone.

After stashing my bags I set out walking for awhile. Where to I had no idea. It was now after midnight and the first train out wasn't until after 6.00am. There was not much to see at that time of night - just clubs, pubs, and *rabu hoteru* (love hotels).

What an interesting concept 'love hotels' are. Japanese houses are not renowned for their privacy, with thin walls, sliding doors, and the fact that up to three or four generations can be living under the same roof. Therefore 'love hotels', rented by the hour, can provide respite for those more intimate moments between frazzled couples or frustrated dates, not to mention secret trysts. But they are not just for things sexual. Rooms are often so well equipped that they are used for entertainment in the form of spas, *karaoke* and/or satellite TV. They also provide an excellent mid-budget option for overnight stays when the price is cheaper. It's either that or the 'capsule' hotels where you can sometimes find yourself slumbering in a space not that much larger than a coffin.

Apparently there are around 37,000 love hotels in Japan and it's estimated that nearly 500 million couples visit them each year. Now for those good on their maths this works out to 1,370,000 couples using a love hotel per day - more than double the <u>annual</u> number of combined visitors to both Tokyo Disneyland and Tokyo Disney Sea. Not that the target consumers would be searching for the same kind of experiences, presumably. These institutions rake in at least four trillion yen (US$37 billion) a year, slightly more than the entire GDP of Cuba. In fact they are so profitable that major investment funds in both Japan and overseas are taking major stakes in them. The origin of these institutions harks back to post-World War II. Simple inns were set up for ladies to 'service' American soldiers in occupied Japan and the establishments were called *tsurekomi* (bring your own woman).

Charles swore by the use of 'love hotels' when travelling and after awhile I was convinced too. At the first place I ever tried the room's sound system had a huge list of soundtracks and radio stations to choose from, and if you pushed a button you could get those particular sounds vibrating the bed. There were foreign stations, international music (Caribbean, Hawaiian, French, Italian, etc.), the sound of a heart beat, a cooking class, counting sheep, a church service, and even an English conversation class. Even allowing for my comment before on entertainment options, I could hardly envisage people coming to listen to cooking tips or English conversation. Or be spiritually enlightened either.

The funniest were the 'alibi' sounds. With these you could turn up the sound and call whoever, making them think you were somewhere else. The soundtracks included traffic noise, a bank, a train station, and a post office. So you could easily say,

"Hi Honey. Yes, I'm running late now. I'm in the shoe store. Yes, soon. Love you too."

Accompany this with some kissy-kissy sounds in conclusion and the partner would never guess. I really liked the books on the bedside table – 'Love Select', where you could dial up for sex aids, and 'Memory Notes' where you could register the details of your time together. Presuming you were actually with someone else. Many of the pages discreetly had names missing, which made sense to me.

Another establishment came complete with food service, *karaoke*, seven channels of dirty movies, and one (yes, only one) 'Mighty Ace' condom. After your time was up you had to press a button to get the price, then send money via vacuum tube delivery system - with the change was returned the same way. Talk about privacy. The last concern I stayed at was amazing. This place had *karaoke*, a 'pokie' machine (one-armed bandit), *usen* world network radio, porno movies, Playstation (obviously for the kids), free drinks, a huge spa tub, a Polaroid camera (at ¥500 per shot) to remember the more 'tender' moments, and a vending machine full of sex toys. I must say that this one (the room, not the vending machine) did cost a small fortune but it was worth it for the bizarre experience.

Back in Osaka I had not yet clicked to the value of *rabu hoteru* so by 2.30 I was sick of walking around and got some KFC to kill some time. I went back to the *eki* about 3.00am and, with naught else to do, tried sleeping outside in the bushes - but it was just too damn cold. In my zombie-like state I went out reconnoitring again and managed to find a 24-hour restaurant where fortunately I could dally a couple of hours over one ¥600 cup of steaming hot coffee. Thank goodness I didn't have to hand over any tips to the waitresses, most of whom looked more fatigued than me. The *eki* was finally coming back to life around 5.30am, and I was a tired and somewhat dishevelled soul as I alighted from the first train to Kansai Airport after 7.00am. I got my tickets, paid my terminal fee, and changed some money. All I needed then was to get out of there plus get about fifteen hours sleep...

37: Toilets, Smokers and Cults

You don't have to die; heaven and hell are in this world too - Japanese Proverb

I thought I might take some time here to reflect on some of the big issues in Japan. Did you know that the Japanese have the longest life span in the world? Yet at the same time they use up one third of the world's blood supplies and have one of the highest smoking rates in the world, particularly for males. Of course there's also the problem of alcohol abuse. But let's not go there shall we?

According to the *New York Times*, Japan is the world's largest importer of cigarettes – totalling roughly eight-three billion in 2001. Japanese smokers also pay some of the lowest taxes in the developed world at only ¥100 a pack. With 600,000 cigarette vending machines operating nationwide in the late 1990's, a ¥250 pack costs the equivalent of eight minutes of work in Tokyo, as compared with twenty minutes in Los Angeles and forty minutes in London. The government earns US$17 billion in taxes from cigarette sales, and what is referred to as a 'tobacco tribe' of lawmakers in the Diet makes sure that there is no serious financing for antismoking campaigns.

Recently in Tokyo they have begun to institute some 'no-smoking zones'. Yet everywhere one goes, lurking furtively deep amongst the shadows, even a few short steps from the no-smoking zone, you can find the glowing ash tips of the *hotaru-zoku* (firefly tribe), as Japanese smokers are often known. This can lead one to ponder - how can the battle against smokers be won? One of these is quietly unfolding at the Ministry of Health, Labour and Welfare in Tokyo. This government agency, which serves as the 'standard bearer' for Japan's antismoking campaign, is discussing whether it should remove automated cigarette vending machines from its premises. The conundrum was apparently set off by a complaint from the ministry's Health Sciences Council, where one council member found it "strange" that a ministry responsible for educating the public on the hazards of smoking should have cigarette vending machines on its site.

From one poison to another, let's discuss cults in Japan – the good, the strange and the ugly.

The separation of church and state is an argument that has been around for centuries in the West since the Protestant Reformation, but has recently raged anew in Japan. Thousands of religious groups in Japan had broad freedoms under the Religious Corporations Law of 1951, probably as a result of the influence of the American post-war occupation. Part of the tension stemmed from the growing power of the Buddhist sect, *Soka Gakkai*, and *Komeito* (Clean Government Party) – its political offshoot. Its new found status even put it on the cover of TIME in November, 1995. *Komeito* now serves as a small part of the ruling coalition of parties, proclaiming that it seeks to influence cabinet decisions in a positive manner.

And isn't that just needed in Japanese politics, although government in Japan is now moving much closer to a transparent two-party system. One recent example of how politicians may get 'confused' with the truth, apart from weapons of mass destruction, is the charismatic and youthful Junichiro Koga. Before his election to a seat in the Diet representing his local Fukuoka district he proudly displayed his resume on the internet, claiming that he had graduated from UCLA in the 1980's. However someone with a keen eye at UCLA pointed out to him that he didn't even attend any classes there.

So he jumped on a plane to America to "consult" with the university and clear up any "misunderstanding". Upon his return to Japan he confessed to being "confused" over what were 'extension courses', that anyone could walk in off the street and view, and what were college courses earning credits. He apparently had attended three different universities in California, none of them actually being UCLA, and graduated from none of them – still being collectively nineteen units short of any type of degree. Koga could at least produce a photo of himself on the tennis team at Pepperdine University. He also stated that, "I was convinced that I had graduated, and I am very surprised about these results." Sacked from his party, he intends to continue on as an independent, and in all likelihood this imbroglio will be forgotten by the next election.

Nevertheless, it appears in these troubling times that religion in any country can either be a servant or master when it comes to political processes. It can also be a very convenient vehicle when needing to win some extra votes, or alternatively, just to practice some good old demagoguery.

On the quirkier side of cults in Japan is the 'Pana Wave Laboratory' cult founded by Hiroko Chino, a 69-year-old female guru. Since the 1970's her followers have moved with her from one place to another across the nation in caravans. They were last seen occupying a 200-metre stretch of a mountain road in Gifu, some 300 kilometres west of Tokyo, with an entourage of fifteen white-shrouded cars and vans. Wearing surgical-style white robes, headgear and facemasks, the Pana Wave members erected white fabric screens along the roadside, and wrapped nearby guardrails and tree trunks in white, claiming that white cloth can help them avoid being exposed to harmful electromagnetic waves. The doomsday sect, whose membership is believed to top 1200, claims the earth is in danger because of electromagnetic waves used with evil intent by communists. Perhaps they would be major proponents of the American 'Star Wars' missile program.

All of their vans are also white and covered with numerous pieces of white paper printed with mysterious whirlpool pattern. Television footage showed the inside of the vehicles as also white with the steering wheels bandaged. As the police kept trying to move them on it became the first major confrontation between a cult and local government in Japan since the ugly *Aum Shinrikyo* (Aum Supreme Truth).

Aum Shinrikyo are the lovely cult people responsible in 1995 for the release of sarin gas in the Tokyo subway system that killed twelve and injured thousands of commuters. This was after they had a June 1994 trial run in Matsumoto City in Nagano where they managed to bump off seven innocent souls and harm countless others. Apparently one of the victims was singled out by the police as the main suspect. At the same time his wife was laying in a coma, the media hounds dubbed him "The Poison Gas Man", leading to hate mail and threats against his life. Eventually by the time of the Tokyo attack the blame shifted to *Aum Shinrikyo*, thereby prompting an outpouring of apologies from officials and the media.

Sarin is a poison nerve gas, twenty-six times more deadly than cyanide, invented by Nazi scientists prior to WWII. One drop of this substance, no bigger than a pinhead, is enough to kill a person. Saddam Hussein also used it to good effect during the 1980's against both Iranians and rebellious Kurds. The trial of their leader Shoko Asahara (a.k.a. Chizuo Matsumoto), who denies any guilt, dragged on for years with little to show for the efforts of the prosecuting team, although by 2002, nine Aum cadres have already been sentenced to hang for their crimes.[5]

Apart from murmuring incoherently, Asahara made virtually no statement at his trial – which opened in April 1996 – since January 1998 when he denied masterminding the gas attack and often appeared to doze during proceedings. Some sort of verdict was expected for him by mid-2003 but it was not until February 2004 when it took more than four hours for the presiding judge in Tokyo District Court to recite guilty verdicts on the thirteen charges against him and finally sentence him to death. It was reported that as the judge spoke, "Mr. Asahara, his trademark flowing black hair and beard now greying and trimmed short, reportedly crossed his arms, smiled, openly yawned, snorted, scratched his head, smelled his fingers, mumbled incoherently and muttered as if reciting mantras."

---

[5] Incidentally the cult, which has now renamed itself Aleph, is still legal in Japan and has 1,650 followers - including about 300 in Russia. At the time of the attack, Aum is believed to have had more than 10,000 followers in Japan, and between 30,000 to 40,000 in Russia.

Why did they actually do this? Apparently the group has some apocalyptic type belief that "all souls should be liberated from evil habits" by killing them as an act of charity. This is one charity I would not want to support. Apparently Asahara also nurtured some deep desire to be king. Could you imagine the kind of parties at the Imperial Palace when other heads of states visited?

Before the subway attack, Mr. Asahara appeared regularly on television and in 1990 he and other members ran for Parliament. After none won, Aum built a commune at the foot of Mount Fuji, and factories to produce weapons and sarin. Members of the cult went to Australia in 1993 and 1994 to test this sarin nerve gas on sheep. They didn't want to appear conspicuous, so they evidently turned up at Perth Airport wearing safari suits and wide brimmed hats with corks dangling from them. The upshot of their quest was that the group successfully exterminated a large number of the sheep with the gas that was eventually to be used in Tokyo and Matsumoto.

There was also a rumour flying around that they had been mining uranium on the property they owned in remote Western Australia in a primitive attempt to manufacture an atomic weapon and in 1993 a large unexplainable tremor was felt in the area. The Australian government of the time didn't act on any of this information. I suppose because Australia is a very big country and is used to the unexplainable (*see:* John Howard and Steve Irwin), as well as its inhabitants and the occasional Asiatic visitor, acting strangely. The Japanese government must have also been blithely unaware. Not that much would have been done much anyway. Some of the punishments handed out are akin to being flogged with a piece of wet spaghetti.

Some people were aware of the danger and were speaking up. At one stage the cult were shown videotape of a lawyer making accusations against them by a local television network seeking comment. Shortly afterwards the lawyer and his family mysteriously vanished. They later turned up in shallow graves about thirty kilometres north of Omi. Punishment was nonetheless meted out in due course to the network for its indiscretion. *The Daily Yomiuri* stated after the ruling was handed down that,

"....the Post and Telecommunications Ministry decided Thursday to issue a "stern warning" to the television station for allowing the Aum Supreme Truth to view a videotape interview with Tsutsumi Sakamoto before he was slain. Minister Ichiro Hino is expected to announce the decision to give TBS a written warning on Friday..."

Wow, what justice. Bet that had the network shaking in their boots.

Speaking of boots, there is an old Australian saying about 'splashing the boots'. This is from the usual literal sense of what happens when a man goes to the urinal and doesn't bother to watch what he's doing. And even sometimes when he does I presume the non-male readers will cry. One cold night back home in Australia my friend Rod and I were caught a bit short and decided to nip into the new public toilets built in one of Adelaide's many fine city squares.

However we were dismayed to find that it was so new a toilet attendant was *in situ* and collecting money for the privilege of use.

"How much mate?" asked Rod, as he bobbed up and down ever so slightly.

"Ten cents" was the reply

Never afraid of being up front Rod simply stated,

"How about you just let me in? Because if you don't I'm actually gonna flop it out here and you'll be the one to clean up the mess."

Rod has a way with words as you see.

"Okay" the attendant reluctantly agreed as he opened the gate, "but next time you'll have to pay."

Of course if we had been in Japan Rod could have "flopped it out" just about anywhere he wanted to, apart from the female toilets. If one does that in Australia you can be arrested, as was a certain high profile AFL footballer some years ago. The act of relieving oneself is much more public in Japan. Which is why toilet doors on the bullet trains contain windows. I guess it's useful if you want to wave to passer-by's. Also because the same doors don't have locks it means anyone wanting to come in can see you and not come in – therefore saving you the embarrassment of being seen. Huh? Even though the Japanese are not afraid to use the great outdoors it's inside the home where toileting really comes to the fore.

The Japanese have moved on somewhat from the hole in the ground and/or squat toilet. *Gaijin* have generally found these kinds of toilets difficult, unless they liked working out on their calf muscles and voluntary sphincter. Even the Japanese seem to have become more used to the idea of sitting down and the attendant comfort it brings. One company recently unveiled a toilet seat that contained,

"electrodes that send a mild electric charge through the user's buttocks, yielding a digital measurement of body-fat ratio."

Not to be outdone another competitor retaliated with a toilet that,

"…glows in the dark and whirs up its lid after an infrared sensor detects a human being."

On the horizon are 'talking toilets' that will be equipped with microchips. These would go beyond music, greeting each new user with a personal message, perhaps a recorded word of encouragement from their mother, boss or teacher.

The *New York Times* reported that the giant Toto Corporation had come out with their new 'WellyouII' model which,

"…automatically measures the user's urine sugar levels by making a collection with a little spoon held by a retractable, mechanical arm."

These results would be sent from the toilet to a doctor by an Internet-capable cellular phone built into the toilet. Naturally a competitor upped the ante by declaring that they would install devices in toilets that would measure weight, fat, blood pressure, heart beat, urine sugar, albumin and blood in the user's urine.

However some civil libertarians in Japan began having nightmares about these 'smart toilets' getting out of control and e-mailing all sorts highly personal information that could up in the hands of terrorists. Or even worse, the government. In an Orwellian 1984 scenario 'Big Brother' could have master computers monitoring millions of bowel movements, checking around the clock to see who has diarrhoea, who is not eating their vegetables and who, God forbid, is using illegal substances. Like the JET participant who leased a plot in his town's community garden – then used it to grow marijuana. He was on a plane back home very shortly after that. So was I. But the important difference was that I was actually coming back. For a few months anyway.

38: Ground Zero and the Road to Mecca

A brush of kimono means they are in some way, destined - Japanese Proverb

Coming back from Australia I ran into a number of friends from Japan who were all connecting onto the same flight to Narita from Kuala Lumpur. Just before we started boarding we were startled by the appearance of a huge group of furry hatted people of unknown ethnic origin attired in very large coats. They obviously had difficulty remembering that Malaysia is situated in a tropical zone, rather than the sub-arctic zone that we imagined they had come from. They looked the types that would be far more comfortable herding a group of yaks through a blizzard in the Taklamakan Desert than in a crowded airport midway on, presumably, their hajj to Mecca. Maybe they were lost and their conversation was proceeding something along the lines of;

Gryswwlfty: "Hey Tyrrewslfty! This is not Miami! The agent said we'd get to change in Miami! I can't use my thong here."

Tyrrewslfty: "It could be. Lot's of white folk staring at us over there. It's hot too. Let's check out those tickets again...."

(Silence while he slides tickets from his Yves St Laurent goatskin purse and checks)

Tyrrewslfty: "Bloody hell! You're right Gryswwlfty – this is somewhere called Koala Lumpy. What kind of a f***** up name is that?"

Gryswwlfty: "I told you not to book through your second cousin. Now I know what he meant by 'Mecca Surprise Package'"

Tyrrewslfty: "Yeah, and those b***** white folk still can't stop staring at us either. Let's go get a beer and some sheep's balls...."

We negotiated our way into Osaka from the airport in the morning, before my companions split for Niigata. I thought about curling up in the bushes outside, just for old time's sake, but quickly dismissed that as sentimental claptrap. Also, if I left at the same time I thought it might be poor form to turn up today, and take tomorrow off - which was the date I was meant to be returning. Okay, I thought it would only be bad if I was actually <u>seen</u>. So, instead I headed off in the opposite direction on the *shinkansen* to Hiroshima. The fare, equivalent to a reasonable size mortgage in Gabon, Liberia or some other similar IMF-challenged country, cost about ¥22,500 return from Osaka. One could get clear across China for that amount – except that it would take six days on a hard-assed seat, eating noodles and listening to the comforting sounds of locals and their hacking phlegm.

Visiting the Memorial Park and Museum in Hiroshima is a fairly sombre experience, regardless of ones view on the validity of the decision to use atomic weapons against Japan. In deference to more recent events it can be easy to forget that this was the place of the original 'Ground Zero'. In a blinding flash, tens of thousands were killed instantly or suffered excruciating injuries, from which some are still dying over sixty years later. Yet this does not even match the intensity of the incendiary bomb attacks on Tokyo, where on March 10th 1945 around 100,000 people died in one raid alone. It's sad that mankind, on all sides of any conflict, can stoop to such depths of brutality. And still it continues today. At the finish of wanderings there I found myself fortunate enough to sound the Peace Bell. A small, but obviously futile, personal statement.

Once back in Osaka I thought I'd have to take the overnight train but managed to get to Toyama in time to catch the last local train out. At least I didn't end up sleeping in the bushes outside. After a long night on the plane and a day to reflect on the virtues of mankind I found myself in a melancholy mood and deep in reverie, wanting to do nothing more than stare out the window. I rummaged through the bottom drawer of my emotional dressing table and found myself wondering what it was going to be like back in Omi. I began pondering about home, about my future, but most importantly like many *gaijin* before me, what the hell was I doing here? In the end I concluded it might just be time for an emotional crash and the sooner I got it over with the better. I slept badly that night and had the weirdest dreams - something like the X-Files on heroin.

The following weekend was the annual Omi winter *matsuri*. Not that I'd been told about it. I just discovered it the next Saturday walking down to the *eki*. Actually it was probably advertised in amongst the surfeit of junk mail that continually made its way into my mailbox, but eighteen months into my time and I was still lucky if I made out more than a few words. Actually, once I saw myself in a town newsletter, but only knew it was about me because it had my picture. And not that good a one either. When I was younger I had distinct muscle tone – a bit like a half-inflated bicycle inner tube. These days it's more like the Michelin man. The older you get, the better you realise you were. Oh, and I made out the word *furendori* (friendly). I asked Yuko for a translation of the whole article but she was rather non-committal on the whole thing. I could've been suspected of embezzlement and/or panty theft for all I know. Did make me rather self-conscious for a little while.

There was quite a throng at the festival - predominantly lots of men and kids with their faces painted. Despite the fact it was still snowing the men were only wearing skimpy shorts and *yukata* and doing strange things with huge bamboo poles. Obviously fortified by much *sake*, they seemed oblivious to the freezing cold and were undertaking quite a bit of shouting and clashing of the bamboo. There were plenty of photographers and news crews on hand to document the whole thing. It was all rather a jolly occasion, despite the fact I had bugger all idea of what was going on. The *grand finale* came when the mayor and other officials began throwing out oranges and sweets to the crowd from a rooftop. Many of the oranges landed with an unceremonious 'splat' on people's heads, or on the road. Conceivably it was payback time to those not paying their taxes.

After the sticky conclusion I continued onto the *eki* to catch a train to Myoko-kogen. By that night I was to feel like I'd been hit by a b***** huge Mack truck – with the driver backing up afterwards to spin his wheels on me. But in between those two points in time there was to be a period of hours that would change my life forever. Literally.

Like many others of my contemporaries around that time I had bought a snowboard, and was heading up to the Ikenotaira ski ground with Todd, Beth (the local English teacher) and several others to try them out. Although I was told I was a 'natural', that didn't stop me from falling over (*see:* crashing) countless times. Usually with little panache. At the end of the day, generally bruised in both body and ego, we indulged in an *onsen* at the Myoko Hotel, before heading out for dinner at the house of a local friend of Beth's.

We had originally planned to retire to Nakago Village for a night of carousing at James's apartment. James, who I first met on the train coming out of Tokyo, had become one of the original diehard snowboarding clan of English teachers in the area. Until this point most of the rest of us had been skiers. However, when his local board of education got wind of our plans they rapidly vetoed the idea. James passed the torch to Beth who could accommodate the hordes in the activities room of her teacher housing in her nearby town of Myoko-kogen. But there were no local restaurants able or willing to take in such a large group of noisy *gaijin*. Beth contacted her friend Michiko and she had kindly offered to cook a stupendous feast for about fifteen of us.

Not too far into the evening repast the *shoji* door slid open and one of the most attractive women I have ever seen stepped gracefully through the entrance. This was Michiko's daughter, Mami. She sat down next to me to chat and the rest, as they say, is history. Mami is now my wife and the proud mother of our beautiful daughter Youki.

39: The Toilet Sled and Free Whisky

There is no teacher for love - Japanese Proverb

In Muikamachi, Giles, whom I was always calling Clinton or Clint for some odd reason, had replaced Betty during the summer. In Koide, the next hamlet over, Bjorn had replaced Jack – much to the relief of the town. Both settled well into their new assignments and had not broken any legs or crashed any cars. But along with some other cultural peculiarities Giles had difficulty adjusting to the traditional 'squat style' toilet in his apartment and missed the usual western style.

One day Bjorn was visiting as winter neared and remarked to Giles about the unusual object sitting under the stairs. Neither had much idea about what it was but Giles thought it may be some sort of snow sled. When Giles indicated that he was not likely to use it Bjorn took it home to try out on the slopes near Koide. He was given some strange looks as he did so but presumed it to be just the usual lot of being a *gaijin* in Japan.

Some time later Giles' supervisor dropped by his apartment. Noticing that the unusual object was missing he asked Giles where he had put it. The supervisor had difficulty keeping a straight face as Giles explained. It turned out Giles had lent Bjorn his 'toilet converter' that a workman was soon coming to install. Therefore Bjorn's sledding on a toilet must have provided some light relief, of the comedy type, for the Koide locals present.

This preceding story was related to me, not without a little embarrassment, at a party one night. On the same night Bjorn was trying to give away a very expensive bottle of whisky which led to one of the strangest cultural insights I have ever encountered. It went something like this.

Across the road from Bjorn lived a nineteen-year old young lady who occasionally dropped by to say hello. One night, well you know how it goes, and one thing led to another. Afterwards she didn't want to leave but insisted she stay the night. Bjorn couldn't convince her otherwise and after breakfast she made the short trip back across the street to home. Later that morning Bjorn sees her mother walking toward his front door.

"Now I'm in for it", he was thinking to himself.
Mother knocks on the door, and before Bjorn can explain, she begins,

"I'm so sorry", she says, "that my daughter was so bothersome last night. She so enjoys your English lessons but after she fell asleep on your couch you were too kind to wake her. I hope it wasn't a problem for you."

Bjorn is obviously standing there speechless. Then comes the kicker.

"So I wanted to apologise for her bad behaviour", and she plucks a very expensive bottle of whisky out of her bag.

"Please accept this whisky as a token," she implores him.

So Bjorn has just spent the night in lecherous pursuits with her daughter, and she's apologising to him? Surely she doesn't believe the, "I fell asleep" line?

But you see the whole truth of the situation didn't matter too much. If the mother believed the daughter and Bjorn agreed with the mother by accepting the whisky then that was what happened, and there would no shame for the family in that. Naturally as this story spread there were a few English teachers hoping they could also help 'save face' for any families in their district with pretty daughters. Purely for the sake on international and cultural understanding mind you.

Nonetheless, even with incidents like these we had to keep our focus. We were in Japan to teach. Not everyone however had great motivation or ideas. I liked to use words, very difficult ones if possible – like xenophobia. It's also a useful word when you're stuck on 'X' during the alphabet game in class

"Now let me see children. How about 'X' for xenophobia? That's a <u>big</u> word isn't it children? Who can tell me what that means?"

Then you pick on the dumbest kid.

Don't laugh. Tom told me he did use it in one class, though maybe in not such a humiliating way….

Naturally, some people had ideas but didn't realise how bad their ideas were. Below is one lesson plan that came to me via a mailing list. God bless this enthusiastic guy. He was obviously trying to be ultra-helpful because he kept e-mailing these things. Unfortunately this was not one of his better attempts. At least he wasn't like the member of the JET mailing list who complained that 'Sesame Street' had no educational value. That guy's mother must have been a crack addict while he was in the womb, or else he grew up on the Planet Zork. It was fairly obvious that some on the list had no life, or relationship, or even comprehension of the real world, outside of their computer.

The lesson coming, getting back on track, you must know was most likely aimed at kids around thirteen or fourteen years old. If I taught this to my students in my current gig I would be most likely unemployed by the next day. They would probably not notice in Japan but I really struggle with defining what the actual educational objectives and outcomes are. Namie Amuro, by the way, was a famous nineteen-year old pop star who later ran off with her thirty-five year old producer - which made us all incredibly jealous. Now presented, getting back on track yet again, is the lesson <u>exactly</u> in the same form (apart from the name) as it passed through my inbox:

****

I really like this type of lesson becuase it leads the students through a discovery of new expressions, allowing them to think about the situation, imagine what the meaning is, and experience an "Ah-ha!" reaction that makes learning fun. In this particular lesson, the two words (?) Uh-huh and Uh-Uh (for yes and no, be careful of stress) are very interesting and funny for the kids. When reading them for the first time, make sure you have their attention, get a gaping stupid look on your face, freeze, and utter.

The class erupted in laughter 3 out of 4 times I tried it. If you have time I think it is necessary to practice usage with a simple yes / no question relay, substituting Uh-huh and uh-uh for yes and no.

Dialog:

B: I'm pissed.
K: What's the matter?
B: I went to Tokyo yesterday.
K: So what?
B: Well, when I was riding on the train, I saw Namie Amuro!
K: No way!
B: Really! I was very surprised. Have you ever seen Namie Amuro?
K: Uh-huh. I saw her on TV. But I never saw her on the train. What did you do?
B: I asked Namie Amuro for her sign(ature).
K: Are you kidding?
B: No, I'm not. But Namie Amuro didn't sign her name.
K: That's too bad. Did you ask for a picture?
B: Uh-Uh. I asked Namie Amuro for a kiss!
K: A kiss?
B: That's right.
K: Are you crazy?
B: No, I'm not crazy. But she didn't kiss me, either. So I'm pissed.
K: Of course! Bob, I think you're really crazy.

****

Now if you were a teacher I would doubt very much that you would think, "What a great lesson plan!" and then run off copies for everyone in the staff room. You would be far more likely to do the Christmas thing and photocopy your bare ass I think. And that may be one of the intrinsic problems of the JET Program. They only hire graduates – not necessarily teachers, and many have little idea of what they're doing. A bit like me. But the buzzword is *kokusai* (internationalisation), so it probably matters little. They mainly just want the *gaijin* mucking it in there with the locals and letting the students do neat cultural stuff like sticking pencils up your bum. Therefore the actual learning of any English can often take a backseat to a wider social and political agenda.

How did the JET Program begin? Well as the behemoth of economic growth rolled through the 1980's the Japanese government was upset by international criticism that it was too inward looking. In August 1987 they took action to correct this (and its burgeoning trade surplus with Western countries) by instituting the Japan Exchange and Teaching Program - one of the largest educational programs ever conducted. Not that there was any 'exchange' of teachers. We're talking purely in the cultural sense. In its first year, over eight hundred graduates from America, Britain, Australia and New Zealand were brought to teach in public schools all over Japan.

Overall the JET Program has enabled many unemployable young graduates of Western universities to continue living a university lifestyle, but with money, and without the study. It also gives the Japanese people a chance to internationalise without actually having to do anything - except maybe harass the young female graduates and/or steal their underwear.

Further discussion on this point can be found in later chapters. Just not in this book. You have to go and look for something a bit more serious if you're seeking profound insights.

40: Victims of Fashion

One kind word can warm three winter months - Japanese Proverb

As the days moved through February the snow continued to be solid on the ground. The banks would lie in large white swathes on the sides of the road tumbling and impinging on the space of pedestrians and drivers alike with each fresh fall. As I traipsed to school one morning I spied what I thought was a high school girl setting out through the white blanket with her skirt hitched up and much of her slightly chubby bare legs showing. As I came closer I realised it was in fact one of my *san-nensei* (Year Three) – soon to graduate and obviously practicing for her upcoming high school debut. *Chugakko* students are not meant to be wearing skirts above the knee but she must have pulled the top of the skirt up above her, ahem, bra to achieve the desired effect. I ran into some others walking down the hill dressed the same way. Their progress through the snow was slow and measured - probably due to the totally inappropriate high-heeled boots they were wearing. One's heels were so high she tottered at an angle that threatened to pitch her face first into the icy pavement at any moment. It was then once again that I was reminded how very good it was to put behind me adolescence and the vagaries of peer fashion.

Not only that, but fashion in Japan can also be life threatening. Take the following example which I found;

"This season's fad for extra long scarves claimed another fashion victim when a Japanese woman fell from her motorcycle after her two-metre long muffler got caught in her bike's rear wheel, police said. The woman was in a coma after the accident but regained consciousness, a police spokesman said, adding that she remained in a serious condition. The student was riding in the western Japanese city of Higashi Osaka when the end of her scarf snagged in the wheel, pulling her back and choking her, he said.

"Long, long scarves became fashionable among young women after (Hidetoshi) Nakata, the football player, wore one that almost touched the floor. Wearing a scarf like that is obviously dangerous for motorcycle riders as well as bicyclists," the spokesman said.

Fashion-conscious Nakata, who plays for Italian club Parma, arrived in Japan for an international match last autumn sporting a long grey scarf, one end of which reached his knees while the other fell to his feet. The motorcycle accident followed a similar incident in November, when a 26-year-old Japanese woman suffocated to death after her long scarf was caught in the engine of a go-cart at an amusement park."

I also suffered a setback to my health, but unmistakably nowhere near on the same scale. Munching on a packet of sweets that week I bit down on what I thought was a hard centre and spat it out. Staring at it something seemed amiss. I scoured my upper molars with my index finger and made a discovery. I had just broken off half a tooth! In the morning Setsuko set forth to hook me up with a local dentist. These were the guys who finally proved to me that deep down all Japanese are really masochists. Yes, not even watching people immerse themselves in boiling water on TV game shows could convince me until I had the misfortune to visit a dentist.

The first problem is actually contacting one. In Omi the three local dentists all took the same days off. I think there was a regular golf date on Tuesdays. The second problem was actually getting an appointment. Seven to ten days is considered a normal waiting time, but in 'an emergency' it could be brought back to oh, three or four days. The third problem is paying the bill, which roughly equates to the same figure as the GDP of a small African nation. What happens in a <u>real</u> emergency I hear you say? Like, if I got my teeth knocked out in an accident with a *karaoke* microphone? Well, I guess you have to wait three or four days to see a dentist like everyone else - if you can actually contact one.

In reality, I can't see what purpose dentists actually serve in Japan anyway. Have you ever seen the average Japanese persons' teeth? Setsuko managed to pull a few strings, probably by letting on that I was anally retentive, and within three days I found myself sitting in a dentist chair and having my first genuine Japanese crown fitted. So now I had a silver smile at the back of my mouth and a substantially smaller bank balance.

Kinya-san came to visit me at school and gave me a new contract to sign but it was extremely ambiguous with several new clauses inserted re sick leave, holidays, etc. Kuriiwa was not being replaced when she was to leave after March and Setsuko intimated they would want me to teach some classes solo in the next year. Suddenly the future was not so clear, and to the disappointment of many, I returned the contract and declined to sign on for another year. I was a bit sad to be leaving, not yet convinced it was the right decision. But for good or bad it was the decision I had made and now I could get on with the rest of my life.

Mami was saddened that I had not renewed but we pressed on. I would visit often on weekends for snowboarding and Michiko would cluck over me like an old mother hen. She apparently had pegged me from the very first night as her future son-in-law. Valentines Day came and there was a box of chocolates from Mami waiting in the letterbox. She sometimes would turn up with flowers for the apartment, drinks for the fridge, books for my library, plus maybe some food, often from Michiko, and/or sweets. She doted on me so, and still does.

This month also saw my last weekend English seminar attended by only four students, the usual suspects – Yumiko, Mai, Rie, and Tomomi. This event involved us bunking in the 'seminar house' at the back of school for a weekend and providing a few hours of intensive English. The girls tried to convince Kato to come but he refused to be the solitary male. A couple more years of raging hormones and he probably would have felt blessed to play that role. Still, it was a lot of fun and the girls were very *genki*. They just fell in love with Joanne who

L to R - Mai, Rie, Tomomi, Yumiko, Joanne, myself and Igawa-san

taught them all very deep English stuff like 'love ratings'. There was no hot water for the weekend and hence we went home smelly and unwashed, but happy, by Sunday lunch.

The weather began to clear up and I hoped that spring was on it's the way. Spring – that time when a young man's fancy turns to what girls have been thinking about all winter anyway. The first assembly of the season was mind-bogglingly boring. I considered getting a cardboard cut-out of myself to set up at the back of the hall. Kanai led the school anthem, which was usually sung at each assembly. After nearly three years in junior high his uniform was getting far too small, and as he flopped his loose wrists around he reminded me of a 'Thunderbird' puppet. This assembly was a practice for the upcoming 50th

Anniversary celebrations. On the day when it arrived there were no lessons, just some music, presentations and the inevitable parades of boring speeches. The hall was hot and stuffy, and lots of attendees nodded off (including me for awhile - hey, when in Rome). One guy spoke for an hour and twenty minutes. Just as well I took a book with me! Still, I guess it was worth it as I got my picture in the photos for posterity...

A full house for the celebration

41: What do you do with a drunken sailor?

To appear like a god and disappear like a phantom - Japanese proverb

One Friday night I sauntered down to the *eki*, on one of my now regular pilgrimages to Myoko-kogen, stopping on the way to buy some flowers for Mami. The kind proprietor of the small establishment was a small but sturdy aging man and his wife. When I entered he extracted himself from the *tatami* mats just behind the counter to serve me and staggered toward me a little uncertainly. As I became a more regular client I discovered that by later in the evening he was settling down for a meal and a drink, and any customers after that time would receive varying service and/or welcomes dependent upon his state of sobriety.

On this our first meeting he engaged me for sometime with questions on where I was from and what I was doing in the town. Patently he didn't read the civic newsletters either. He regaled me for some time in Japlish about how he used to be a merchant sailor, and had visited Adelaide on occasions. Just as I was beginning to carefully calculate the distance, space and time before I missed the train (one minute to pay and receive change, three and a half minutes to hurry up the street and around the corner with a twelve kilogram bag, thirty seconds up the stairs, one minute to buy ticket – if no-one waiting, one minute to the platform) his wife appeared from out the back of the shop. As he continued on she kept on telling him to shut-up and apologising to me (in Japanese) because he was drunk. Some things, like nagging, are inevitably cross-cultural…

It was now getting into March and I was conducting my last classes with the *san-nensei* (Year Three's) who would soon graduate. I sadly bid them all, well nearly all, farewell and good luck. Some of the female students from Class 3.3 came into the classroom and gave me a sad little speech before they left. That was sweet. Another year of saying goodbye. As I said before, that's just the lot of a teacher. The lessons for other classes were also quite easy as we wound down toward the end of the school year. The Year Two's were just working toward presenting their English skits. One student, Otsu in 2.1, told me "*daisuki*" (I really 'like' you) when I was giving her a hard time. You can't help but think, "That's so cute". I was pretty sure that she was the one who had scrawled the love hearts on various stationery objects near Utatenami *yochien*. Or perhaps it was just another local resident with broad affection for someone with the initials

'N.K.' The *kyoto-sensei* from Omi *yochien* was also leaving and when I dropped off some *omiyage* for her she promptly shed a tear. I like to think I did at least <u>some</u> things right during my tenure.

Todd arranged for a group of *gaijin* to be involved in Matsudai *matsuri*. On the Saturday evening this entailed dressing up in skimpy *yukata* then running about with portable shrines yelling a lot. You have probably guessed by now that most of these winter festivals involve a lot of shouting, a modicum of semi-nudity, and a s***load of alcohol. I resolved to keep a flask of Bundaberg Rum down the front of my loincloth to keep warm but was still working on the logistics of how to stop it falling out.

Once at the festivities, carrying the shrine from point A to point B was the easy part. However then we had to circle around in front of the crowd for ages and continue chanting. Most of us were put on the least fit team who had to stop and rest all the time. I was the tallest in my group and therefore had to bear an inordinate share of the load on my shoulders. We also made up some new chants which I'm sure had never been used in that context before. I'm not sure what the locals made of, amongst others, "Aussie, Aussie, Aussie, Oi, Oi, Oi!"

Afterwards we were taken back to a local hall for an *enkai*. Sometime over the duration of the evening I discovered that Todd had entered myself and a number of other people, without my knowledge, in a race through the snow and up a nearby mountain to Matsudai Castle. And it was no easy stroll, but a strenuous race over two and a bit plus kilometres to a shrine on top of the hill. I was given number 99, which I thought was a good sign. We had to march in the parade first, so Steve and I livened it up with an 'Australian march' and a bad hung-over version of Waltzing Matilda. Maybe we would have sung Advance Australia Fair if we could remember the words. It's a little unfortunate that probably 80% of Australians can't remember the words to their own national official anthem.

After the preliminary speeches the starting gun sounded and I found myself in a crush of more than five hundred competitors, some of whom had been training for months for this event. Everyone jostled and fought for position as we ploughed along a narrow path that was covered in snow over half a metre deep. And just to add to the fun we were not making a direct run up the mountain. No, first we had to navigate a circuitous obstacle course of ropes, snow walls and the like. I was absolutely knackered by the end of the first round of obstacles. Urged by a gathering of *oba-chan* shouting encouragement I gritted my teeth and then decided.... "Bugger this, coffee is better than a premature heart attack". They'll never call me 'King of the Mountain'. I casually loped off back to the change hall and think I had the distinction of being the only DNF. Too old, too slow was my excuse. It was all a tad much for me and in the holidays shortly thereafter I lay on the beach in Guam to recover.

42: The Ghosts of Children Past, Or Ode to My *Jitensha* II

It is by riding a bicycle that you learn the contours of a country best, since you have to sweat up the hills and coast down them. Thus you remember them as they actually are.
- Ernest Hemingway

Spring had arrived in all of its gorgeous colour and the cherry blossoms were blooming. The new school year was upon us and, with my looming departure, I now found myself as a 'lame duck' at the school. I'd been cast onto the end of the teacher 'island' away from Setsuko and opposite Matsumoto-san the office lady. Staff pictures were taken the previous week while I was away and had already been distributed - without an inset or mention of me. Now the wheel was already spinning on 'Meet the *gaijin*'. Soon the new winner would be announced and it would be their turn to be feted and bombarded with questions and comparisons. A new white face, a new look. But in the end it seemed we were all the same - just with different names.

Having quite a few new teachers was also a bit disconcerting. I walked in early the first morning, shouted my "*ohayo gozaimasu*" and found a sea of unfamiliar faces staring and shouting back at me. I didn't recognize anyone! Plus, like the last year, I had to search for my desk before I could sit down. At my first class with '3.1' I found Saito was sitting next to Sunohara. Saito and Sunohara were best mates, despite the fact that Sunohara at fourteen years of age was as tall as me and probably heavier. Saito was in the vicinity of five foot nothing and forty kilograms if he was lucky. When they stood up at the start of class the optical illusion made it look like Saito was still sitting down.

That afternoon I went down to the city office to sort out some things and found that Tomoe was not working there anymore. She had been 'temporary' for at least three years, and then as soon as she decided to get married it was *sayonara* baby. When I asked Yuko about it she said that it was fairly standard practice. Naturally, there were no 'temporary' male employees.

Springtime also granted me opportunities for some last rides. Along the way I could feel the rhythms of the countryside - people working in the fields and going about their lives, snow still on the mountains, fisherman by the ocean, the green growth of spring breaking through now that the snows had passed. Truly providing those warm fuzzy moments in life. From Itoigawa, through Nagano-ken and onward to Tokyo there lay the old *shio no michi* (Salt Road) – an ancient path where salt was borne between the Japan Sea and Tokyo via Matsumoto and Kofu. I tried to find the remnants of the old road but eventually had to give it up as a lost cause. Even the locals I asked along the way appeared to be ignorant of it. Or more likely it was just my bad Japanese. Eventually I found myself lost, rode up a mountain, had to turn back because it was closed and then went careering over the handlebars on the way down.

Springtime would also bring a new bounty of fresh fruit and vegetables. In this humble author's opinion Japanese fruit and vegetables tend to be all far too expensive. More than once students commented that, "Nicholas-*sensei* likes bananas." That's because they were imported from the Philippines and were far cheaper than anything else I could buy. A famous Nagano apple will set you back at least ¥500 because the farmers put special bags on them while they are ripening, then later get up and polish them <u>on the tree</u>. It could be said, "An apple a day keeps you poor". Vegetables tend to be usually strange, mostly bitter, and all expensive. But in springtime you will find people who construct roadblocks by parking their cars all over narrow mountain roads.

Sometimes these hunters and gatherers can be even more effective than the Chinese who, in any random mainland supermarket, routinely manage to block an entire aisle with a single shopping cart. If, for example, the Australian government really wanted to keep out the illegal hordes in their leaky boats, they could employ a few mainlanders armed with shopping carts; they'd only need about two dozen to block the entire north-west coast. Anyway, after parking these people proceed to act like mountain goats in search of elusive 'mountain vegetables'. These still taste strange and bitter, but are less expensive - unless you take into account the exorbitant motor vehicle running costs.

On my next ride I went higher into the mountains noticing obvious signs of the recent snow. Clearing marks, fallen trees, and the like - all being overshadowed by freshly sprouting ferns and trees. Shortly after passing a small village in obvious decline I spied an old building and went back to have a look. It turned out to be an old *shogakko* that was now serving out its years as a sawmill. No one was around so I wandered in for a peek. Up the rickety wooden stairs and past shuttered classes I found an old mural painted on the wall. Many years ago some young local children would have taken great delight in painting it. Now it lay dusty and unseen. I stood in front of it feeling dispirited. In a few years time the same will likely happen with the school at Utatenami[6] and maybe even later Ichiburi. Maybe some future teacher will wander through them like I did trying to commune with the ghosts of the children past contained therein.

---

[6] In fact when revising this chapter I was informed that both Utatenami *yochien* and *shogakko* had closed at the end of March 2004 due to declining enrolments. It made me incredibly sad.

Setsuko later told me that village was Hashidate which means 'built up bridge'. Too bad the place was falling down. She was impressed that I'd taken an interest in the old school and figured it must have closed at least twenty years ago. I would've thought ten at the most.

Further up I decided to take a left turn and ended up at a fast flowing river. There were steps heading up the hill so I followed them and came to some dams, rapids, and waterfalls. It was quite spectacular. I wanted to cross the main stream but to do so I had to abandon shoes, top, camera, and gloves. It was bloody cold but I made it across and back. When I returned there were some town employees surveying the newly installed steps. I ended up having my photo taken standing in the stream. I don't know what they thought of me and where the picture was published I'll never know. I was quite surprised by the work put into the area. I wouldn't think they would have a lot of visitors there. Just maybe it was something to do with the LDP, fiscal stimulus and the need for votes (as discussed in Chapter 8).

I left there and as I climbed higher noticed that *sakura* were still blooming. In fact some had not even got out of bud yet. Snow started to appear by the road as I gained altitude. As I traversed the shoulder of one range I saw that the snow on the other across the valley was still quite thick. It was getting close to sunset by the time I reached the top of the range. I had hoped to take the alternate road down into Toyama-ken but it hadn't been cleared of snow yet. I either had to take the winding route down into Oyashirazu or turn back. Having already travelled the former trek once before I decided it would be better to turn back. Rugged up but still freezing, and with Enya playing sweetly through my earphones, I rocketed the return twenty kilometres in about one-fifth of the time it had taken to get up. I glanced over my shoulder for what would probably be the last time at the North Alps; their mantles still shrouded in snow.

My trusty wheels had provided so many of my special memories of Japan that I felt we had forged some kind of bond. As the time of my leaving drew closer I found the legend of my bike and its rides had spread throughout the prefecture. It seemed like people were lining up to buy him. Even Fukushima-*sensei* was quite keen to adopt it. I thought it strange that a Japanese person would want so something so obviously well used. As I mulled over the offers I procrastinated. I knew I couldn't keep it, but the break would be tough.

Tom in Itoigawa was the eventual lottery winner, and the last I saw of the bike was as Tom rode him into the distance down Route 8. Later, apparently, he just disappeared one day. Was it stolen, or did it sense my absence and like an old dog go away to die? I would like to think it was the latter. I hope it didn't end up in a *gomi* pile, or lies abandoned in a field, but rather that somewhere in the mountains near Omi lurks the spirit of a dirty green and white mountain bike. And now that I'm gone perhaps, just perhaps, others will see him like a ghostly apparition freewheeling out along *shio no michi* and through the back blocks near Hashidate....

43: Going from bad to worse

The war has developed not necessarily to Japan's advantage
- Emperor Hirohito

One of the constant dilemmas for those in the teaching profession is coming up with original and stimulating lesson ideas. And so it was for the *yochien* and *shogakko* teachers who were called upon each month to come up with novel concepts for teaching English. These were a mixed bag of good and bad, but usually fun nonetheless, apart from 'Toolman Teacher' in Utatenami.

These could include speeches, games, physical activities, cooking, drawing or crafts, such as *origami*. This is another of the traditional Japanese arts. I've always been such a weakling that I've continually searched for ways to prevent getting the crap kicked out of me by more assertive males, or in some unfortunate cases, females. When I was around thirteen I tried to scare bullies off by claiming that I possessed, "…a black belt in *origami*." This didn't work because even if the bullies were that stupid, they could assert afterwards that they had kicked the living s*** out of a black belt holder. "They're not that tough" they would declare, flexing their biceps to the cooing cheerleader girl as I lay senseless and prostrate at their feet.

For those not aware of the whole concept of *origami*, with this you get to fold little bits of paper into the likeness of other bits of paper. I quite like *origami*, even with the pain it originally inflicted upon me, because I used to do folding tricks for a living back home. But I eventually gave up when I got kicked out of a kid's party for folding a dog into the shape of a balloon.

I would have liked to have had an activity based on *pachinko*. The best way I can describe this is as 'Japanese pinball'. You see these parlours with their huge garish neon signs everywhere, but they seem even more popular in Niigata-ken. Perhaps because it's easier to get the hard currency back to North Korea from there. I tried it a couple of times but viewed it as nothing more than a very popular and more expensive way of playing with your balls.

Many people are obsessed with *pachinko* and there are even a number of professional players who make a living from the machines. Like gambling anywhere they can also be the source of friction, fraud, job losses and marital troubles. In 2003 Kyodo news agency carried a report that Takashi Chiba, the deputy governor of Akita Prefecture which borders Niigata Prefecture, resigned after admitting to playing *pachinko* instead of helping to deal with a powerful earthquake in his prefecture. Mr. Chiba was "…enjoying a game of *pachinko*…when the earthquake struck. It injured about 100 people, damaged buildings, roads and railways and could be felt as far away as Tokyo, about 280 miles to the south. Officials said that Mr. Chiba, who had an official car waiting for him outside, contacted the prefecture's disaster agency by mobile phone, but decided to keep on playing the game. He left when he learned the emergency had been upgraded, about an hour after the quake first hit."

Mami and I took ourselves for a tour around the local area near Omi one fine spring day and we found ourselves on part of *shio no michi*. As we did so we admired the rice planters now out in full force. Everywhere we saw the farmers bent over in the fields that had only recently shed their cover of snow. About eight kilometres up we came to our first destination, the Fudo *daki* (waterfall). This was an awesome sight, particularly with all the water from the snow melting. I couldn't believe I hadn't been to see it before. We began talking to one of the workers there who directed us to an old village further up the hill that was now mostly abandoned. Several of the remaining traditional houses were in a state of disrepair. In Japan it often appears that every scrap of land is used up but most of the surrounding rice paddies here had succumbed to overgrowth. Yet still a couple of wizened *oba-chan* and *oji-san* sat out the front of their houses indulging in their daily chores and seemingly happy to allow at least fifty years of progress down the hill pass them by.

As we continued on up to the *Hisui* (Jade) Gorge the scenery was really spectacular. The rain earlier had cleared away and now it was bright blue skies. The water pumping through there along the Kotaki-*gawa* was amazing. We collected some rocks that we thought could be jade and took them home with us. When we took them to the mineral museum in Omi the next day to be checked we were informed that it's illegal to take rocks from there. Technically, if they turned out to be jade we could get arrested. It was safer just to fossick for any jade on the beach that may get washed up. I discovered that a small stone that I'd picked up off the beach when I first arrived was jade and the museum staff kindly said they would polish it for me for free. Celebrity status in Omi did help at times.

By the time we left the gorge we were getting hungry. We bypassed one restaurant on the mountain and headed to Kotaki but discovered there was little there. Making our way further to Hiraiwa we still couldn't find any restaurants. All of the *onsen* hotels were empty because their hot water supplies were destroyed by the earlier floods and had never been restored. One *oba-chan* related to us that during the flood they had to be taken away by helicopter. They had no open restaurants and the whole place seemed like a ghost town. We had just about given up and were on our way back to Itoigawa when we noticed a small shop. We bought some instant noodles and other supplies, and the sympathetic lady proprietor supplied us some hot water. We sat out overlooking the river and hungrily consumed our plastic lunch. Intent on an *onsen* we headed for Renge Spa high in the mountains but were stopped by snow about a third of the way up. Eventually we drove back down to the coast for an *onsen* at the Itoigawa Hotel. Being a holiday weekend the price had for some strange reason tripled. Must have had something to do with penalty payments for staff.

With less than two months now to go some 'stuff' hit the fan big time. In all my time in Omi I had never received any income or wage statements. I requested some information on my taxes and pensions and found the town staff was mystified by the request. Shortly thereafter it came to light that I hadn't been paying any taxes. In an ultimate show of incompetence the town revealed that they had not been aware that they should be paying taxes for me. I almost cried when I was informed, as I could be liable for a bill of several thousand dollars when I arrived back in Australia. Not only that, but I had missed out on some of my pension money too. It had to be close to my most distressing experience in Japan I think, but it was actually to go from bad to worse. At first they went with the concept of *mokusatsu* (taking no notice of someone). The Japanese had tried this one after America dropped the first atomic bomb. It obviously just doesn't work - and I was about to begin my own warfare.

A few days later Setsuko came back to school after a meeting with the town office and informed me that they wouldn't pay my taxes. I could just "…pay them in Australia instead". Thereafter any notion of goodwill was lost as I battled through meetings without resolution, along with faxes and calls to the education offices in Tokyo and Joetsu. Setsuko took up the struggle on my behalf and said that she would try hard to make sure that the problems didn't surface again with Peter (my replacement). Then she asked me to stay. She should have done that before I signed my papers. Too late alas. Some time later the town told me they would pay my taxes - after I paid them first. I informed them, rather curtly, that I wouldn't do it. Then Setsuko stepped in and offered to lend me the money, nearly ¥500,000. An unbelievably magnanimous offering.

To relieve my grief the next day was in stark contrast. It was one of my favourite times of the month - Ichiburi Day. On the way to the station I posted off a cheque to the Australian government that cleared away my student debt. A good start to the day. As I walk down the road from the *eki* some of the *yochien* kids spy me through the windows and begin to scream my name. This alerts the others and by the time I reach the door the assembled throng are in a positive lather. As soon as I step into the *genkan* they are all over me before I can even get my coat and shoes off. Yesterday is behind me for the moment as I remember what made being here worthwhile. We pass a wonderful morning with lots of fun and hugs. Even the new *san-sai* (three year olds) are getting in on the act. Despite everything else I know that leaving them in July will break my heart.

It was raining lightly but still warm as I left after lunch. As was my usual want I strolled down to the beachfront. I sat down under a shelter near the toilets and gazed at the mountains for awhile. There was a mist rolling over them obscuring the fresh green spring growth. In the foreground hawks were circling, and in the distance I could hear the sounds of crows and a passing train. The peace it invoked displayed a sheer disparity to the turmoil of the day before. The lessons at *shogakko* went well in the afternoon and I went home much more the happier. As I walked back to the *eki* I noticed with sadness that the last old original house with thatched roof had been demolished. Yes, it was rundown, but you think someone might have wanted to restore it. The Japanese have a strange attitude to aspects of their history. They respect the past but at the same time seem eager to junk it and embrace the new. Well, in a material sense maybe.

On the weekend my friend Kiminori took Hang, Tom and myself to Matsumoto. It was a nice day but very long. I got woken up about 5.30 by rescue helicopters. Apparently somebody else had drowned in the Hime-*gawa* and they were still looking for the body. Had they ever thought about rubber dinghies? Our first stop for the day was - a radish garden. A <u>very big</u> radish garden. And there were the usual hordes of tourists there wandering around and buying lots of *omiyage* – radish hats, radish sake, radish ice-cream, radish dressing, radishes carved like penises, etc. I guess there was even a bit of *wasabi* in there somewhere, seeing it's made from radish. I didn't see the attraction myself, but I guess it's one of those cultural experiences. From there we were also taken to Matsumoto Castle and Zenkoji Temple in Nagano. The latter was just bedlam. There was meant to be a special image on display that they only roll out every hundred years or so. It must've been the lump of wood with *kanji* written on it out front that everyone was fawning over. The gathered devotees bowed, prayed, scraped, and inserted coins in any of the cracks they could find. It was good to finally escape before Kimi returned us via Hakuba village.

On the Monday morning I had to go to the town hall with all other government employees for a free health check. I gathered around chatting with some of the others while we waited for the medical staff to take a blood sample, along with our blood pressure. Next they checked our eyesight and presented everyone with a cup for another sample of you know what. Then you left that on a numbered tray (your number naturally) outside the toilet. It was quite humorous to see all the different coloured samples sitting right out there in the open. After that they took an x-ray and cardiogram. This was serious stuff. In what other country would you get this kind of preventative health care?

Afterwards I headed up to the office to check on the continuing progress of our negotiations and discovered that my airfare payment had been summarily revised downward as well by a substantial sum. I was so torn. I adored my students and my apartment by the sea but I despised the inert bureaucracy. I knew it was time to move on.

44: A Very Public Intercourse?

Bad and good are intertwined like rope. – Japanese Proverb

The inviting orange peaches sat warming on the tree in the early morning sun, and naughtily I plucked one as I passed by and savoured it slowly. As I wiped the juice from my stubbled chin I rested on the crumbling moss covered wall of the local temple which seemed to groan unsteadily under my weight. Though spring was here there was still a slight frost on the surrounding grass. Above me, carved into the cliff face of the valley side were the remnants of an old Buddha figure – its cherubic face long disfigured by the constant pounding of wind, rain and snow. I stood up slowly and stretched. The morning sun was just breaking through the clouds and it felt good on my face. The day seemed like any other, but later that would prove a fallacy. It would be a day that would change my life. Indeed a good many lives. In just a few short minutes the communist planes from across the sea would scream in over the waves and change the lives of the townsfolk forever. There would be no reporting of this tragedy. Government spin doctors would see paid to that…

As I sat reading this in a trashy novel I was under-whelmed in its ability to keep me awake and soon found myself snoozing. I woke with a start and realised that if I were to dally longer I would miss the train to Naoetsu where Tomoe's wedding was being held. Halfway to the *eki* I realised that in my hurry I had forgotten my jacket but it was too late to turn back now. I didn't have any good shoes but figured it didn't matter, as I would have to take them off anyway.

Once on the train I had some high school students, who I wasn't acquainted with, being rather friendly. One came over, stood in front of me, pointed to Joanne's *futon* - that I had borrowed and intended to return before I went to the wedding - and said "*sugoi*". After that she just stood there. I didn't know quite what to say. Did she think it was a good idea to carry a bed around? If so, did that mean she wanted to have a quickie with me? Would I enjoy a bout of public intercourse with this fairly unattractive young girl? Wouldn't there be some kind of law against this - even in Japan? But after a while of staring at each other, as I pondered these questions, she just gave up on waiting for a reply and walked away. However, when we went to get off at Itoigawa she and her friends started on basic English phrases.

One girl said, in very broken English, "My name is Julie Green. I'm from California".

"*Honto?*" (Really?) I replied.

"No, it's a joke" she replied, and we all laughed.

They followed me up the stairs chattering and giggling, then bade me farewell with a hearty "*bai, bai*".

When I arrived at the Washington Hotel in Takada I wasn't sure exactly where the wedding was. I wasn't invited to the formal reception but only the less formal *nijikai*, which was due to start around that time. I asked at the desk and the not so helpful staff vaguely pointed up the stairs. I went up to the second floor ballroom and heard something going on so I peeked through the crack in between the doors to see if it was the room I was looking for. Suddenly the doors flew open and there I stood at the main entrance of the grand ballroom with about two hundred Japanese faces all staring in my direction. The three video cameras and enough lights to film 'Ben Hur' swung around to highlight me *sans* jacket and wearing hiking boots. You must understand that Japanese weddings are very formal, very expensive and have the budget of a small art house Hollywood movie – if such a thing still exists. I had, in my usual bumbling way, committed a truly stupid act and stumbled into the formal reception still in progress. Tomoe was just giving a speech and after being momentarily flustered, stopped to introduce me. After the applause died down I was beckoned inside, given the bride's father's seat, then some food was hurriedly located and placed in front of me. I really would have preferred to crawl into a hole and die instead.

Later we were all led upstairs and released balloons, some with well wishes for the finder. The *nijikai* followed soon afterwards but didn't last very long. They were taking Polaroid photographs of everyone on which we had to write a message. I posed like I was being strung up with my tie and wrote, "*Omdeto gozaimasu*. The bungling *gaijin* strikes again".

That evening I went drinking with some friends in Niigata City. Just about everyone else left for a love motel around 3.00am but I was crashing at Aaron's place. I caught a taxi then realised I hardly had any cash left. I went as far as my remaining cash in my wallet allowed, then had to walk the rest of the way to Aaron's. Along the way I considered shop fronts. "Maybe I could sleep here. Just for a little bit. It wouldn't be <u>that</u> uncomfortable." I was feeling great but just very tired. To be intoxicated is to feel sophisticated - but not be able to say it. Others of a similar level of difficulty would be 'indubitably', 'preliminary', 'specificity' and maybe 'cinnamon'. An even greater level of 'things that are very difficult to say when you are drunk' would be:

I suffer from passive-aggressive disorder,
Nope, no more booze for me,

Good evening officer, isn't it lovely out tonight?,
*No matter how much I drink, these clothes are **not** coming off,* and
I just really don't find you attractive.

I finally negotiated my way on unsteady legs to the house, crashed soundly and woke in the morning with a horrendous hangover. After much searching I finally found where Aaron stashes his aspirin, as he was spending the weekend elsewhere. After an hour they hadn't taken effect, so I took some others. This rather foolish action gave me some anxiety because I started to feel quite faint. I had visions of Aaron finding me dead face down in his *genkan*. "Dead of drug overdose" would be the rumour, but at least the Omi bureaucrats could stop worrying about my tax bill.

I got taken to the tax office in Itoigawa and went through a long convoluted meeting. They sorted my taxes for two years and would eventually sort out the last few months just before I left. Kinya-san said there was some late tax penalty to be paid as well, but said he would fork out for that personally. It was another kind offer that so epitomised him. I'm not sure who eventually paid for it. He also assured me that the town had informed him they would pay the taxes direct to the tax office, which showed a rare display of bureaucratic logic. Never underestimate the power of stupid people in large groups. Finally, after another bout of yelling, fights, meetings, faxes to Tokyo and losing face all round I also was also to be paid the full amount for my airfare, rather than the 50% as originally proposed.

I had my final morning with the 'Tazawa Terrors'. In actual fact they were pretty well behaved for my last visit. I was presented with several gifts, which varied from elaborately made origami flowers to a ripped open sweet box with nothing inside. One kid had made copies of the five shapes I had been teaching them. At least one had obviously been paying attention. I taught Year Two at the *shogakko*. At the start of the lesson they sang "Kookaburra sits in the old gum tree" which I taught them last year, and then we sang "Head, Shoulders, Knees, and Toes". I think I'll go to the grave with that jingle still swimming around my brain. The rainy season was upon Omi now

Yes kids – just one more time!

and leaving was coming toward me like a freight train with just on three weeks to go.

Late that night as I sat watching TV I changed channels and found a live cross to Kobe. Just a few weeks before Jun Hase, a mentally handicapped boy in Kobe had been brutally murdered and decapitated. The case had captured the attention of the nation and the news bulletin was showing that the killer had been arrested - a fourteen year old *chugakko* student. The impact of this act had even been felt in Omi. All the *shogakko* kids were bunching together on their walk to school and at least one parent was always with them. Of course anything like that was very unlikely to happen in a tiny rural location like Omi, but you couldn't help but think that Japan in general had lost a kind of innocence. The PM promised to act on any shortcomings in the education system that the investigation showed up. Yeah, sure thing Mr. Prime Minister - and tomorrow I'll skateboard to the moon!

45: "The time has come, and so I face the final curtain…"

Start spreading the news. I'm leavin' today. – Frank Sinatra

And so now it was July - my last month in Omi. I had started handing out my 'farewell sheets' on which students could write me notes and quickly had a couple of replies back. One trusted that,

"In the end, I do hope you will be successful as an ALT or a human being."

All responses I received were positive and reflected the wonderful nature of the students I had been teaching. The collection stills reside in a box in Australia as a treasure house and fragrant memory of my time in Omi. If I tried the same thing in Australia with the average student many respondents would make sure to include a number of words, mostly of four letters, that cannot be printed here.

Additionally many of the students were happy to collect my cast-offs as I sorted through the collected debris of two years. Mitsuru Nomoto from the '3.1' class came around with a couple of his mates to collect my surfboard. Setsuko didn't approve because he had been "a bad student", but reflected that; "Taking up a sport might help him". Unless of course that sport catapulted him head first into the *tetorapoto* during a typhoon.

Saying goodbye to the younger students at the various *shogakko* and *yochien* was tough. At Utatenami I gave the kids some coins and they returned the favour with various gifts. I also left my frisbee behind for them, which they were rapt about; as that was something we'd always had fun with during my visits. Surprisingly I managed to get through without any tears. Five-year old Masaki was obviously upset and clung on for a long time in the hug goodbye. At Utatenami *shogakko* we had a 'Tanabata' (star) *matsuri* and we all tied our wishes to some bamboo. As I rode off down the hill all the teachers and the students gathered to wave goodbye. As I negotiated the curve at the bottom of the hill I waved one last farewell – then fell off my bike. Of course all the kids laughed, though not noticing the huge chunks of flesh missing from my hands and knees.

As I packed and readied boxes to be posted back to Australia I found myself having to leave so much extra space for gifts from students. There has been so much thought and TLC put into many of them and I hated having to be randomly discriminatory by throwing some out. A lot I just put in a box to be left at Mami's house so that I could sort them better when there was much more 'distance'.

Yamada-san sent me a jar of sesame butter and Miyuki from the Idobata class took me to Itoigawa to look for track shoes, just one of the many farewell gifts they would provide for me. On the way she was explaining about the serious accident she had two years ago. As she did so she turned onto Highway 8 veering into the path of an upcoming speeding van. As my fingernails dug deep into the dash I was grateful not be part of her next one.

Sweet farewell notes from the kids continued to trickle in. Most gave them to other teachers to pass on but a handful were game enough to hand them over personally. Tomoki Hirano issued me hers and said, with her usual smirk, "This is love letter for you!" Asaka Yagi from Year One was very happy that I liked cooking and because I had let her know that, yes indeed, I do have a teddy bear. There were surprises too. Yoichi Umezawa, a quiet student, came to me with head down and silently handed me a fan as a surprise farewell present. He didn't say anything - just shoved it in my hand as I left class. Still reluctant to speak but the gift said it all. Rie presented me some wind chimes and put above her attached 'print club' sticker "I like you", which I guessed for her was a final declaration of her 'admiration'. She said, also expressed by other *san-nensei*, that she wanted for us to "graduate together". It's a pity, as I would've really liked to have stayed and seen them through to graduation. Tomomi endowed me with a fan beautifully inscribed with golden Buddhist sutras, then asked why I was leaving. At the moment, with such outpourings of gratitude, I wondered myself.

That evening I sat by the bedroom window and stared out into space for a long time. The rain had eased and the lights of fishing boats were dotted all along the horizon. It was hard to believe that in a few days I would have this view no more. Once again I was at that melancholy and reflective stage. I had to leave sometime I guess, and now was as good a time as any.

The night before my farewell ceremony at the *chugakko* Mami and I had dinner with the Kinya-san and his wife, Yuko and her husband, plus Tomoe. The men wanted to kick on to a *nijikai* for one last time but I was unfortunately too buggered. At the school farewell ceremony Rie gave a short thank you speech in English on behalf of the student body. Afterward Yamada gave me flowers and I didn't carry through on my threat to kiss him, merely shaking his hand. The roles were meant to be the other way around but Yamada had 'chickened-out' on the speech and left Rie in the hot seat. I asked some of the teachers what they thought of my farewell speech to the students then realised the futility. Stupid me! Did I really think they would tell me? That silence was something I wouldn't miss.

Another thing I knew I wouldn't miss about Japan was the low entrances and doorways. In Japan doorways are built for the tallest median Japanese person. I guess that this is about 165 centimetres. Unfortunately I'm 185 centimetres tall which enabled me to have close and unsolicited attention to the abeforementioned fact more times than I wish to attest to. A Canadian friend, Ewen, who is about 200 centimetres in height, just gave up and wore a heavy bandanna when inside his apartment. It was disturbing to be in a place like Japan when at my age the peripheral vision starts to give out. I now have so many bumps and dents on my head that if my body is exhumed by archaeologists in a few thousand millennia they will automatically presume that I had met with some grisly and slow death. To a phrenologist my head would have the same effect as ball bearings in Stevie Wonder's braille books.

In the days before I left I gave *kocho-sensei* a gum tree that I had grown on my porch from a seed and which I hoped would grow happy and healthy in the s***** climate. I cleaned out my desk and locker, and then after my farewell speech to the staff *kocho-sensei* presented me with the usual farewell gift of ¥5,000. I felt like the waiter who gave great service and got a lousy tip. That was my point of view though. I know the great depths of their tradition provided different meaning for them.

Chris Connor, the original ALT in town, dropped by the school in my last week so we had a chat for awhile. It was interesting to hear some of his stories, how some things had never changed, and why some things would never change. Kinokawa was with him, unfortunately looking more sickly and geriatric than ever, and he didn't seem to really want to talk to me. I gave out *omiyage* to Fukushima and Setsuko. Fukushima laughed when I gave him my *didgeridu*, an aboriginal music instrument. I could never play the thing but surprisingly Atsushi, Yuko's husband, could.

My farewell Idobata *enkai* was a lot of fun and the food was good. Everyone was so unbelievably nice. I received a horde of wonderful thank you letters, plus an equally large plethora of expensive gifts. Igawa got quite drunk because he thought he wouldn't have to play baseball the next day due to rain. He was wrong. After leaving the restaurant we discovered that the heavy rain had stopped and we were greeted by a clear star-filled sky. We finished off at the 'nine-ball' *karaoke* box near the Hime-*gawa*. I sang a few songs including "Leaving on a Jet Plane" and an emotional "My Way" as a finale in which they all tried to join in with.

The next day I had to front up to the Board of Education to offer thanks and say goodbye. I brought another tree to give to the mayor, but got confused with the order of things and gave it to the head of the board instead. Oh well. I hope I didn't offend anyone. Staff took me into an office, where I presumed the mayor would meet me, but unless the mayor had changed it wasn't him. No matter - I just gave a little speech anyway and whoever he was seemed appreciative. The town staff all walked me to the door and waved me goodbye. They were probably thinking "Boy, are we glad he's leaving!"

I took some time on the last morning of school to post the rest of my boxes and the friendly post office staff had now become my firm friends over two years. In the afternoon Setsuko took off early and didn't bother to say goodbye. I guess she'd already given me a gift and was not sure how to react given our ups and downs over the years. Fukushima was more effusive in his farewell. Finally around 4pm I got up and said my final good-byes. The newer teachers bade me a fond farewell. The older teachers present didn't seem like they could be bothered. About eight staff followed me down to the *genkan*, shook my hand and gave me a final *banzai*. Riding down toward the underpass for the final time I passed three solitary *san-nensei* who shouted after me their last hearty "bai-bai". As I came to Route 8 I spied Rie waiting for her bus, so I rode over to say so long. I wanted to give her a hug and wish her all the best, but there are things you just don't do - particularly in Japan. So we just shook hands and exchanged farewells.

On the last morning Kinya-san and the utilities people turned up at 9am to do the final readings. He said they would give Peter the incoming teacher the option of moving to a single man's apartment where the cooking would be done for him. I thought it was good that he would have an option, but also annoyed because they just couldn't shrug off the feeling of male domestic helplessness. Mami loaded up her car with my final possessions and departed for Myoko after they left. At 2pm, after one final check, I closed the door on Casá del Klar - my home for two years. I deposited farewell *omiyage* for the neighbours in their letterboxes then set out for the *eki*. I had lunch with Yuko and Atsushi at Yamada's. As we sat at the counter for one last bowl of steaming hot *chiyashu ramen* Yamada-san began to cry, plaintively bemoaning the loss of "her best customer". Others began to assemble outside and so it was now the time had come to make my way to the *eki*.

46: Farewell, Blue Sea, Farewell

Remember that here all is enchantment, - that you have fallen under the spell of the dead, - that the lights and the colours and the voices must fade away at last into emptiness and silence.
- Lafcadio Hearn

FRIDAY: After a few traumatic months the time had finally come. It seemed like so long ago I had come to this tiny town precariously balanced between the sea and the mountains to make my temporary home. Where had the time gone? There I stood at the gate as the familiar announcement came,

"Naoooetsu... Naooooetsu... Platform Number One, Naoetsu train soon leaving"

A blue and white local train coming from Toyama City slides in alongside Platform One. This was a trip I had made countless times, yet this one was to be very different.

Visibly missing amongst the gathered crowd were many I thought may have come to bid farewell. I almost felt this was the defining moment - about those who you have touched or those you didn't. There are those that turn up at the *eki*, those who write you sad letters - long, short and/or incomprehensible, those that give gifts from the heart, those who call you just one last time, Yamada-san the elderly *shokudo* owner who cried when I told her I'm leaving Omi. Now she stood outside her little shop as I walked up the stairs to the platform, waving and dabbing her eyes with her small white handkerchief until I disappeared from view.

I reflect on my first day at the school. I had walked in sweating from the humidity, my shirt sticking in a most clammy and unattractive manner to my skin. How come it can snow in winter, yet still be so stinking hot in summer? Another one of my great questions to ask God when I finally meet him. There greeted me the famous bundle of 350 essays to be marked - and so began the two years of my journey into the mysterious world of teaching English in Japan.

Early on I had lamented to other *gaijin* how much easier the job would be if we didn't <u>actually</u> have to teach any students. At the end of two years they were the part I treasured most - young and old, big and small. From cute little Yuki-*chan* at Utatenami *yochien*, who one day looked up at me with her big brown eyes and simply said '*daisuki*' (I love you), to the even cuter mountain climbing *oba-chan*, Mitsue Kitamura, at Tuesday night *Idobata* class, who was forever plying me with fresh vegetables from her garden. They were what had got me through the rough times. I had even missed the prefectural farewell with the governor to teach one last class. I hoped I had been able to impart something to them during my time. I knew they had to me.

On my last day the school had generously parted with ¥5,000, less than the price of an *enkai*, delivered by a bowing *kocho-sensei* who I hardly knew. It seemed so meaningless in all that had gone before. Even now, I still had much to learn about the Japanese. As I strode from the staff room for the last time there was the teacher who didn't even bother to look up from his desk in acknowledgment. But the Idobata class were there at the *eki* in strength - and still loading me up me with gifts I couldn't even hold onto.

They all walk down to the platform with me to say their goodbyes. Sato-*san* hugs me in a spontaneous show of un-Japanese like public emotion. I dally for a few short moments, savouring the moment, before I step aboard. The whistle of the stationmaster rings out, the doors clang shut behind me, and they all continue to shout and wave goodbye. Bemused passengers look at me awry wondering what all the fuss is. As the train rocks slowly away I feel a little ambivalent - sad, but maybe not overly so. Over the last few years I seem to have left so many people behind in so many places perhaps I was becoming too hard.

I look for the last time at the *chugakko* as the train passes by, and framed behind that the mountains I have loved so much. So many times I took my bike up into those North Alps making new discoveries, getting lost in the awesome beauty of its nature. Days of sunshine, days of rain. How I would miss them.

To the left there is a slight glimpse of my apartment block. Not mine anymore, soon to be someone else's. Tall, grey, forbidding - once referred to by the indomitable James as, "…classic 1950's communist Romanian style architecture". Now the memory of that remark brings a brief smile to my face. Yet, it is the only place I will ever live in that has a sea view at the front and the mountains at the back. Grand views of God's great vista on tap. Well, maybe apart from the Denka cement and chemical factory…

Neither could I ever expect again a plethora of smiling Japanese housewives clutching plates of sandwiches, fish and rice to beat their way to my door concerned for the poor hapless *gaijin* bachelor. "How does that poor man survive by himself?" they must have thought to themselves.

As I pass over the surging Hime*gawa* I am leaving finally after two years. Where have they gone? It's been so fast. Maybe I regret leaving a little, but know it was the right thing. In a melancholy mood I stare out the window all the way to Naoetsu. Itoigawa, Nou, Nadachi - all the familiar names come and go. On the Japan Sea a typhoon is building and the sea lashes the coastline as the train continues to speed me away. I begin to feel like a man who had fallen in love but never realised it until after it had been lost.

Later I will spend my last weekend with Mami near Mt. Fuji, and I change trains to Takada so I can wait for her to finish work. I wander aimlessly as time seems to drag its heels. In and out of the convenience stores, discovering a small temple I've never seen before, one last look at Takada Castle. I sit on the bridge at the park and a few colourful carp come to the surface, mouths open, hoping for a feed. As they disappear back into the depths disappointed they remind me of many who have crossed my path in these two short years. Often appearing briefly yet leaving an unforgettable impression. Some wanting something, others just curious.

As I wander down Nakamachi I find some wet cement and casually carve my initials. I step and admire my handiwork. Will it be the only real mark I ever leave on Japan?

SUNDAY: My last night in Japan. We are caught in a traffic jam with everyone crawling toward Tokyo. Eventually near midnight we find a place near Fujino. In a *ryokan* (Japanese style inn) we sleep in our *yukata*. It seems appropriate.

Time for goodbyes

MONDAY: We wake at 5.15am and Mami takes me to the *eki*, getting worried that she wouldn't find it. She tries to book me on the 8.00 express out of Tokyo but it's full. Before the train to Tokyo arrives we have the inevitable sad goodbye. A passer-by offers to take a photo and Mami is embarrassed because of her red eyes from crying. She can't stand to watch the train leave and I watch through the window as her figure disappears down the grey stone steps in the early morning light. I touch the glass trying to frame her outline - but it's gone too quickly...

I'm late changing at Tokyo station and the killer instinct of Tokyo kicks in. What did I hear Tokyo described as? I think it was, "L.A. without the guns". I decide to get on the express, as I figure they won't be able to kick me off until Narita anyway, and I move around trying to avoid getting my ticket checked.

The airport is like ants around a honey pot. How will I get through all this? I have problems when I eventually reach check-in because the routing had been changed to go via another two cities. All formalities take a long time, my cheap bag carrier is collapsing under sixty kilograms of luggage, and I only make it to the plane with ten minutes to spare.

The first leg is to Malaysia and I'm finally able to watch 'Kura', a beautiful movie that I had always wanted to see but could not find with subtitles. I should've really tried to learn more Japanese. Well, perhaps I should've done a lot more things...and less of others. I keep hearing the familiar names of Niigata (Kashiwazaki, Shibata, Shiozawa, Nozumi, Kamadegawa, etc.), and see the familiar snow country, and finally a wave of emotion comes over me.

The young boy and girl actors also remind me of my munchkins who I always adored. Every Wednesday morning was like a bonus for me. Three hours of hugs, games, laughing...quickly followed by a collapse into exhaustion. I had struggled under the sheer volume of lovingly hand made farewell gifts I had received from them on my last visits. When the young boy dies in the movie I think about one of my *yochien* kids who had died a short time before, and it increases my sadness. In a period of contemplation I think of Mami and spend some time writing her a letter. Finally the plane banks in leftward over the Adelaide Hills and I spy familiar landmarks. This is it - home.

LIFE AFTER: The transition is not difficult. At home I'm subsumed in so much study and peripheral activities that I have little time to miss Japan. I find myself still in the introverted mode. My home is my fortress. I stay there and keep to myself. The view out my front door is now a disused vegetable patch, full of weeds. I don't go around telling Japan stories. Nobody much would want to listen much I think. Better maybe just to get on with life.

I grow fatter, but also fitter as I ride my bike regularly and rejoin my old basketball team. Dodging trucks and cars in peak hour traffic on Main South Road I laugh to myself. Kinya-san and the Board of Education would have a fit if they saw me doing this. How many times was I told not to ride down Highway 8 to my visit schools? Too many to remember. "*Abunai*", they would scold me. Sure the Japanese truck drivers were crazy but I was prepared to take that risk. I could see their point though, I mean, who would want to send their one and only resident *gaijin* home in a lead lined box? It just seemed to me that too many things were dubbed *abunai* by Japanese society in general.

A couple of boxes arrive for me and my housemate is more than amused when he sees them covered in ¥20 stamps. I open them up and reminisce as I unwrap the *Japan Times* from around each item.

A family friend, a deputy school principal, tells me of her troubles with some Japanese exchange students. She remarks that one was caught with a 'porno' *manga* (comic book).

"What would your mother say?" she asks him.

"My mother sent it to me" he replies.

I try to keep a straight face. A Japanese girl begins to attend the local church. They ask me to speak with her but I protest,

"...really, I can't speak Japanese".

"Well, you speak more than anybody else here..."

Fair comment. Somehow we get by in Japlish. I want to cook some Japanese food, particularly *yakisoba*. I locate many Japanese imported foods in an Asian grocery and spend sometime reading the labels in English. So that's what I was eating all this time I think to myself in bemusement. And on it goes...

NOW: What do I think about now? Sometimes my fellow teachers, sometimes the old townsfolk, sometimes my perception of what I once had. I'm sad that I didn't develop many close friendships - even amongst the *gaijin*. Mainly I guess due to my geographic remoteness and the influence of prevailing cliques. It matters little, *shoga nai*, all will go with their lives and I with mine. The Land of the Rising Sun graciously accepted us all, for better or for worse, and affects us all in different ways.

Do I miss Japan? I sometimes feel that I don't talk about it or think of it often. If I'm just finishing writing a book about it then that's probably not exactly correct. But in most ways life has just gone on. My time in the little town by the sea was not something permanent. I have moved on, got married, started a family and a whole new life in yet another country. It just was a way station on my travel through this earthly existence.

What could I say that I learnt there? Many things. Some good, others maybe bad. Sometimes I was the gentle traveller, revelling in the differences from whence I had come and trying to learn, adapt, accept. Other times I was the raging bull of *gaijin* indignation, battling to overcome the brick wall of chain-smoking, teeth-sucking bureaucrats and their standard explanations of, *muzukashii* (too difficult). I tried over and over to reconcile the paradoxes of Japanese society. How could one be so gentle yet so rude, all at the same time? I was never going to change Japanese society. Then again, why would I want to? It is not mine to change. I will leave the *gaiatsu* (bullying) to others. I have left and the changes are in me. It is most likely I will never know of the influence of those whose lives I have passed through. Yet that is true of wherever I go, whomever I teach, whomever I cross paths with.

Regardless, though I have left Japan, it will never leave me. I will remember the smiles of countless small children, and the song of the train whistle from the nearby tracks. I will never forget the taste of *ramen* in old Yamada-san's little *shokudo*, the refrain of "*bai, bai*" from the students each school night as I cycled home, nor the sight of thousands of *sakura* trees in bloom. As years pass I remember Japan each time I stare into the face of my wife and children - or maybe even get a cheque from my publisher.

On hot summer nights I sometimes sit on the doorstep listening to traditional Japanese folksongs and all the memories come tumbling back. I know that in time any distant bad memories will fade away, only the good will remain, and I will only recall the time in Omi - my little Japanese town of the blue sea, with a special fondness. I guess that's exactly how it should be...

47: A Post-script. Same Stuff, Different Day

Travelling carries with it the curse of being at home everywhere and yet nowhere, for wherever one is some part of oneself remains on another continent.
- Margot Fonteyn

In France in the late 1800's there appeared a peculiarly localised illness that only lasted a few years. Young men would disappear from Paris, and then turn up quite a few weeks later in Moscow, completely unable to explain how they got there. Probably some of Napoleon's men felt much the same way in the winter of 1813. Then again, the winter was so cold it was most likely impossible for them to feel anything. Like, "Oh hello, where did my toes get to then?" Our moves have been somewhat more calculated and, at most times, we've generally been aware of what was happening in our particular dimension.

By the time this book comes off the presses it will have been quite some time since we washed up on the rather polluted shores of the *Huang Pu* (Yellow River) that, after a reasonably lengthy journey from inland Wuxi, discharges itself into the Yangtze River and East China Sea. Along the final stages of the Yangtze Delta you find the rapidly re-emerging metropolis of Shanghai. This is the city that possesses the famous 'Bund', a store of legendary 1930's tales, a towering new skyline, and an economic base that accounts for more than 20% of China's fast growing GDP. It is the latest 'hot' destination for business, capital and of course grubby English teachers, all in search of a buck. Here we came to this great city to take up international school positions via a stint back home in Australia. In Omi I was the only *gaijin* in the town. In Shanghai I am the only person without a mobile phone.

Distance wise it's only a relatively short way to my little town of Omi on the Japan Sea coast. Two and half-hours by plane and then the train ride. Just about as quick as the journey from Sapporo or Nagasaki. Culturally there are similarities too, but *inaka* was never like this! Each day instead of a leisurely ride up the hill and under the railway line to my *chugakko* I find myself dodging crazy bus and taxi drivers plus fellow cyclists - some carrying all manner of bizarre loads, following the ladies with 'night soil' carts down back alleys and wishing for one of those wonderful face masks to keep out the pollution.

But there are benefits too. So many people speak at least a smattering of English. I can communicate with the vast majority of fellow staff members - Western <u>and</u> Chinese. There are malls, foreign food stores, English language magazines, local markets, and any kind of restaurant you could hope for. In fact I think we eat at more Japanese restaurants here than we did back in Niigata. And there's a Starbucks, plus a host of fine foreign restaurants, right opposite the school.

But, the curse and/or blessing of the expatriate, so many things are still the same. I fumble through my broken and basic phrases to many of the locals. I stare at the writing trying to discern characters (oh, for *katakana* and *hiragana* in Chinese). There's nothing to watch on TV - unless you can afford to rent a place in one of the mega-expensive ex-pat compounds with foreign satellite TV, or choose to discard principles and purchase a pirate system. The bicycles, shirts and shoes - but not the doorways, are generally all too small. I have to cope with the occasional culturally shocked and/or dysfunctional westerner. The checkout ladies using three bags for two items. Impossible travel agents that can't release prices and won't confirm. Bizarre pizza toppings. Men peeing in the street. And don't even get me started on the bureaucrats.

For many *nihonjin* the people and places of China evoke bitter/sweet memories of what Japan once was or seems to be losing. With many poor, but seemingly happy. People with a strong sense of community. Industrious, intent on putting what is behind. Building a better way for themselves and the generations to come. A people with a destiny, self-belief, knowing that they will one day achieve a standing in the world that is rightfully theirs. Like *Meiji* Japan of the 1800's, China is gobbling up technology and modernisation from all over the world, and the world is once again taking notice of the land that even Napoleon Bonaparte referred to as, "the sleeping giant".

We love living in the Middle Kingdom - apart from having to skirt the occasional rabid anti-Japanese protests. We have travelled widely and then started our family here. Everywhere one goes there is new construction and new things to see. Things can change almost in a matter of days. The progress is truly amazing. Shanghai will surely be one of the great cities of the 21st Century and we have been rapt to be part of its rebirth.

But regardless of any of this Japan is still always in our minds and hearts. One day we will return 'home' again or maybe to some other exotic location. Then I'm sure we will miss China and inevitably compare what is the same and what is different, what we miss, all those things we are happy to have once again, and what we are glad is behind us. Such is the lot of the traveller. That's all a matter for another book - maybe...

References

A great big *arigato gozaimasu* to the numerous parties who contributed to this book, either willingly or unknowingly. Some material has been culled from amongst the hundreds of e-mails and articles still in my files that I trawled through for research. However, during the transfer from my old computer to the new (e.g. from one that worked rarely to one that generally works most of the time), it was unfortunate that in a number of cases the files did not travel well. Hence, a number of names, e-mail and web addresses, dates, places, titles, and/or other distinguishing features were no longer attached to the remnant. Wherever possible references are as listed below. The important thing is that at least I have tried to show that I have actually done some research. Then again, it doesn't matter if I 'sexed' up any parts – I can always perhaps get a job at the intelligence gathering wing of the British Labour Party and/or certain well known media outlets.

Books and articles:

Arthur Jones, 'Mad for Maladies', That's Shanghai, 12/2002

Bill Bryson, 'In a Sunburned Country', Broadway Books, N.Y., 2001

Dave Barry, 'Dave Barry Does Japan', Fawcett Columbine, N.Y., 1992

Deborah Picker, 'Touring Tokyo – Japanglish', Boulevards New Media Inc., 1995-6

Haruki Murakami, 'Underground', Vintage, London, 2003

Hideo Takamura, 'The Face of Japan', Time Inc., Tokyo, 1997

Howard Tomb, 'Wicked Japanese for the Business Traveller', Workman Publishing, N.Y. 1991

Jack Seward, 'Japanese Eroticism, A Language Guide to Current Comics' Yugen Press, Houston, 1993

Japan National Tourist Organisation, 'Hello Japan', Tokyo, 1998/1999

'Japan', Lonely Planet Publications, Melbourne, 1995

R. Baimbridge, 'Face Down in the Grasslands', That's Shanghai, 11/2002

Tom Clancy, 'Debt of Honour', Harper Collins, London, 1995

Unknown, 'Japlish', Niigata JOHO, Issues 3 & 4, 1995/96

Yoshimasa Otsuka (Ed.), 'Japan Almanac', Asahi Shimbun, Tokyo, 2002

E-mails:

'Lesson plan', via JET-L e-mail list, 12/1996

'Sexual Harassment in Schools', via JET-L e-mail list, 2/1997

Internet Source (unknown), 'The Five Levels of Drinking', by Larry Miller, via e-mail, 7/1996

Klutch Baseman (a.k.a. John Williams), 'Amwayville', via e-mail, 9/1996

Rob Conrad, 'High School Swingers', via e-mail, 5/1997 & 'Story', via e-mail, 3/1997

Todd Stafford, 'RE: More news', via e-mail, 11/2002

News Sources:

Australian Broadcasting Commission, (http://abc.net.au/news):

'Japan Cracks Down On Used-undies Salesman', 1st November 2002

Asia Times (http://www.atimes.com):

'Politics in the paddies', 1st October 2003

'Japanese sickos 'buy it' from American psycho', 7th February 2004

'Death penalty for a fallen guru', 28th February 2004

'Japan, land of rising poverty' 11th February 2005

Financial Times, (http://www.ft.com), app. 8th March 1997

Japan Today (http://www.japantoday.com):

'The wacky world of love hotels', 22nd October, 2004

Mainichi Daily News (http://mdn.mainichi.co.jp)

'The Wackier World of Japanese Ice Cream', December 4th, 2004

News Corporation, (http://news.com.au):

'No damage done, says Howard', 4th December 2002

'Japan readies for cult attack', 11th December 2002

'Japanese keep cash under futon', 1st January 2003

'Scarf almost kills bikie', 22nd January 2003

'Cult still a danger in Japan', 11th April 2003

'Bizarre cult raises concern', 1st May 2003

New York Times, (http://nytimes.com):

'Turning Japanese: It Takes More Than a Passport', 29th November, 2000
'Young People Feel a Chill in Japan's Hiring Season' 1st April, 2002
'Japanese Masters Get Closer to the Toilet Nirvana', 8th October 2002
'Teaching Japan's Salarymen to Be Their Own Men', 27th November 2002
'Get Off Those Sidewalks, Smokers, and Go Inside', 29th November 2002
'More Advice for Curing Japan's Ills', 9th February 2003
'As Japan's Women Move Up, Many Are Moving Out', 25th March 2003
'Man in Schoolgirl Uniform Held on Robbery', 4th May, 2003
'Official Resigns Over Postquake Pinball', 31st May, 2003
'Japanese Workers Told Drop the Formality', 30th October, 2003
'Volunteers in Japan Give Mount Fuji a Makeover', 7th December, 2003
'Body Left Outside Shop For Two Months' 15th December, 2003
'Japan's New Homeless, Disdain and Danger', 17th December, 2003
'Never Lost, but Found Daily: Japanese Honesty', 8th January, 2004
'After 8-Year Trial, Cultist Is Sentenced to Death', 28th February, 2004
'Japan Seeks Robotic Help in Caring for the Aged', 5th March, 2004

Reuters Press (http://reuters.com), app. 10th April 1997

Shanghai Star (http://www.shanghai-star.com.cn)

'Dancing in the Shadows', 22nd January 2003

The Daily Yomiuri (http://www.yomiuri.co.jp), app. 28th March 1996

The Japan Times (http://www.japantimes.com):

'How Japan's JET program got off the ground', 14th June 2000
'Weakened Gangsters, Japanese Mafia Struggles', 2nd February 2004
'Japan: pink heaven for traffickers', 2nd February 2004
'Pendulum Swings on China vs. Japan', 4th February 2004

ISBN 141204897-4